Deadbeat
vs.
Deadbroke
A Guide To Getting All Children
What They Deserve

Simone Spence

Deadbeat vs. Deadbroke

Simone Spence

Eggshell Press

This publication is designed to provide accurate and authoritative information in regard to the subject matter covered. It is sold with the understanding that neither the author nor the publisher is engaged in rendering legal or accounting services. If legal advice or other expert assistance is required, the services of a competent professional person should be sought.—From *a Declaration* of Principles Jointly Adopted *by a* Committee of the American *Bar Association and a Committee of Publishers and Associations*

Although the author and publisher have researched all sources to ensure the accuracy and completeness of the information contained in this book, we assume no responsibility for errors, inaccuracies, omissions, or any inconsistency herein. Any slights of people or organizations are unintentional. Readers are encouraged to consult an attorney for specific applications to their individual situations.

Published by Eggshell Press
P.O. Box 850294
New Orleans, LA 70185
1-888-390-1950
info@dontgetmadgetpaid.com

Library of Congress Number: 99-90151

Spence, Simone.

    Deadbeat vs. Deadbroke : a guide to getting your children all that they deserve / Simone Spence.

       p. cm.

    Includes index.

    ISBN 978-057-8140759 (alk. paper)

    1. Child support—Law and legislation—United States. 2. Attachment and garnishment—United States. I. Title

  First Eggshell Press Edition June 2014

important

If your children are not receiving sufficient financial support from their non-residential parent, then you, as their primary caregiver, have the right to utilize any legal means necessary to get that parent to do so. What you legally cannot do, and should not do, in the best interest of your children, is to deny them the opportunity to have a relationship with their other parent. Understandably, when a non-residential parent refuses or has an inability to support his or her children, the parent who bears the responsibility may become frustrated and angry. Sometimes they become punitive towards the other party. Use that anger to enforce your child support order, not to keep your children away from their other parent. If the non-residential parent is abusive in any way, or you feel that he or she is emotionally unhealthy, then take steps to protect your children during visitation. If your children are not to have a relationship with the non-residential parent, let that parent make that decision. Let your children love both of their parents, but at the same time, insist that they be supported financially.

contents

items

acknowledgments

first I would like to thank my husband Mark and my daughter Storm for agreeing to read my material and for being brilliant sounding boards. Thanks to Xander for being a good sport and allowing me to plaster his face on the mock-up cover while the actual cover was being designed by my amazing designer, Rahel.

Thanks to the readers of my previous books. You are the reason book number three has been written.

A thousand thanks again go out to my husband and my children. Without their love and support, this book would not have been possible. Yes Skylar, the book is finally done.

preface

Some things change slowly, some things change quickly, and some things never change at all. This certainly applies to those who have gone through the child support process only to find themselves going through it once more. Maybe you had additional children with a new partner who also turned out to be less than enthusiastic about supporting his children, maybe you find that you are now helping a friend through the process or maybe it's the same old deadbeat, up to his same old stuff but now the game has changed, and he has a new set of tricks up his sleeve.

My first and second how-to collect child support books (1-800-Deadbeat: How to Collect Your Child Support; and Deadbeats, What Responsible Parents Need to know about Collecting Child Support) were still selling like hotcakes, when the economy began to take a downturn in the fall of 2005. Although the Dow didn't officially fall then which caused economists to officially declare a recession sometime in 2008, the big housing boom went bust long before that. This is when the game began to change and brought some new rules, and with new rules, new strategies must be born. Prior to the housing bust which began in the fall of 2005, one of my favorite tactics to collect from a deadbeat which I wholeheartedly encouraged my readers and my private clients to take advantage of, was moving to foreclose on real estate owned by the offending non-payor. The process began by the parent who was owed the money filing a lien against the property, followed by writ of execution and impending threat of following through on the foreclosure. It was always one of my very favorite tactics because at the time most home owners had some bit of equity in their homes. If the property was successfully foreclosed, and there was sufficient funds received for the property – enough to cover the amount of the arrears – the full amount of the unpaid child support would be set aside to satisfy the child support debt. A strategy such as this would never be implemented unless we knew in advance that there was money (equity) to be had. The beauty was that 99% of the time, the property would never be foreclosed. Somehow the non-residential parent (NRP) deadbeat would "find" the money to pay –up the arrears. (Imagine that!) The property was simply being held hostage until that point. The important things and the only things that mattered were one – that the NRP had a new-found respect, awe and fear of the residential parent (RP) and he knew that she meant business and two – that the past due child support would be paid.

About 70 percent of the information in this edition is new, thanks in part to feedback from thousands of readers who read the first two books. Some wrote to me personally by sending handwritten letters via snail mail post or via email, many others posted comments on my website www.dontgetmadgetpaid.com and Facebook page at www.facebook.com/pages/Child-Support-Solutions. Some reoccurring comments were, "Your book saved my family", "Your book helped me to keep my house...feed my children...changed my life...saved my life"!

Here are some of the changes from the first two books that you will find in this edition:

NRP's

You will find throughout the book that I refer to the parents who live away from their children the majority of the time as the NRP's (Non-Residential Parents). In the first two books, I referred to them as the NCP's (Non-Custodial Parents), the AP's (Absent Parents), or even the NPP's (Non-Paying Parents). Among the thousands of questions and comments from my readers, there were a few from fathers who were offended by these terms because either they did have custody – but not the same custody that the mother enjoyed (maybe joint legal but not residential, maybe some variation of joint residential or split), or they otherwise felt that while they were not there daily that they were clearly not absent from their children's lives. Some of the dads spent a lot of time with their children whether they lived close or far and some of the dads did not spend a lot of time with their kids – whether close or far. They all chose to complain equally stating the position that to call them out as non-custodial or absent was an injustice. My primary decision to change that reference and to refer to dads as Non-Residential Parents is to honor those dads who are indeed parenting on the front lines alongside moms. My secondary decision to change that reference is to get it out of the way so that it cannot be used as a smokescreen by some parents to deflect from the fact that there are child support dollars out there in the billions and parents that don't want to pay and they must be stopped. Some of these parents are just vile and evil and purposely evade payments, some engage in small "manipulations of the system" distorting facts and truths and believing (or telling themselves that they believe) that their manipulations are not so bad, and others just cannot get over the fact that it is not about them. The world does not revolve around them, the payments are not about the ex and they need to get over the paranoia because the world is not out to get them. I will not change the term NPP (Non-Paying Parent) because it is what it is. In the introduction chapter which follows I explain when and why I stick to males (dads) when referring to NRP's and females (moms) when referring to RP's (Residential Parents). I want to also be clear that in no way am I backing off of deadbeats. I am here to hold a mirror up to the faces of all deadbeats in support of the moms and dads that are raising the children despite them.

Skip Tracing

Locating the non-paying parent has become easier than before. For all of those parents who were able to use my techniques 12 and 13 years ago to seek out the deadbeat who didn't want to be found, we are now full throttle in the technological information age and if you have just the smallest inkling of what you are doing you can find nearly anyone, anywhere, anytime. There are different levels of the lengths that deadbeats will go to in order to not be found and I discuss these in depth in Chapter 8, locating the NRP. I have outlined different "phases" of disappearance and most people can be found quite easily when you apply the proper techniques to each identified phase. Some people will require a bit of the brick and mortar approach (old skip tracing techniques) to locating them and you will find that some of my old techniques still appear but there are also many new ones.

The Economy

The economy has gone haywire since I wrote the original content for "1-800-Deadbeat: How to Collect your Child Support" and "Deadbeats, What Responsible Parent Need to know about Collecting Child Support". People have lost their jobs, their homes, their life savings and many are hanging on by the skin of their teeth. That does not mean however that NRP's have no means to pay their child support and cannot pay, even though that is what some of them will tell you and what many will like to have you believe. Does it mean that for some NRP's? Of course it does. Does it mean that for all NRP's? Of course it does NOT! What it does mean is that if you are a parent on the collecting end of this drama that you have to become even more vigilant in your pursuit. Do not become battle weary. Do not give up. Leave no stone unturned because the parent on the opposite end may be working his rear off, working night and day to hide his income and assets. He may be digging holes in his yard at night to deposit cash, he may be engaging in underground employment opportunities, creating bogus LLC's, working off of the books – you name it. I have dedicated an entire chapter to this because that is how pervasive the problem has become. I can't tell you how much work you will have to put into solving your problem, but I can tell you that 83% of the parents that have followed my techniques have succeeded. My job is to explain your options to you – your job is to make the decisions.

Non Residential Parents POV

In my first two editions I did not address the perspectives of the NRP as I perceived them. All of these years later, my perceptions have not changed. What has changed however is that the NRP's have sought me out in order to tell me just what they DO think and they are spitting mad about the whole thing. I was very careful (or so I thought) to place a paragraph in the beginning of each of those books to address the hot issue that this child support thing – this deadbeat thing – is only about the children. I don't care if you are a mom or a dad if you are court-ordered to pay support you have an obligation to make that happen. If you are not court-ordered, you still have an obligation to that child and to the person you created that child with. Like it or not. If you made the baby then pick yourself up – pull up your big boy drawers or big girl panties and do the right thing. Man or woman. Dad or Mom. Unfortunately, it seems that most of the angry ones passed by that paragraph because I have been called a man-hater for about 14 years now.

The Kids

It's no mistake that most kids who come from a two-parent family are generally better adjusted and prepared to enter the world on their own and become productive citizens, than kids who come from single parent homes. Two parents mean two sets of eyes, four arms to hug and hold and maybe two incomes to sustain and provide. This does not mean that kids who come from single parent homes can't and don't succeed;

all other things being equal – in many cases they just don't have the same opportunities as their peers from two-parent homes. What then happens when the single parent who depends on the child support can't seem to get her hands on it? For example, most of us seek to provide our children with as many opportunities as possible to help ensure their happiness and success. You want to provide a safe and comfortable home for them; food and clothing, and maybe sports and music play a part. You need to pay for all of these items, do you not? What if the RP's income cannot cover it all? Who suffers as a result?

Originally, it seemed proper to address child support only in my how-to-collect child support books. In practice however, it made some readers block out some of the other good messages as well. Since men seem to be on the paying end of the support issue, most of them didn't think that the books were for them. We should all keep in mind two things in mind. First, that the support is for the benefit of child though it is paid to the mother and second - both dads and moms can be deadbeats. The world does see too much of both but the nature of the beast is that more dads than moms are deadbeats because residential custody typically goes to the mother. But that's fodder for another guide or article.

introduction

Probably the most important part of the introduction to this book is the following paragraph:

> *If your children are not receiving sufficient financial support from their non-residential parent, then you, as their primary caregiver, have the right to utilize any legal means necessary to get that parent to pay up. What you legally cannot do, and should not do, in the best interest of your children, is to deny them the opportunity to have a relationship with their other parent. Understandably, when a non-residential parent refuses or has an inability to support his or her children, the parent who bears the responsibility may become frustrated, angry, and sometimes punitive toward the other party. Use that anger to enforce your child support order, not to keep your children away from their other parent. If the non-residential parent is abusive in any way, or you feel that he or she is emotionally unhealthy, then take steps to protect your children during visitation. If your children are not to have a relationship with the non-residential*

parent, let that parent make that decision. Please try to separate love from money. Let your children love both of their parents, but at the same time, insist that they be supported financially.

Blackstone, 1750

The history of child support *orders* and the *enforcement* of child support has been an outrage since the day "family law" first entered the legal system. Historically, the majority of residential families have not had *court-ordered* child support, and those receiving child support orders have rarely been awarded enough money to care for their children properly. Theoretically and by design, child support awards should be sufficient to mimic the same economic advantages a child would have if his or her parents were together as a couple. In addition, once the court has ordered child support, most *residential parents* still have a hard time collecting all child support monies. Some families are able to get partial payments, while other families receive no payments at all.

Fortunately, not all residential families experience the economic abuse of child support evasion. The sad truth is, however, that only 25 percent of families that have child support awards ever collect all that they are owed.

This book is not written to tag men or non-residential fathers as deadbeats, although some of them are. It is written for any residential parent, male or female, who needs help getting financial support for his or her children. Eighty-seven percent of residential parents are women. The remaining 13 percent are men, grandparents, and others. There are deadbeat dads, and there are deadbeat moms. In some instances both dad and mom are deadbeats. It does not matter what gender the deadbeat parent is, the object of this ball game is to get financial support for the children. That stated, for the sake of simplicity, this book will use male gender pronouns when referring to *non-residential parents* and female gender pronouns when referring to residential parents. Similarly, gender pronouns will be consistently applied to other roles, such as lawyers, caseworkers, and judges.

Some of the techniques in this book, when used properly, may cause embarrassment to the deadbeat. Some techniques can cause a businessperson to lose his credibility and some can cause financial ruin. If you are at the point where everything else you have tried is working and you can't get across to him or her that your expectation of the financial payment cannot and will not be waived, well then it just may make sense to go for the jugular and use some of these options that I lay out and which are available to you. Not every mom or dad will feel the need to go for the jugular and they may not even have to but you should know your options. A parent that is not paying child support should not be blatantly permitted to carry on with his life and enjoy a comfortable lifestyle as if there is no obligation or if he does not take the obligation as seriously as he should. Paying a portion of the child support obligation is not the same as paying it all and paying none at all is just downright dirty. A residential parent should feel little sympathy for someone who has to be dragged into court before he will financially support a child. If anything, the residential parent should liken themselves to a hero because in the long run that is exactly what you are. You will be a hero to and for your children. Unfortunately, many residential parents are ashamed that they have to force their child's other parent to pay. After all, supporting his own flesh and blood should be something that he wants to do. That shame is misdirected when it is internalized. The parent that is not paying should be the one to own the shame. Others do not want to cause the other parent to become angry. It's a common misconception that a non-custodial parent will be more likely to pay child support if not forced to and if the amount of child support is low or if they allow the non-residential parent to provide "in-kind" payments to the child as opposed to paying the support directly to the residential parent. Many times non-residential parents will want to buy the children clothes and other items in lieu of paying child support directly to the residential parent. While buying things for your children is always wonderful and kudos to the non-residential parents that go above and beyond their child support obligations (they are a rare but a wonderful breed), that is not child support and it should not be allowed to be considered as such. Remember child support is not just for the clothing and food that a child needs, it is also for the roof over their heads and the light bill and the water bill and everything else which is received for their benefit. So it is not the same to allow a lower child support obligation because the non-residential parent provides 'gifts'. In the long run the children are being cheated out of a better daily living life and the residential parent is being cheated as well. If the non-residential parent in the end does not really pay their fair share, the residential parent in the end is the one who must make up the slack.

These ideas are not new. According to Blackstone, an eighteenth century jurist, judges would award nominal child support awards in the belief that there would be little animosity towards a lower amount. That process of thought only causes more difficulties. Children suffer due to a lack of economic stability and often even the lower amount of money is not paid. That tactic did not work two hundred years ago and it does not work now. To award a low amount of support trivializes its necessity and meaning.

Sometimes residential parents just give up, feeling that they want to raise their child on their own, without any help from the other parent. But be assured that by getting child support you are doing the right thing for your child. Children deserve support from both parents and the problem will not go away on its own. Part of the problem with residential families enforcing their child support orders has been the lack of support from our government. Bureaucrats can talk themselves blue in the face over solving this issue of parental responsibility, but it has been around for centuries and not enough has been done to change it. We as a nation have not decided whether child support is a legal or moral issue. Should financial responsibility for our children be a matter that we readily enforce legally like other civil monetary disputes, and if so, to what degree? Or should we allow parents to manage these matters between themselves?

There's the rub. It is a case of "free exercise of families," meaning that families have the choice of how they want to interact with each other, versus "public moral ordering," meaning that the government can decide what is best for families. Should each family decide for itself if, when, how, and how much child support should be paid, or should the government ensure that it will be done? You can see how it becomes a dilemma. Whose moral codes and culture considerations do we use when deciding child support? As long as child support is considered a domestic or a family issue, the nation will be split on how it is viewed.

As mentioned before, the obligation to support one's children has been around since the eighteenth century and developed in the nineteenth century under family law. Up until the nineteenth century, fathers were awarded *custody* of their children. This is largely due to the fact that since women did not work outside of the home, they were unable to financially support children. In the late nineteenth century, women began to get custody if they had some visible means of support and if the father was at fault in the divorce. At that time, industrialization and the growth of factories moved production out of the households and off the farms so as to require less help from the children of the household. Women also at that time began to take paid-labor positions, despite public disapproval. Soon thereafter, for reasons still under debate by historical scholars, the Social Security Act of 1935 was created and included both Old Age Insurance (Social Security as we know it) and Aid to Dependent Children. Aid to Dependent Children (ADC) was created to replace a mother's pension or mother's aid program that had been created to provide assistance to "deserving widows," single mothers, and their children. In 1962, ADC was renamed AFDC (*Aid to Families with Dependent Children*). The AFDC dole remained low until the mid-1960s. From 1965 to 1973, AFDC nearly doubled its participants and expenditures due to the rise of out-of-wedlock births, divorce, and the civil rights and welfare movements. The government took notice.

In 1974, the federal government established *Title IV-D* of the Social Security Act to set up federally mandated, state-implemented agencies to aid residential parents in obtaining child support awards and collecting from non-custodial parents. The government's main priority in establishing Title IV-D was to the residential parents who were on AFDC, not to residential families on the whole, although non-AFDC families were allowed the same services. The program was developed to collect child support from non-residential parents so as to lessen the financial load on the federal government. When written, it was "directed at the goal of achieving or maintaining economic self-support to prevent, reduce, or eliminate dependency." Other amendments of the Social Security Act are the Child Support Enforcement Amendments of 1984 (CSEA) and the Family Support Act of 1988 (FSA). Both were aimed at strengthening child support enforcement practices through establishing paternity and the collection and disbursement of child support payments. Among other things, the FSA also required that states establish and implement mandatory child support *guidelines* to produce some level of continuity with child support awards. Seemingly, child support enforcement has had congressional support. However, the federal child support program no longer provides overall cost savings. That was its original goal, to provide cost savings to the federal government by forcing parental responsibility. The federal government supports the costs of the program, while states receive income from it. In fiscal year 1993, child support collections totaled $8.9 billion while administrative costs of the program exceeded AFDC collection by $278 million, or 3.1 percent of total collections. Because the original goal of cost savings is no longer being realized, twenty-five million children are owed in excess of $100 BILLION in overdue child support.

The time has come to take matters into your own hands. You cannot wait for a system that is in need of repair to collect your child support. Caseworkers are overloaded. While you can still use the services the government has to offer, you must also be your own advocate and you should choose the services that you want to have and decline the ones which prove to be of no benefit to you. Remember, your caseworker is there to earn a paycheck—you need to put food on your table and clothes on your child's back. Of course there are caseworkers who do outstanding jobs for their clients and really do care about what happens to them and do their best to do great work. At the end of the day, however, it still is just a job for them. They will go home to their life and you will be stuck with whatever condition – good or bad –your support order has been left. No matter how wonderful your caseworker may be, no one can be a better defender of your case, than you. Your caseworker may have literally a thousand other cases. It does not matter where you are in life right now. You can be a TANF recipient, independently wealthy or a well to do business owner, your child still needs and deserves financial support. If you do not need the money to raise your child, then put the funds into a college or trust account for your child's benefit.

chapter 1:

why you need this book

Even though you may think that all is well with your child support order at the present moment, you can't be complacent. Danger can strike at any time, at any place, and can come at you from any and all directions. For example, while I was writing this chapter, the following email came in from Debbie, a mom (her real name has been changed to protect her case) and a reader of my first book *1-800-Deadbeat: How to Collect Your Child Support*.

Dear Simone:

I am trying to enforce my child support case through CSE (Child Support Enforcement) and thought that I had finally gotten somewhere with it because at the end of the call I was given a direct phone number to the woman I was speaking with and she was very helpful. She put my paperwork into the legal division of the office and also gave it to the person who initiates the levies. She indicated that she would get back to me by the end of the week with results and a follow up. Well, it has now been almost 3 weeks since I spoke with her and I have not received a call as of yet. I called and left a message for her last week and I left a message today. I still have not received a return phone call. In the meantime, I found out that my ex's house is for sale. I have a judgment filed in our county. My ex says that it is not a lien against his property but that it's a lien against him. I went to the clerk's office today and I was told that the judgment that I have "acts like a lien" against him. I don't even know what that means. I asked to file another lien and I was told that I can't file a second lien on the same case and that a lien against the property has to be filed by child support enforcement and that I should give them the info. I told her that child support enforcement does in fact have the information. CSE has every bit of information on my ex including his business, his home, etc. Meanwhile, during the time that CSE has had my case, he has been able to obtain a business license, liquor license and wine store franchise. He also managed to lose all of them during this time frame. He has been able to sell 3 ATVs, a trailer, a van, and now he's trying to sell his house. I told them that I have a separate court order from my last hearing because the judge ordered him to pay about $7,000 in insurance and medical bills. I was then told that because the order doesn't tell him he has to pay by a certain date and isn't specific that I cannot act on the court order and implement the judgment. What good is the order, then? Anyhow, I'm getting nowhere. Please let me know what it will cost for a consultation with you.

A lesson learned: You never know who you are going to encounter at CSE or at the clerk's office. Some people will be helpful and will do what they say they will do –such as return phone calls and some will not be helpful, will not do what they promise and won't give you the time of day. Some will give you correct information and some will give you bad information either because they do not feel like doing their job that day or because they are simply just clueless.

YOU NEVER KNOW WHEN AND WHAT CIRCUMSTANCES ARE GOING TO CAUSE YOU TO REPEAT STEPS YOU MAY HAVE ALREADY TAKEN, GO IN NEW DIRECTIONS IN PURSUIT OF YOUR CHILD SUPPORT OR EVEN CAUSE YOU TO START FROM SCRATCH – GROUND ZERO – IF THE DEADBEAT OWES A GREAT DEAL OF MONEY BUT YOU CAN'T SEEM TO GET YOUR HANDS ON ANY OF IT OR IF HE DECIDES TO DISAPPEAR. REALLY, REALLY, DISAPPEAR. YOUR CHILD SUPPORT ORDER IS NEVER TRULY SAFE OR WELL OR STABLE. IT IS SUBJECT TO CHANGE AT ANY TIME. BE PREPARED, BE PREPARED, BE PREPARED!

Fortunately for Debbie, she had previously put into practice many of the strategies from my book. As a result, the first time around she was able to place liens on bank accounts that she located which belonged to her ex and was able to cash out. Because he still didn't pay voluntarily after having his accounts wiped out, the arrears built up to a significant amount once more and Debbie had to go after him again. This time around, he was on to her bank levy strategy and no longer kept cash in his name in bank accounts. From reading my book, Debbie learned how to levy bank accounts and she knew that she can place liens on personal property which she tried to do when she visited the clerk's office. In this case her strategy needed to be tweaked a bit so that she could get around the "gatekeepers" at the clerk's office. They were being helpful but sometimes they gave her the correct information and sometimes they did not. What Debbie needed was to be able to point the clerks in the right direction so that they could help her sufficiently. They wanted to help her but had never encountered someone like Debbie before. She seemed to have a better handle on procedures to further her case than they did. She needed to help them to help her and she needed to move fast because her ex was shuffling and transferring assets left and right. In

3

order to win this battle, she had to remain one step ahead. She contacted me for a consultation just in time.

The above is just one of countless numbers of child support near-disasters my readers tell me about, leaving their stories on my webpage www.dontgetmadgetpaid.com and my company Facebook page, www.facebook.com/pages/Child-Support-Solutions. Some readers – not yet organized and without their own personalized strategy – send me unhappy stories as a warning to others. Frequently, the parents have successfully created child support strategies and wish to share their happy experiences of collection and express gratitude to me for having someone on their side who understands their situation. The purpose of this book is to assist you as you work towards creating your own successful strategy so that you too will have satisfactory collections if it comes to that.

Think of this book both as disaster insurance and a step by step guide to filing your insurance claim if the unthinkable happens. If the levee near you has not yet been compromised, this material can advise you of the potential dangers of living in the flood zone and point you in the direction of higher ground. If the storm has hit, the levee is falling apart, the water is rising and will hit your front door sooner rather than later, I can show you how to build a raft using materials in your home so that you can save yourself and your children. If the water has already invaded your home and has risen to two feet in your living room, danger is here. I can show you how to get out of the house and remind you to take your important papers with you. Remember that just because the levee has never broken before, does not mean that it never will. That's the nature of most disasters – they never call for an invitation before they show up.

You need this book if everything is fine with your child support order…

You may have a child support order and your ex may be dutifully and responsibly paying on time each and every month. You can rely on the arrival of the check. It never bounces. You use that money to help pay your monthly expenses and afford the life you have carved out for

4

yourself and your kids. There are many times when dads are regular payors and then something unexplainable happens and they fall off of the wagon. Most times you will never know what occurred to create this change but you will have to deal with it and many times it is an unexpected, unpleasant and most unwelcome change. You may suddenly be confronted by:

- Your ex getting remarried. Many men feel enormous pressure when they take on a new wife. Now added to the responsibility of supporting their first family, they are now shouldered with the responsibility of supporting a second family as well. The burden is great and life would be just so much better if only he could shave off a portion of what he sends to you every month. After all he's not even married to you anymore . . .

- Your ex has a new girlfriend that he wants to impress. He is in love again and wants to shower his new lady-love with gifts, flowers, candy and romantic weekends away. You and your monthly checks have become an albatross around his neck. AND. . . . he's not even married to you anymore.

- He gets together with the boys at the gym. In the locker-room they all assure him that he's paying far too much money and that he is being taken advantage of. They would never submit to a gold-digger the way that he is submitting to you. He begins to see their point.

- He loses his job. He finds a new job but it doesn't pay as much and although he applied for a downward modification, the courts will not allow it because the decrease in salary does not fall within the guidelines allowing for a decrease in payments. His pockets begin to feel pinched.

- He is just tired of being broke.

You need this book if your child support order is already broken...

Deadbeat vs. Deadbroke

You already have a child support order that is not worth the paper that it is written on. He's not paying, or he is not paying the full amount or he's playing games with you or with you and the court.

- He's shortchanging you every month. He's supposed to pay $800.00 and sometimes he pays $250.00, sometimes it's $375.00, last month he only paid $150.00. You are expected to take it and deal with it.

- He's manipulating the system. His locker-room buddies have taught him well. He has learned a trick called "straddling overtime" which basically means that when a court date is approaching he knows just when to dumb down the overtime so that it does not show on his pay stubs. This way he can report a lower income and pay less in child support. Straddling is only one of the very many tricks he has learned along the way to keep the courts and you out of his business and out of his pockets.

- He downright lies to the courts about his income. He willfully does not report all of his income and knows that the courts will not pursue it unless they are asked to by the RP. Problem is that if the RP does not know her rights or how to subvert this type of behavior, so he gets away with it.

- He hides assets. His cash is not in his name, his car is not in his name, and his house is not in his name. He is broke. On paper. Somehow he lives like a king.

- He's penniless. Truly penniless. Not "faking it" penniless. He is unemployed, he is living with his grandmother, he just got out of rehab, he's in the hoosegow, just got out of the hoosegow, he is disabled, disjointed, disenfranchised, discombobulated, dejected . . .

You need this book if your child support order is dead on the vine…

He has not paid you a cent in years. He is not in communication with the kids. No one has heard from him. You are confident that he is not dead but he may as well be . . . for the moment.

- He has disappeared
- Or, he has made himself invisible

Could any of this really happen to you?

The mental damage from worry and fear can be more devastating than a physical attack. So don't worry about any of this happening to you unless:

- You don't have any children
- The man that you have children with works for your family's business and so you are certain that he will always have a job, that you will always be able to garnish his pay and that he will never quit.

Otherwise, this can happen to you and you should be concerned. The fact of the matter is that this happens to women in all walks of life. Wealthy women have just as much trouble collecting child support as their peers who are poor and rely on state public assistance programs. Child support evasion is not a socio-economic disease. The more money a man has – the more likely he is to fight tooth and nail to protect it. Make a random list of twenty women with children that you know. On the average, 14 of them will at some point be on the receiving end of child support. They may or may not be receiving it through a state CSE agency. Of those 14 women, on average, only 25% of them (3 or 4) will ever receive all of the money that is owed. I have always said that if you shake your friend, family, associate and neighbor tree hard enough, you will get women with broken child support orders falling out in batches.

One of the child support cartoons that I had created for my company to use on tee-shirts and mugs and the like is titled "It's 10pm, do you know where your child support is?" It shows two children at home in their living room in front of the television set. The couch is ratty-looking with holes and tears and the television has an old-fashioned analog antennae hook-up, except that instead of an antennae, there is a wire hanger affixed which is being used to hopefully pick up whatever signal that it can.

Although this was a cartoon drawing which is meant to be funny and to provoke a laugh, what it portrays is not comical. According to the National Association of School Psychologists there are 1.5 million divorces per year which involve children and presumably child support orders. This doesn't include the children born outside of marriage. That's a lot of children who are possibly living a lower standard of life than they deserve to be and worse, possibly doing without a lot of the basics in life.

When a deadbeat disappears

Many parents contact me and they say that "they have tried everything" to locate their deadbeat or that the CSE agency "can't find him" and so there is nothing that anybody can do to help them. To the average person that may seem to be true. To someone like me who has been in the business for as long as I have and has helped as many parents as I have through this process, I know that 99 percent of all people can be found. This is a claim that the average private investigator will make and it is one that I agree with. It doesn't matter where they have gone or the lengths that they have taken to hide and disappear, they can be found. That being said, the smart ones also know that unless you have a whole lot of money and/or a whole lot of time, the more that they do to cover their tracks, the more likely that you will become *battle weary* and give up along the way or run out of money that you want to spend to chase your money. If you want to be successful in finding your deadbeat there are really only two things that you need to have. In the absence of cold hard cash (and lots of it) to lay out to a private detective, one is fortitude and the other is know-how. This book is designed to give you the know-how that you need based on the 4 levels of disappearance that I have created:

Level One: Very basic. 98% of deadbeats can be found within days when they disappear under a level one. Yet, they have disappeared to the extent that it would take a private investigator (PI) several hundred dollars of your money to track him down. When they move they won't leave a forwarding address, they change cell phone companies from the one you knew them to have, they work off of the books.

Level Two: It's getting warmer. This is a deadbeat that means business. He has done his homework and he knows that it would cost you several thousand dollars to find him if you hire a PI and he is banking that you are not going to spend that money. Considering that not all PI's are good PI's and that the only thing that drives them is M-O-N-E-Y, you could go to one or two or three before you find the one that will put out for you. At this point, the deadbeat is shredding his trash, he does not have utilities and telephone bills in his name. His vehicles and home may be in someone else's name or the name of his business.

Level Three: It's downright HOT in here. I am not going to lie to you. If you have a deadbeat in level three, you are not going to find him through any traditional measures. In addition to hiding from you, he also keeps his information private from his bankers, his lawyers, his doctors and the IRS. At this level, not even Santa Claus would be able to find him on Christmas Eve to deliver a puppy. You would have to pay a PI a considerable amount of money to find this cat. If he already owes you a considerable amount of money, you might consider it a wash. You might – or you might want to consider some of the other tips/tools and points of leverage that I have learned, taught and have used with success along the way…and none of them involve hiring an expensive PI.

Level Four: If your deadbeat is at this level then he is in the Federal Witness Security Program (which some people incorrectly call the Witness Protection Program), or might as well be. He has burned all of his bridges, he has no contact whatsoever anymore with family and

9

friends. He receives no magazines, or newsletters, belongs to no clubs or hobby stores. He is dead to the world. This might work in your favor though. If he is dead to the world, then that means that the time is ripe for you to file the claim with the life-insurance policy that you have on him and collect your child support arrears that way. Dead is dead, right?

But I have a lawyer

When confronted with a problem collecting their child support, many RP's think that hiring an attorney to collect from their ex or to represent them in court on an enforcement motion is the way to go. If you have a deadbeat on your hands that is driving you back to court or has driven you back to court time and time again, some parents fail to see the folly in this train of thought. Similar to the difference between the parent and the type of case that works well within the CSE agency constructs and the parent and the case that CSE cannot help you with – it is the same construct.

If your ex is fairly easy to collect from – he is the type to have a regular job, he is fairly responsible, he loves his kids and couldn't imagine not being in their lives just so that he could avoid paying you, then this is the type of guy that you can hire an attorney for because you will get somewhere and chances are he just wants to get through this thing the same way that you do.

If CSE can't help you – if they have told you that you have to find him and then bring the information back to them, if they avoid you and you are constantly begging them to file paperwork for contempt proceedings, if you find that you are constantly going through that proverbial swinging door and banging your head on a brick wall, then it's going to be the same thing with your attorney. The only difference is that you will be paying through the nose for this back and forth and at $250 per hour on average, I can tell you that you are getting nowhere and you will get there really fast. You will also get there a lot poorer. Now if you can afford one and you can afford to take the risk that after laying out a $2500.00 (or so) retainer, and investing in 10 hours of legal work that you most likely will not have any resolution after your ex files motion after silly motion (which you must answer by law) purposely in order to run you ragged and run you out of money, then by all means find a lawyer. Good for you.

I still must caution you however to not count solely on their expertise to get your money. Family law is not an extremely lucrative field, especially when it comes to the collection of child support. Many family law attorneys are not aware of most of the tools in this book, or more importantly, they choose not to utilize them. If you are going to use an attorney, read this book from beginning to end and next time you have a conversation with him, ask about a few of the things that you have learned. You may be surprised to find that you now know as much as, or frighteningly more than, your attorney. The knowledge that you will have once you have completed this book will take you far in your pursuit of child support.

I don't want to brag but there are attorneys who are using my previous books as a research tool and a base to write their own books! I am not going to call them out publically but if you contact me by email I will share that information with you.

What makes this book unique?

- *Author's qualifications* – This is my only business. Since 1995 when I decided to make collecting child support easier for other moms like me, I have been engaged full time in the child support business. I do present lectures about the benefit of self-representation when collecting child support; I write about all aspects of child support and the process, I have been running a company since 2002 which teaches parents how to successfully self-represent. I have helped nearly 10,000 parents to collect over $11,000,000.

- *No Ranting or raving* – Okay, maybe just a little ranting. But this is not a beat up on anybody book -except maybe generically - speaking out against deadbeats who are not taking care of their kids. I know that there are "reasons" that some people use as reasons that they don't pay their support or why they have a problem paying their support. I explore some of those reasons in the book. This book is about content and solutions. Indeed, learning about some of the reasons may provide some of the solutions that we are in search of.

- *No Gender Bias* – This book is for any parent having trouble with collecting on his or her child support order. I repeat- This book is for any parent having trouble with collecting on his or her child support order. It is geared for the RP; this is true because my focus is to get parents to remember that this is all about the children. What are we doing and what can we do to continue to give the kids what they need so that they can succeed.

- *Up to date information and advice for the year 2014 and beyond* – Any book written prior to this date will be obsolete when it comes to skip tracing, e-mail accounts, LLC business protections, child support motion procedures and documents. Of course no book can offer online up to the minute information but laws, procedures and tools and tricks of the trade are constantly updated and on the move.

How to use this book

With each chapter I will take you step by step through everything that you need to know. I have tried to write the material in a very easy to read and understand format without *legalese*. This book is designed for the everyday mom or dad to pick up and read and be able to get going on their own without any additional help. I do my best to explain terms as I go along but there is a glossary in the back of the book. If you come across something that you do not understand, please stop and check the glossary.

You will find that there are motion documents throughout the book. These are actual documents that you can use. They are not specific to each state, so if you intend to use them you will have to customize the blanks as appropriate. This is explained in the book. If you want state specific documents, of course you can check out my website:

`www.dontgetmadgetpaid.com` to get these documents. All documents have been reviewed and approved by legal counsel.

HOT TIPS FOR PARENTS

The book is written so that you can read the chapters in order or you can feel free to skip a chapter if you do not feel that it applies to your situation and move onto the next. I do encourage everyone to read each chapter because the book is chock-filled with tips and tidbits throughout and though the main subject of a chapter may not apply to you something within the chapter may or it may give you an idea as you begin formulate your own battle plans. Otherwise, feel free to jump ahead as you see fit and skip chapters as your leisure. You can always double-back another time.

HOT TIPS FOR CASEWORKERS

Feel free to utilize Chapter 8 to help your clients locate absent parents.

HOT TIPS FOR ATTORNEYS

The search engines in Chapter 8 are not just parents and caseworkers. They will work for you, as well. Consider having your paralegal to run the searches, or better yet, hire an intern and make their primary responsibility locating absent parents and discovering assets and income.

chapter 2:
establishing your child support order

I once met a man many years ago (let's call him Larry, though that's not his real name) who had a child out of wedlock with a woman he loved. The relationship did not work out but he promised that he would support their son, and he did. After we had met and as I grew to know Larry as a person and our friendship evolved to the point where I could ask such personal questions of him, I learned that the child support check that he sent to his son's mother every month was the first debt which he paid. It was then followed by the regular list of bills such as his rent, car payment, insurance payments, food, etc. Being in the business that I am in, I was intrigued and had to know more. Typically, most NRP's, if they are paying the child support at all, begrudgingly write the check. Not because they don't love their children and don't want them to have what they need, but writing a check and saying goodbye to a large chunk of your money every month as you send it off to your <u>ex</u> is not a pleasant experience for most of the NRP's whom I have met. It's generally not a time for celebration.

After nosing around some more, I further learned that they did not have a court-ordered child support agreement. They had never gone to a child support court or to any hearings and neither of them had sought the advice of a lawyer. They sat down at the kitchen table one afternoon when she was about 6 months pregnant and she told him how much money she thought she might need to help offset the increase in expenses she expected to have and what the child might need. He took that dollar amount (which was actually a good estimation on her part), added a third and from that point continued to write a check to her every month. They had what is known as a *voluntary* agreement. It worked great for them for nine blissful years. For nine years the boys' father would write a check to his mother. For nine years, she would cash that check and the month would continue on until the next check arrived and the ritual continued. Sometimes the mother would ask for additional money if there was something special that their son needed or wanted and the father would always come through. Theirs was an agreement that most separated, divorced or otherwise "split" parents could only wish for. They did not play visitation wars and "screw me, I'll screw you" retaliation games with child support. Then the day came when the father discovered that his son was not his son at all. The father had been the victim of paternity fraud. A nine year hole had just been punched into his heart.

The rest of this story will be told in Chapter 3, "The Importance of Paternity Testing; What Both Parents Need to Know". There was major drama around what happened next with the continuation of the child support and visitation of the "son" with his "father." Meanwhile, the story of voluntary child support payments that I just told is not the one which you will hear most often. The most common story is the one of Marsha, who I wrote about in my first and second books. When Marsha and her son's father, Doug, separated, they agreed that he would pay child support to her directly instead of going through the "child support system". In her mind, it would be less of a hassle because she would always know when she was going to get her money, and she thought that it would cause fewer ruffled feathers. She didn't want Doug to become angry with her for "dragging" him to court and then decide not to pay anything at all. And, who wants to go to the child support agency and wait around all day anyway? She had visions of an unemployment office or a welfare office in her mind, and she didn't want any part of it. She somehow felt that she was doing something wrong if she had to ask for help to get child support for her son. Her ex made regular child support payments for about six months before the money abruptly stopped coming. For six more months he promised that the money would come, but, of course, it never did. Marsha did not know what to do and no one she asked knew either. She never thought that her ex would do anything like that. She trusted his word that he would pay the child support because he promised, and she almost lost everything that she had because of it. The majority of the times, *voluntary agreements* do not work. Typically, the NRP (non-residential parent) pays on a regular basis and then for whatever reason, the payments either stop or they do not come regularly anymore. I have found that this occurs most of the time for two reasons: one, the NRP is dating or in a new relationship and his priorities have changed. He may want to purchase a new car, take a romantic vacation, get a better apartment or buy a house. The NRP parent may also simply decide that he thinks that he is over-paying and has been for some time. Instead of taking the matter up with the RP (residential parent) and having a "kitchen-table" conversation as the parents did in my first example, they take matters into their own hands and seeking to gain control over their perceived problem (and sometimes the RP), they stop sending the payments. They may begin to insist that an accounting of the child support money be provided to them (which is neither legal nor reasonable) and when they don't receive it - again, payments cease.

It is not uncommon for the NRP to use child support payments as a means to control the RP. Child support payments have been used as a means of punishment, reward and control. If the NRP does not approve of a behavior by the RP, they may withhold payments in order to

Deadbeat vs. Deadbroke

"punish" them. Payments might be made on a timely basis and without dispute if the NRP hasn't felt hassled recently. Either way, they are both forms of manipulative behavior and are attempts at controlling a situation and the RP. Whatever the reasons the NRP may have for engaging in such manipulations, it is wrong and the RP and children should not become a part of it. In my last two books, "1-800-Deadbeat: How to Collect your Child Support" and "Deadbeats, What Responsible Parents need to know about Collecting Child Support", I wrote that a RP should immediately get a child support award from the court system following the break-up of a love relationship (separation, divorce or otherwise), or when a child is born out of wedlock. Generally, my thoughts have not changed, except that I will now add some exceptions to that rule.

Keep in mind that there will always be men like Larry. He was a good, responsible and loving father to the end. He loved his son, did not take a back seat when it came to parenting and supported his child sufficiently. He was not the type of man who hastily tied up his tennis shoes as the color on the pregnancy stick slowly turned blue or ran to his computer to change usernames and passwords on the bank accounts when his significant other mentioned the possibility of a separation or divorce. You will be in the best position to know if the father of your child will be more like Doug, from my Marsha and Doug example or whether he will be more like Larry. Remember Doug and Larry both entered into *voluntary agreements* with their ex's. Doug's ex ended up chasing him because he did not come through, but Larry paid every month and his ex could depend on the check arriving on time. How can you tell?

Unless your pregnancy was the result of a fling, you should know the father of your child better than anyone. You are probably familiar with his moods and the character traits that he has presented. Ask yourself – is he self-centered or selfish? A bit on the narcissistic side? You have been warned. Does he tend to listen to and believe whatever his parents say...and they never liked you to begin with? You have been warned. Are his locker-room buddies/boardroom buddies behind on their own child support payments or always complaining that they have to pay? You have been warned. Yes, there will always be the good guys – the dads who do the right thing. Those are the dads who would never let their child go without and who would choose to send $50 of their last $100 to their child's mother for a pair of badly needed sneakers, rather than to keep it all to himself. They are out there and they make great fathers, not just because they take their responsibilities to financially support seriously but because they also take their responsibility to parent seriously. Be careful not to paint all NRP's with a broad brush, but do take a close look at what you might be dealing with.

This means that the RP has the responsibility to be smart about all of this. It is your responsibility. I now advocate that a "kitchen table" conversation be considered at the very least prior to running down to the court to file any paperwork. If you could get the NRP "on board" with child support payments, then great. Having this conversation is not different than two attorneys hammering it out prior to a divorce. It has to be hammered out one way or the other and **if** it's possible for the parents to do it and come up with a fair and appropriate child support payment, then everyone benefits. Before any kitchen table conversation can happen however, you must prepare yourself. A RP should not accept just any old number thrown at them simply because you are at the table. You must know what your monthly expenses are expressly for your child and you must know what your household monthly expenses are. A portion of the household expenses which your child consumes can be claimed under child support guidelines. Find the formula which your state uses to calculate child support (there is a list of states and their formulas later). Once you have listed all of your expense items and calculated related child support figures according to your states formula, then it's time to double-check your work, ensuring that all "T's" have been crossed and "I's" has been dotted. You are now ready to invite your child's NRP to the table. There is a method to all of this madness…a strategy in it all - if you will, and if navigating the child support process and getting what you need for your child requires anything at all, it certainly requires strategy…and "know how."

19

Deadbeat vs. Deadbroke

The mistake that a lot of residential and non-residential parents alike make when establishing child support orders is that they really don't know how much money it takes to care for, raise and support the child or children. It leads to misunderstandings, disappointments and anger. Lots and lots of anger. The RP may become angered because often they feel that they are left holding the bag. If not enough money was ordered to be paid (or offered at a kitchen table conversation) then unless the RP has enough resources on their own (or be willing to take a second or a third job or dip into their savings or retirements accounts) to take up the slack that the other parent rightfully should be providing, the child suffers because there is not enough money to go around to cover items such as living expenses, school expenses, medical coverage and heath related bills, clothes, food...you get the picture. The NRP is angered because he/she does not have a full understanding of what is needed and they wonder if the money that they are sending to the RP every month is being squandered. They may ask themselves – "Why does a child need more than $300 a month"? They may have an idea of where the money goes but until the numbers get broken down into line items and is in front of them, most NRP's are clueless. I've heard some NRP's remark that the entire child support check is being spent on personal items for the RP, like salon treatments and new clothes. This is not to say that this never happens because of course there are some irresponsible RP's out there. In my experience however, that is not usually the case. A study of non-payment (fathers) demonstrated by Kenneth Eckhard and written about in *"Divided Children"* showed that if women and their children had to live on what they actually received in support, only 3 percent of them would be above the federal poverty line. One third of women separated from their husbands go on public welfare. Women and children thus bear the normal economic brunt of divorce (separation, never married), and one researcher concluded that even though the average divorced father's real income drops 10 percent, his needs are reduced, so he really is better off financially.

I am not claiming that if you have a kitchen table conversation that it will work for you...or even that they should take place at the actual kitchen table. You can meet at the coffee shop, a friend's house or even over "Skype" or some other free video-conferencing service. Some parents will "get it" after the numbers have been laid out for them, and some won't. Some won't care what the numbers look like and will find any and every reason that they can to avoid paying up. If that happens to you, don't fret because the purpose of this book is to provide you with all of your options so that you and your children won't be left in the lurch. *Voluntary agreements* will not work for everyone. By the end of this chapter you will have a better idea of what your expenses are as a result of being a RP. If you are offered an amount that is not fair and you are not able to renegotiate it with the NRP, you can then decide what is in your best interest – whether you should accept it or go to court. If at any time you have reason to believe that the NRP will not provide you with agreed upon payments on which you can rely, you should always get court-ordered payments. Period. Not wanting to trust your financial future to someone who may or may not pay your child's support on time is a sound reason to go through the court system. Once you have finished reading this book, you will know how to pursue someone who has not paid their child support to you and there are lots of sound reasons for preferring to have your payments sent directly to you and bypassing the "system".

Many parents do not understand the difference between a basic child support order and a child support order in which the parent received requested deviations from the basic order and thus more money for necessities such as extra-curriculars, additional health care costs, work-related child care, etc. The list which follows will help you to determine what your child's needs are and what amount of money is necessary to meet them. Usually people forget the little things that add up to great sums of money in the end, such as weekly allowances, school lunches, and school trips. Then there are things that sometimes are not considered in the first place, but should be; for example, life insurance on the NRP. The list provided will help you to determine what you spend, or will be spending, in an average month to care for your child. Go through the list on the following pages and fill in the blanks as they

21

apply to you – but first, a word or two about basic child support obligations and deviations...

Child support payments cover the basics – including but not limited to important items such as food, clothing, and shelter...Lifestyle choices are secondary but can be seen as equally important. Some parents may want their children to play sports or take music lessons or attend private school and these items can be factored into the child support agreement as well. Presumably we all want what's best for our children but that happens to be a very individual thought process as well as very specific to what benefits the child would have had if the parents remained together. That is why it is crucial that you understand what is allowed under child support guidelines, where a parent can ask for a "deviation" from the guidelines, and what you can expect kitchen from the process. It is only then (not before and hopefully not after) that you initiate your kitchen table conversation. Example: if the RP is going to be a working parent, this is important to know and to factor into the process because more than likely unless that topic is raised, work-related day care or child care or babysitting will not be factored into a basic child support agreement, even though it is allowable. If your kitchen table conversation fails, you will already have the tools in place (because you have already done your research and your work) to move forward with a case in court. This research and work prior to filing your case is something which needs to be done even if you plan to bypass the kitchen table conversation and go straight to court because if you are filing pro sé (representing yourself) the courts will NOT be able to aid you in your case. They will not give you the guidelines or explain to you about deviations or listen to you drone on about how you want your child to attend private school. More often than not, in many areas, they won't even give you the appropriate paperwork to take home and *think* about the information that you need to provide. They expect you to complete the paperwork right then and there in front of them, or in a waiting room, within your time slot allotted, with other people, screaming babies and toddlers running all around you. No pressure, right? Who can think clearly under those circumstances? Not to worry though, we are going to cover how to get a fair deal when the courts are trying to pressure you so that they can get on to their next client. In all fairness, though I have painted a less than wonderful picture of that process, you really can't blame the people behind the bullet-proofed windows because these people are swamped. This gives you more reason to educate yourself about your rights or the process you are involved in or it will be an undertaking.

I have seen cases when a residential parent was granted $40 a week for child support (or offered $40 a week by the NRP and then accepted it). Before you agree that any offer is a fair offer, do your due diligence. Usually people forget the little things that add up to great sums of money in the end - such as school lunches, school trips, haircuts...Then there are things that sometimes are not considered in the first place, but should be. For example, there may be extra medical expenses that are not covered by an insurance plan, or if you have a sick child, an endless amount of co-pays which adds up to hundreds of dollars a month. The following exercise will help you to determine what you spend, or will be spending in an average month to care for your child. Go through the list and check off the boxes as they apply to you. Then in the space provided, enter the amount that you pay for each on a monthly basis. For those items which you don't buy monthly per se` but consistently (like clothes for your child), take the amount that you spent over the past year (hopefully you have receipts or can dig out your bank and/or credit card records), average it out and use that number. Keeping yourself organized around these money issues is going to be extremely important throughout the child support process. You have to prove that you are spending the money or will need to spend the money, that the money is necessary; and that's just to get a fair amount awarded – whether it's through the courts or via a kitchen table conversation. If you should ever have to go after your money because it's not being paid (in the case of a voluntary agreement), then you will have to prove this all over again to a court of law in order to receive a proper judgment. This process will not end until your child has graduated from college and you have collected every last cent of your money.

Deadbeat vs. Deadbroke

To get you excited about the possibility of a successful kitchen table conversation, let me share with you the true story of popular radio personality Michael Baisden. Baisden, who was divorced from his wife with a young daughter, was quoted as saying that if he had known how much money that his ex-wife needed to spend to support their daughter every month, he would have gladly paid her more child support much sooner. It took a kitchen table conversation, initiated by his ex-wife, for him to understand that the basic child support amount that he regularly paid was just not sufficient. Upon seeing the numbers for himself, he volunteered to increase the amount he was paying.

Child-Related Expenses Checklist

Rent/Mortgage   _____

House/Apt. insurance   _____

Taxes on home where child resides   _____

Water/Sewer   _____

*Repairs on home where child resides   _____

Gas/Electric   _____

Phone   _____

Garbage   _____

Food   _____

Household supplies   _____

Clothes – for the child   _____

Laundry/*Dry cleaning – for the child   _____

*Clothing repair – for the child   _____

Car payment – if the car is used to transport
     the child anywhere   _____

Car insurance – if the car is used to transport
     the child anywhere   _____

*Car repair - if the car is used to transport
     the child anywhere   _____

Public transportation – if you do not own a car   _____

Day care – if it is "work-related"   _____

Baby-sitters – if they are "work-related"   _____

Child-Related Expenses Checklist (contd.)

Medical insurance payments _____

**Health care not covered under medical

insurance plan (co-pays, deductibles…) _____

Dental visits _____

Vision visits _____

Prescriptions _____

***Private school tuition _____

School supplies _____

School trips _____

School lunches _____

***Dance, music lessons, etc. Extracurricular

activities _____

Barber/Beauty shop _____

***Religious affiliation fees _____

***Religious Schooling _____

***Books/Magazines (other than school supplies) _____

***Pets _____

***Vacation _____

**Gifts to others _____

***Allowance _____

Total: _____

*In some states the RP must meet a minimum threshold for health care not covered under medical insurance plans before the non-residential parent is required to contribute. The median amount for most states with this threshold is $250.

**These items would have to be recurring items which can be calculated on a yearly basis so that a fair and reasonable amount could be added to the child support order. They are not normally added into the basic child support award but the guidelines allow for deviations to include them if they make sense and if you can prove your case in court by demonstrating necessity and a history of previous payments.

***These items relate to lifestyle. Not all families are accustomed to providing private school tuition, enrichment activities, or religious affiliations which come with a fee. Not all families want to provide these "extras" for their children or deem them to be necessary. However if these extras were the norm prior to the divorce or break-up or if based on your own personal lifestyles it would make sense that your child would participate and enjoy the enrichments, extras and the benefits which some parents feel come with private or religious schooling, etc, then you have a case for child support deviations in court to have these items included in your child support order.

Now that you have a better idea of what expenses you incur as you raise your child, you may not want to jump at the first offer of financial support you get. At the same time, it does not give you the right to pad your expenses to try to get more money either. I've see that happen too. Besides, knowing your expenses is only a starting point. You have to know what to do when you have the information. The first thing you must do when you are ready to file for child support is to decide whether you want to handle your case yourself or if you want to get a lawyer or to have the state to work your case for you. However you decide to handle it, the procedures remain the same. The only difference is that you retain complete control of your case if you do it yourself, but you will also have more legwork to do on your own. If the state handles your case, you end up at their mercy while they work the case on your behalf. It can be slow and since they are the ones who will be filing motions with the courts, you will largely remain in the dark and will have to push them to advise you of any progress made. You can at any time decide to change paths if you choose a method that does not seem to work for you. If you have decided to let the agency collect your support, you can take the case back from them at any time (provided that you are not on welfare), and vice versa. The methods that you use to enforce your child support order can remain the same regardless of who collects the money.

Which path should you use? It's a personal choice and only you can make that decision. If you want complete control of your case and don't mind some of the headaches along the way, collect your support on your own. If you don't mind giving up control of your case and would rather if someone else did most of the legwork for you, even if it does take forever and a day; then let the agency work on your behalf or hire an attorney, if you can afford one and if you can find one whom you can trust who will work swiftly and will get the job done sooner rather than later and will keep you informed every step of the way. Most people do opt to have the state child support agencies collect their support for them, mostly because they do not know that they can do it themselves and they wouldn't know how. This book should change both concerns. Keep in mind that it is your choice and you can change your mind at any time. If you are working with an attorney, you can still receive benefits from the state agency. Likewise, if you are handling your case on your own you can receive benefits from the agencies. Many RP's are routinely told that they cannot have it both ways, but that is not true. Be sure to speak with someone who knows – your caseworker may not.

The first thing that you must do when you are ready to file on your own (pro sé / self-represent) for child support is to locate the family court in your area which handles such proceedings (if you want the child support agency to file for you, then locate the nearest child support agency). Every state has several child support enforcement agencies and family courts that are obligated, by law, to help you obtain a child support award. The child support agencies are also obligated to enforce your child support order once you get one but remember that they will control all filings and procedures and most of the time, simply provide you with "updates". You will be informed on things such as when you need to appear in court but you will most likely not be informed of anything going on behind the scenes. Any paperwork they collect or any information about the absent parent they obtain will not be provided to you as a matter of course. I wish that I could just tell you the name of the agency or the court division to make it easier for you but they are named differently across the country. If you have a difficult time finding the correct office (being misdirected seems to be a rite of passage), a fail proof method is to call your local welfare agency and ask them for the proper address and phone number for your filing purposes. Be sure to be clear about your method (whether you are looking for the family court to file pro sé (self-representing) or whether you are looking for the child support agency to file on your behalf. Don't let this make you nervous. The only reason I suggest this is because while the child support agencies and the welfare agencies are not directly related, they do work together at times. The reason is because many RP's end up on welfare because the NRP does not pay child support. In fact, most of the families receive the benefit because they have not been able to collect.

Once you have made your decision concerning how you want to collect your child support and how much control of your case you want to have or not, the next step will be to have a court date assigned. In some areas a hearing officer or a magistrate rather than a judge will hear the child support case, but it could be either. You and the absent parent will be notified of when you must appear in court, and when you do, an Order of Support will be entered. Child support that is ordered will be retroactive to the date that you filed your motion in the family division of court or at the child support agency, and sometimes that could be a month or two. That means that the absent parent will owe you for several months already! For example, let us assume that you filed a motion for child support on July 1, and you finally got your day in court on August 15th. If the hearing officer awarded you $75 a week in child support, the absent parent would now owe you six weeks of child support, or $450! So if you are going to file for financial support for your child, the sooner you do it, the better. If you can sense that I am clapping my hands excitedly and reaching my fist out so that we can "fist bump" together, you would be correct- and non-apologetically, I might add. Let me explain. If a RP has been saddled with the responsibility of financially supporting (and mentally and emotionally and physically...I might add) a child or children on their own because the other parent has yet to step up to the plate, then they deserve to be "reimbursed" for the other parent's share. The retroactive child support does just that. It's not giving the RP anything that he or she does not deserve...or has not paid out of their pocket already. The retroactive child support is a small victory for a RP and gives a small bit of hope that from this moment on maybe the situation will improve.

How child support is calculated

Before 1988, judges had considerable discretion when formulating child support awards. Because of that, wealthy NRP's sometimes paid very little, and poor NRP's sometimes were ordered to pay more than their monthly income. The biggest tragedy, however, was that in most instances child support awards were inadequate to meet the true cost of raising children. Thankfully, in 1988, federal *legislation* was passed (Family Support Act), which ordered all states to establish a guideline for determining child support. This helps child support awards to be more fair and realistic. Every state was ordered to adopt one of three formulas. The chosen formula was a guideline, however, and if you can prove that the amount you would receive as a result is insufficient, you may be able to get a higher amount through deviations from the guidelines.

Formula #1 Income Shares

The Income Shares Formula considers the income of both parents and assumes that they will equally share the costs of raising their child together. The goal is to base the support on the concept that the child should receive the same level of financial support that he would have received if the parents lived together. The income of both parents is combined. A chart listing the support amount for that level of income is checked. The support amount that each parent pays is then prorated according to his or her income. Thirty-three states, Guam and the Virgin Islands use this formula. The following is a complete list of states that have adopted the income shares model:

Alabama	Arizona	California
Colorado	Connecticut	Florida
Idaho	Indiana	Iowa
Kansas	Kentucky	Louisiana
Maine	Maryland	Michigan
Missouri	Nebraska	New Hampshire
New Jersey	New York	North Carolina
Ohio	Oklahoma	Oregon
Pennsylvania	Rhode Island	South Carolina
South Dakota	Utah	Vermont
Virginia	West Virginia	Washington

An example based on the income shares formula is listed below:

RP's monthly earnings	$823.00
NRP's monthly earnings	$2,650.00
Combined earnings total	$3,473.00
Percentage of RP's share	23.7%
Percentage of NRP's share	76.3%
Child support OBLIGATION	$488.00
Work-related child care costs	
(a deviation from the basic guidelines)	$170.00
Total child support obligation	$658.00

Deadbeat vs. Deadbroke

Formula #2 Percent of Income Formula

The Percent of Income Formula uses only the NRP's income to determine a child support award. It is the easiest method to use since all that is done is a simple mathematical deduction. For example, Wisconsin deducts 17 percent of a NRP's gross income for support of one child. That figure increases slightly for each additional child. In Tennessee, however, the percentage is 18 percent and it is deducted from the NRP's net income, and, as in Wisconsin, the percentage increases slightly with each additional child. (Gross income is the amount of salary that a person receives before taxes are taken out, and net income is the amount of money that a person is left with after taxes are deducted).

The states that use the percentage of income formula are:

Alaska	Arkansas	District of Columbia (Washington, D.C.)
Georgia	Illinois	Minnesota
Mississippi	Nevada	North Dakota
Puerto Rico	Tennessee	Texas
Wisconsin		

Formula # 3 Melson Formula

Only three states have chosen to adopt the Melson Formula. Unlike the other two guideline types, the Melson formula sets aside a "self-support reserve" for each parent before determining their ability to pay. What it does is allow each parent to subtract the dollar amount from their salary that is needed to keep them at poverty level before child support payments are considered. Once each parent's reserve amount is calculated and subtracted from their salary, child support can then be determined. The three states that use the Melson Formula are:

Delaware	Hawaii	Montana

Once you have listed your expenses, have run your numbers and have a solid estimation of what your basic child support award will be, (including any deviations which you might ask the court to include), such as work-related child care and college expenses just to mention two, you might consider approaching the NRP.

Before you do that, keep in mind a few things:

1. Deviations often are calculated at a different rate. The judge, magistrate or hearing officer may decide to call it 50/50 or he or she may decide to calculate it at the same rate which was used to determine the child support.

2. You will want to read this book from cover to cover before you have any kitchen table conversations, complete any applications for child support or speak with an attorney. The reason is because there will be information throughout this book which you may want to consider regarding your case and you don't want to jump the gun, as they say, and act before you have all of the information that you may need. Remember, winning your case for your children will be about information and strategy.

3. Always remain as calm, cool, and collected as you can. It may be very difficult at times, especially when you want to shout your head off or wring somebody's neck. You will always get more honey away from the bee if you do not kick the beehive.

Deciding to have a kitchen table conversation with the NRP can be a nerve-wracking thing to do, especially if the two of you are not on the best of terms. You could also simply be nervous about the whole thing and blow it because you forget what you want to say or can't seem to find the words which seem appropriate. Because of this, I have created a "script" that you can use in this situation. You don't have it use it but it's a good way to get the conversation started if you are not sure how to do it. Feel free to use all of it, parts of it or none of it all, but I have always found that that it's good to have your talking points in order.

Deadbeat vs. Deadbroke

A kitchen table conversation might go like this:

RP: I would like for us to go over the expenses which will be incurred for (child's name). I have made a list of regularly occurring basic expenses such as food, clothing, rent/mortgage, health insurance payments, as well as expenses which occur less frequently such as medical co-pays and deductibles, eye-glasses when they are lost, broken or otherwise need replacement, payments for sports teams, etc. Let's look at your income and mine and try to come up with a fair agreement between us.

NRP: You don't trust me? You don't trust that I will take care of my own children? I don't need you to tell me how to take care of my kids.

RP: It's not that I don't trust you; I just think that it will be easier this way because we will both know what is expected of the other and we don't have to waste our time guessing about it. Meanwhile, it's better for (children's names) because we will both know that they are being provided for and that we have both been a part of that decision making. It's for everybody's protection. I want you to feel that you are a part of the process and that I am not the only one making decisions and I want to feel secure knowing that my financial future has been protected. I don't want to have any misunderstandings.

NRP: What is this really about? You know that I have always been there for you and for the children.

RP: I just want to make sure that we have as little to argue about as possible. I am sure that we will not agree on everything. I am sure that there will be times that we are stressed out – we do not need to argue about something as silly as money. I would rather not ask you for money when the children need something. If I have adequate and regular support coming in, I will be able to budget accordingly.

The guidelines work well for most people if the amount turns out to cover everything your child needs…(AND if both parents come to the table honestly submitting information on income…*all* means of income, assets, occupations, current addresses, etc. If the NRP does not come forth with information or come forth themselves, the RP can *serve* him/her with papers requiring them to produce what is needed). Frequently, parents forget what they spend on their children. If you have already gone through the process and received a child support order that you feel is too low because you have forgotten too many items, were never told to include certain items in the first place (which happens very often) or maybe you learned that the NRP was not honest about their income initially; you can try to get your child support order *modified*. Chapter 5 deals with modifying child support orders.

Here are a few items which parents tend to overlook when they are making their lists. By no means is this list conclusive, you have to look at your own family situation and circumstances and be prepared to prove your case for each item. Some are usually seen and some may not be such as if your child requires special needs for a wheelchair, for example:

- Mental health visits
- Medical care not covered by insurance (co-pays, deductibles)
- Dental care
- Eye glasses
- Braces
- Accommodations for special needs

Two items which require special attention are healthcare and life insurance.

Health Care

It should be made clear in any agreements made who is the responsible party for providing health insurance coverage for the child. Typically the NRP covers the child through a qualified *medical child support order.* This requires that the employer's group health care plan provide health coverage for the child. The employer can charge the NRP for any premiums.

Life Insurance

Many parents overlook the importance of having life insurance written into their agreements. If a tragedy were to occur and the NRP parent were to die prematurely, it could launch their children into poverty. Usually the court will order the parent who pays support to obtain the policy on himself or herself to ensure that payments can continue for the benefit of the children. Look at it as "child support insurance". It may be something that the RP has to request. In some states it's automatic and they "get it" and in some states you have to ask for it and be prepared to prove the need. The best way to do this is to either have the RP listed as the beneficiary of the policy since they are the ones who will be raising the children and have the need for the income or to name the children as the beneficiaries but the RP as the adult custodian of the policy.

Duration of the order

Child support awards are not final. They can and should be reviewed every two years. All three guideline formulas recognize that children become more expensive as they grow older, so the two-year review period allows for the RP to request an increase. Likewise, if there is a change in circumstances where, for example, the NRP received a windfall through a raise or otherwise increased his or her income, the child support order can be changed. Chapter 5 will cover the ground on modifications.

There is no one particular age when a child support order expires. Just as there are different state guidelines which determine how child support is calculated, each state has their own guideline as to when child support ends. Some states say that it ends at the legal adult age of 18. Some states say that it ends at the age of 22 – as long as the child is a full-time student, and there are varying ages in between and beyond with varying reasons.

Check my website www.dontgetmadgetpaid.com for a listing of states and their emancipation rules.

The old okie doke

You've all heard of the "old okie doke", haven't you? That's the stuff that you shouldn't fall for when folks try to pull something over on you. Here are three okie dokes to be aware of…

- <u>The default okie doke</u> - Sometimes NRP's think (and sometimes they will tell the RP parent this to frighten them) that if they don't show up for court, that they can get away with facing a child support award against them. They will say that they didn't receive the paperwork and make up all kinds of other stories and believe – or try to make the RP believe that they can get away with this game. All states require that the *respondent* or *defendant* (depending on the paperwork that you are looking at) be provided with a certain time limit in order to respond to the claims against him or her in the child support petition. If the respondent (or defendant) does not respond and does not appear, a *default judgment* can be entered against him or her which means that the RP would automatically win the case. Notice that I said that the judgment *can* be entered and not *will*. Most times those considering child support cases automatically enter defaults without being asked to but sometimes you have to actually ask. Sometimes, unless you ask for it in your initial petition, it will not be granted. My clients know to cover all bases and to ask for the default in the event of a "no-show".
- <u>The procrastination okie doke</u> – There are some NRP's who never show up with the proper paperwork and never respond to court requests for *discovery*, yet they insist that they do not have the income and assets that you suggest that they do and they cannot make the payments which you request. They make it

very difficult for the judge to come to a fair and appropriate conclusion for the child support matter...and they know that. The court has the power to give you an order for temporary relief while your child support order is pending. You will have to prove your case (prove your child's need) and prove that the NRP can pay but you can receive this by making a formal request.

- The IRS tax exemption okie doke – For income tax purposes, the only parent legally able to claim the child(ren) as exemptions is the parent with primary custody and who the child lives with most and who supports the child most financially. Simply being a parent who pays child support is not enough according to the IRS. I know that there are many parents who are splitting that privilege but according to the IRS and they are the ones who make the rules on this, not the family court – the family court just follows them – or should anyway. If the RP agrees to allow the NRP parent to have the deduction, they must complete a special form – IRS form 8332 and submit it to the IRS along with their tax statement for Uncle Sam's approval.

HOT TIPS FOR PARENTS

If you want to have the child support agency file your case on your behalf, call and ask that they mail the application to you. There is a federal law that states that, as of October 1993, applications must be provided within five days if they are mailed or upon request if you visit the office. Keep in mind though that if you choose to pick up the application, depending on the agency, they may not allow you to take it home and complete it.

The following insider tips for caseworkers and attorneys may be valuable to you as well, especially if you will be filing pro sé or simply want to stay on top of things with your caseworker or your attorney, if you have one.

HOT TIPS FOR CASEWORKERS

It may be helpful to request that your client provide the following information at the first meeting rather than requiring that they provide it later. It's basic information but it will get your clients moving in the right directions.

Intake documentation:

1. Birth certificates for each child

2. Your identification

3. Your Social Security Number

4. Child's Social Security Number

5. Other parent's Social Security Number

6. Last known address of other parent

7. Last known employer of other parent

8. Any information about assets owed by the other parent

9. As many current photos as you can find of the other parent

If paternity has not been established, additional intake information clients should also provide:

1. Records of any money the NRP has given to your client for the child

2. Records of any gifts that the NRP has given the child

HOT TIPS FOR ATTORNEYS

In addition to the intake information:

- Prepare your clients. Tell them that when they enter that courtroom that they are really on stage. As their attorney, you are orchestrating a production – as is your adversary. He who puts on the best show, wins. It's not a dramatic Shakespearian production about death, but it sure is something quite close to it. It is dramatic and it is about life.
- Remind your clients that the filing of a child support case means that they are essentially suing the other parent. People don't like to get sued and sometimes they tend react negatively. Steel them for the onslaught which may occur.

If you are looking for suitable language for the health insurance provision, try this:

_____ (NRP name) shall obtain suitable health care coverage through an employer for the most reasonable cost, for minor children _____ (children's names). Out of pocket health care costs which are not covered by insurance will be prorated according to the states guideline of percentage of income, which is currently 70% for _____ (name of parent) and 30% for _____ (name of parent). These payments shall be made within 30 days of the presenting of the bill to either party. Both parties must promptly execute and deliver any documents to ensure timely payments of insurance claims, medical bills or reimbursements to the other party for medical bills paid. In the event that the paying party fails to maintain insurance, that party must pay all health care expenses for the child.

I also suggest that you consider including language for confession of an automatic judgment if the paying party does not pay up within the 30 day period. You know your jurisdiction and whether there's a good chance that it will fly. I have many clients who have used it successfully.

If you are looking for suitable language for the life insurance provision, try this:

For the duration of the child support order, _____ (name of NRP) will obtain and maintain suitable coverage in the amount of _____. The beneficiary of the policy shall be the minor child(ren) _____ (names), with _____ (RP name) listed as the adult custodian of such polices. The NRP will provide the RP with a copy of the policy and annual proof of payment of the premiums.

chapter 3:

the importance of paternity testing: what both parents need to know

Statistics:

According to the Office of Child Support Enforcement Report FY 2012:

- One out of every four children born in the United States is born out of wedlock.
- Only 25 percent of RP's parents who were not married at the time of their child (ren)'s birth obtain court-ordered child support.
- 75 percent of RP's who *were married* to the NRP parent at the time of their child (ren)'s birth obtain child support orders.

According to the research study "Measuring Paternal Discrepancy and its Public Health Consequences" by the *"Journal of Epidemiology and Community Health"*, 2010; 59; 749-754:

- Three out of ten of alleged fathers are not the biological father at all. (*that's 30%*)
- Approximately 300,000 of these paternity tests are performed every year.
- Approximately 90,000 men are falsely accused and held responsible for children who are not theirs and for child support payments.

According to the Office of Child Support Enforcement Report FY 2012:

- Over $110 **BILLION** currently owed in past due child support
- 11.3 **million** parents (mostly women) are owed past due child support
- 17.4 **million** children are affected

❖ It is estimated that over 50% of parents who have a child support order as a part of their divorce decree (they are pro sé in court, have volunteer agreements or work with an attorney) do not make applications to their local child support agency and many of them are owed current and back support, which make these statistics much higher.

❖ These statistics do not take into account parents who have given birth out of wedlock and have not sought a child support order through the agency, though they are entitled to the support.

What do these statistics suggest? They suggest that we have a lot of problems. We have moms who are naming the wrong men as biological fathers of their children, sometimes purposely and sometimes not. We have men who have been named fathers who are not the fathers and are paying child support and men who have been named as fathers who ARE the fathers and have *not* been paying child support. For the sake of simplicity, for now we will focus on those parents who are not paying child support. For now, it does not matter whether they deny paternity or not. Another okie doke to be familiar with is the – (using my best TV talk-show host, "Maury" voice) I am <u>NOT</u> the father – in hopes of being able to avoid child support payments. Paternity testing is always available to named fathers if they truly want to know the truth about the paternity of a child if they have been named. If a named dad fell for the *other* okie doke – the you ARE the father – from a mom desperately in need of a father to give to her child (and maybe to collect child support too) have him to check my website www.dontgetmadgetpaid.com for a full state by state listing of *paternity disestablishment* guidelines. Each state has procedures and guidelines on becoming free of such an entanglement. Later in this chapter there will be more about how both men and women can avoid getting themselves into the sticky paternity mess to begin with. It is much easier to avoid the problem than it is to try to repair the problem. For now, we will focus on the non-payors of child support and how, if they have made a game of it, how to beat them at their own game fair and square. First, I want to share with you how dad Larry from Chapter 2 fared in his paternity fraud case.

Remaining consistent to the end, Larry decided that while he knew and understood that he had been swindled by the woman he thought had given birth to his child; he did not want to consider any possibility of a paternity fraud case. This case was many years ago and as of this writing there remains to be no laws on the books which provide relief to men who have been taken advantage of by unscrupulous women. The phrase 'paternity fraud" has been coined and there are a lot of angry (and rightfully so) men out there. I expect that soon there will be some bit of legislation written expressly for cases like these. For now, the law assumes that named fathers will protect themselves by requesting paternity tests if they are not married to the mother at the time of conception. Larry did consult with an attorney and the attorney explained all of this to him. He also explained that Larry could nonetheless file a civil lawsuit against the "mother" and sue her for fraud. Suing her for fraud would be a way around the law, allowing him to possibly recoup the nine years of child support without a law being on the books specifically designed for that purpose. Larry reasoned that suing the mother and winning his case would only bring financial distress upon the boy he had come to love and to call his "son". Instead, Larry wanted only to carry on and continue to be a part of the boy's life – just as he had for the past nine years.

"Tiffany" (not her real name), the boy's mother, had her own idea of how things should proceed. She hired an attorney and had a letter sent to Larry demanding that he continue to pay child support as he had for the previous nine years. The letter continued on to inform Larry that because he is not the biological father of the boy, that he had absolutely no parental rights. He could no longer make decisions on his behalf, he would no longer be consulted for his thoughts and opinions and he could no longer have visitation rights but because he had *"held himself out"* (represented himself) as the boy's father for nine years and because the boy had no other father in his life, Tiffany was making the case that it was in the best interest of the boy that child support continue. This was from the same woman who initiated a successful kitchen table conversation nine years before. Major Drama. As you might imagine, Larry was sick and beside himself. He also did not have a leg to stand on. Maybe he could have then sued to be named as the *"psychological parent"* or the *"de facto parent"* of this child and thereby regain his visitation and the right to be a part of his life. Who knows if he would have won his case? What he did know is that the situation was a mess and likely to turn into an even bigger mess. In the end, he did what she really wanted him to do...he walked away...with a broken heart and tens of thousands of dollars poorer.

Larry's story underscores some of the reasons that establishing paternity is not to be overlooked. Other reasons point to the RP's whose past due child support dollars are reflected in the statistics above and what can be done to get them paid. The reasons are endless…sending kids to camp, being able to buy new sneakers when they are needed, and assuring that the lights turn on when they flick the switch in their house after school…

Once we are done with our reasons and the "why's" that it is so important to know and understand your rights and responsibilities of paternity and paternity testing, we can move on to parents receiving fair and appropriate child support awards and enforcing them. We can discuss the details of teaching RP's the fine art of how to determine if the NRP is a deadbeat (and if so how to pursue him or her) or if he or she is really just deadbroke and couldn't give their child a dollar if they wanted to. There is a difference. Some NRP's shirk the system, their responsibilities and their children in the process. Some NRP's are having a hard time getting by. There are ways and means and methods to manage both and it always begins with paternity. Who is responsible for these children?

Marriage

If a woman was married at the time of her child's birth, the law assumes that her husband is the father of her child. We all know (or have heard) that sometimes this is not the case. Unless we want to begin to discuss the lives of people of which reality TV is born, for the sake of simplicity, let's just say that this is so. In this case, there are no paternity issues. Paternity is established by law at the time of birth. I have known some cases where a father has questioned paternity of a child while in the middle of divorce proceedings. I do not personally know of any cases where it was found that he was not the father, although I am sure that it has happened. In fact, a friend told me recently that it happened in her family not too long ago.

Deadbeat vs. Deadbroke

Unmarried

If a woman was not married to her child's father at the time of birth, she will need to establish paternity in order to receive court-ordered child support. This means that she will have to prove who fathered the baby. Child support payments can always be paid voluntarily by the father (and hopefully established via a kitchen table conversation) but as discussed in Chapter 2, it may not be recommended in some cases. I knew of a father who paid child support to his ex-girlfriend based on a voluntary agreement that they made. According to him, they did not need a formal order. "Whatever their daughter needed, their daughter received". While that sounds very wonderful, I always wondered if they really split their child's expenses fairly. The mother had custody of the child and lived in a different state. Even with court-ordered child support awards, the RP usually ends up taking on the lion's share of the load. I don't want to diminish this father's loving participation in the raising of his daughter at all. In my experience, however, unless some real numbers have been raised and reviewed, whenever a number gets pulled out of thin air because it sounds "about right" or the parents choose a "whenever a needs arises it's fulfilled" philosophy, instead of a budget which has been pre-ordained, someone (and usually it's the RP) gets the short end of the stick. Does it happen all of the time? I bet not. Does it happen frequently? You betcha.

On the other hand, I know and have known many fathers throughout the years who bent over backwards to do much more than their fair share. There are several ways in which to establish paternity and as mentioned in Chapter 2 - it's a personal judgment call about *how* you do it and only the parties involved can make that call. My only suggestion is that you consider it carefully and choose the option which works best for you and your circumstances.

Why establish paternity?

Establishing paternity is important to everyone involved. It gives everyone rights; mom, dad and the children alike. Remember Larry? In the end, Larry found that he did not have any rights whatsoever. Don't be like Larry.

- **Identity:** It's important for everyone to know who they are and where they came from. Our ancestry creates us both genetically and culturally. We are the sum totals of our ancestor's genetics.
- **Health:** Medical histories are important. Knowing whether your father and the men on your father's side of the family have a history of prostate cancer can possibly be a life or death situation. Also consider that some non-life-threatening medical conditions are genetic. What if your child develops a condition that neither the mother nor the named father as? Imagine the horror of an emergency room visit for your child which leads to the discovery that his or her blood type is not possible with the blood types of mom and named father. Or that the allergies that the child has are genetic but cannot be traced back to either parent on record.
- **Financial support:** Paternity must be established before a child-support order can be entered. There are varying ways to establish paternity, being married to the child's father at the time of birth is only one of them.
- **Parenting time:** Without legal establishment of paternity, a named father does not have any rights to the child (ren) which could make visitation, custody and the ability to make any decisions on the child's behalf, a problem.
- **Benefits:** A child with established parentage is entitled to benefits such as health, inheritance, social security, and veteran's benefits.
- **Public Assistance:** Similar to child support, paternity must be established before parents are able to benefit from some

assistance programs. At the very least, the applying parent must agree to be of aid and assistance to the agency as they attempt to establish paternity of the child.

Three pathways to paternity

Outside of marriage there are three pathways to establishing paternity.

- **Acknowledgement of Paternity (AOP):** I wrote about the easiest way to establish paternity in my first two books; it's during what I call "happy hour." That is when the child is first born and lying in the nursery at the hospital. Cute as a button. The entire family has gathered around and friends have come from near and far to see the new baby. Of course, proud Papa is standing by grinning ear to ear, almost intoxicated by the miracle of it all. (Look what my seed has sprung!) This is the time that most fathers would proudly announce their fatherhood. This is "happy hour". Have him sign the birth certificate then and there. By putting his name on the certificate of birth he is admitting that he has fathered the child. In most states, that will be all a woman needs in a court of law to give her child a "father" without having a DNA test. Along with the birth certificate will come a form probably called an *"Acknowledgement of Paternity (AOP)"*, which must be signed by mother and father and provided to state officials by the hospital, birthing center, midwife or other official uninterested party. Any party to the AOP has 60 days from the date of signing in order to rescind (take back) their acknowledgment. After 60 days, the acknowledgment can no longer be rescinded but it can be challenged on the basis of fraud (lies), duress (force) or mistake of fact. An AOP does not provide for child support, custody or visitation. To receive any of those, one of the parents must make an application to the court. The paternity phase, however, has already been bypassed. The AOP is not a legal document but it is filed with the court system because the named father agreed to the paternity. The child now has an "official" father on record.

- **Paternity Agreed Court Order:** When parents agree about the paternity of their child and want to bypass the DNA testing phase and get straight to setting fair and appropriate child support orders, custody agreements and visitation schedules, they can enter into a paternity-agreed court order through their attorney, child support agency, local DA's or family court office (if they are pro sé). It is an official court filing and the results of a kitchen table conversation can be brought into the court and entered into your agreement or the agreements can be hammered out in court. The Paternity Agreed Court Order is a legal and binding document.

- **Paternity Petition:** If there are any doubts as to the paternity of a child, DNA testing can be ordered through a paternity petition filed with the court. Once the results of the test have been received and it is positive, the named father now becomes the biological father. DNA tests are over 99 percent accurate. Either parent can request a DNA test to prove the proper parentage. If a test is ordered by the court due to a mother's petition and the father does not appear for the test, a default can be entered and the named father can become the biological father with all of the rights and obligations that a biological father has. Items such as child support, visitation, custody and medical support can now be sought.

DNA testing...If the genes don't fit – you must acquit!

There are many different types of tests that can be administered. They involve testing the mother, the named father and sometimes the child too. There are also tests which can be performed in utero, which means while the woman is still pregnant.

- **Chorionic Villus Sampling (CVS):** Is performed by inserting a catheter into the cervix and taking a small sampling of cells from the placenta which formed from the egg when it was fertilized. The cells have the baby's DNA and it can be used for positive DNA testing. This test can only be performed within the first (approximate) 8-14 weeks of pregnancy.

- **Amniocenteses:** A small sample of amniotic fluid is taken with the use of a very long needle and an ultrasound. Like the CVS, this DNA test is just as accurate as a test taken once the baby has been born.

- <u>**A word of caution:** It is my job to provide you with your options; it is your job to decide how to manage your paternity matter. I personally would never have either of these two tests performed because for one reason, I am not a fan of catheters, two – I hate needles and they use very, very long needles and three, because I would be afraid that the test might somehow affect my pregnancy. These tests are not without risk. You might choose to make a different decision. I suppose the reasons you may feel that you need the test are important too. If you think you might want to consider this option, certainly discuss it with your doctor first.</u>

- **Buccal swab sampling:** The most common type of paternity test today, in most states, is a form of DNA *matching* called *buccal swab sampling*. In this procedure, a long Q-tip type stick is rubbed along the inside of the mouth of the mother, the named father, and the child to collect cells which determine DNA. The swabs are sent to a lab, where the DNA of the named father is compared with that of the child in question. This test, along with other genetic procedures that can be performed, can determine fatherhood with up to 99.99 percent accuracy.

- **Other tests:** Other common tests include the blood test, when blood is drawn from both parties, and umbilical cord sampling, where part of the umbilical cord of a newborn is sent in for testing.

These tests are familiar to most people. What the majority of people do not know is that paternity can be proven even if the named father is deceased or has not been seen in years. Let's say that you become pregnant and you and your boyfriend are madly in love and planning to be married even though his family has expressed their strong dislike of you. Before your wedding day, a terrible accident occurs and your boyfriend is killed. You were not married to him so the law cannot assume that he fathered your baby. His family doubts your boyfriend's paternity and will not help with your expenses. Meanwhile, bills are piling up and you do not have anyone to help you. To add insult to injury, your boyfriend was very well off. What do you do? Simple, you either have a *family calculation* study ordered by the court (which tests the named father's family members for matching DNA), or you have *forensic paternity testing* or *abnormal specimen testing* performed. These are tests that can be done at the medical examiner's office before your boyfriend is buried (by emergency court order of course). If he has already been buried, you can order that his body be exhumed (removed from the ground), and tested for DNA matches. Sounds gruesome, I know, but desperate times call for desperate measures. If it will keep your child out of poverty, it is well worth it. Obviously, time would be of the essence, so you'd better act quickly.

Now let us imagine that your boyfriend is not dead, but instead says that he will die before he admits to you or anyone else that he is the father of your baby. In fact, he says he will refuse to take a paternity test so that you cannot prove his fatherhood. Do not let this type of threat keep you from establishing paternity for your child. He is trying to make you believe that if he does not take a test, you cannot prove his fatherhood, or maybe he really believes that himself. The fact of the matter is that you have the law on your side. If you file a paternity petition against the named father, he is legally obligated to show up for the DNA testing. If he does not show, he automatically loses, and you win, by *default*. You have not confirmed that he is the father, but you have won your case by default because he did not show up to defend himself and prove that he is not the father. You can then begin your pursuit for court-ordered child support because of course— a kitchen table conversation is not going to work in this circumstance. The only way the father can get out of having a *judgment* for child support entered against him is if he takes the test and the DNA does not match. This will be the only thing that will prove that he is not the baby's father. So if the named father threatens to refuse testing, do not let it bother you one bit. Just smile, finish reading this book so that you are amply prepared, and complete the paperwork as quickly as you can.

Now let us imagine that you do not know who the father is. You were dating two men at the same time. You slept with guy #1 for the last time three weeks before you slept with guy #2. A month later you are pregnant, and cannot be absolutely sure who the father is. In this case, both men are possible fathers and you will have to have both of them tested. Either that or you can have one of them tested and when the results come back in that he has zero possibility of fathering your child, it's time to call the other father in. Remember, if you have only slept with these two men, one of them will be excluded <u>completely</u> as being the father of the baby, and the other will be proven to be the father. If you lose your paternity case it could mean only one of two things. Either there is third man who needs to be tested, or the lab somehow went awry. You can ask to have the test repeated, but the labs rarely, if ever, make mistakes.

Bombshell Development in Prenatal DNA Testing!!

There is a fairly new testing procedure for DNA testing while pregnant. Not only am I happy to be the first to announce this new procedure nationwide by providing the 4-1-1 but I am so thrilled about this test and the possibilities that I am sponsoring a nationwide bill to ask that *everyone* with a possible contested paternity suit have the opportunity to take the test and have it admissible in court. Let me explain:

- **Non-invasive fetal prenatal DNA testing:** Is a newly developed test in which the pregnant woman's blood is used to gather a sample of the baby's DNA. It is a simple blood test between the mother and the named father. This new method has been reported by the New England Journal of Medicine, is widely available, and would fast forward us all out of the 1970's when the only methods available were the amino and the CVS. It's been over 40 years – we could use new in-utero paternity testing procedures. There are greatly reduced health risks to the mother and unborn baby, and the potentially life-changing benefits of resolving paternity before the baby arrives. Think of how legally identifying the father of the child during pregnancy could change everything. Let's start with - no more paternity fraud. The moment that a man is named as a potential father, with a simple blood test, he could be ruled out. No more child support payments paid to anyone on a fraudulent basis. No more Larry's to discover after nine years that his son is not biologically his. Consider how it could change child support payments for the moms and children who rightfully should receive it and who could begin to receive support earlier because the named father has fewer opportunities to use delay tactics. According to the US Census Bureau, 27 million children in the United States reside in fatherless homes. That's 1 out of every 3. With this bill more children will know who their father is sooner, rather than later. For those men whose tests are positive and they did father a child, it could mean that they begin to take responsibility sooner.

I am so excited about this bill. At the end of this chapter I have included a copy of the petition which will be sent to the White House. At the moment, the court system does not recognize this test so it is not legally admissible. I am going to jump off this soap box now but if you are interested in mailing in a copy of the petition to me to the address listed in the back of this book, please do so. If you want to go online and sign your name in support, that's even better.

If you will be proceeding with DNA testing and have an attorney, he or she will prepare the necessary paperwork to get the tests ordered so that paternity can be established for your child. If you do not have an attorney, you must contact your local *child support enforcement agency*. See the appendices in the back of the book for a listing of these central offices or if you are acting pro sé, you will be filing paperwork through your local family court. Depending on your income, you may have to help pay for the tests. If you are *indigent*, you will not be asked to pay for the tests. In most cases, you are not asked to pay for DNA testing. It usually is made the responsibility of the named father. At this point you may be asking yourself why anyone would bother to go through all of this. That's a good question, and there are some very good answers. Once paternity has been established, children born out of wedlock have equal benefits to those who were born within a marriage. This means that they cannot be discriminated against for any reason. If one child is entitled to two peas, then the other child is entitled to two peas. For example, if a woman had an affair with a married man, her child would be entitled to the same medical and life insurance, Social Security benefits, veteran's benefits, if any, and rights to inheritance. You will want to establish paternity even if your boyfriend does not have a job. Just because he does not have one today, does not mean he will not have one for the rest of his life.

Chapters 9, 10, 11, 12, 14 and 15 will explain how you can get child support from someone who does not have a job. At first it must be determined if he or she really does not have a job or if they are just *saying* that they don't have a job. You also must determine if they are as broke as they say that they are or if they do indeed have a job. Is it one job or two? Is it one full-time job and a part-time off-the-books business which brings in more income than the job? Questions, questions, questions. Chapters 9, 10, 11, 12, 14, and 15, will help.

There are some women who choose not to establish paternity for their child. They are well aware of the benefits that their child would receive, but to them the drawbacks are more serious. By proving paternity in court, you are forcing a father to assume the responsibility of fatherhood – or at least the financial responsibility. The other side of the coin is that the father now has a parental right to that child. So he may then, if he has not already, file an action for *visitation*. Some mothers fear this because they do not want the father in the child's life; in some cases because they feel that the father is mentally unstable or abusive. Without legal paternity, a named father cannot exercise any rights to see or have any involvement with his child. This is a rather personal decision, and each state has laws which determine how much time is allowed for paternity to be established. Keep in mind, however, that the child will not be entitled to child support or other benefits, and you will be on your own financially. Also keep in mind that the suspected father can take you to court at any time for paternity and visitation. You might as well beat him to the punch and allow your child the benefit of having two financially contributing parents. If you are truly concerned about the safety of your child, you can ask for supervised visitation. Be sure to have a good reason for asking for it in the first place. Using visitation as a means of punishment and control in the same way that some fathers use child support as explained before is unfair to the child.

Some suspected fathers will use visitation to threaten the mother of the child. They may say that if the mother takes them to court for paternity, they will take her to court for visitation of the child. Sometimes this is enough to cause a mother to reconsider her options. Keep in mind, however, that a father has a right to see his child, so he may end up taking you to court at any time. Do you really want to live with this hanging over your head? Besides, any father, or named father in this case, who would make that kind of threat really has no interest in his child anyway. So threats of visitation, or actual visitation, would probably go away as quickly as they came.

If you are unsure of your child's paternity and would like to find out before going through an embarrassing court procedure to do so, there are DNA tests which you can perform at home. These tests will reveal the paternity and are the same tests that the courts use. The drawback is that while you will have the paternity of your child answered (and generally in a shorter period of time than it takes for the courts to do it); the results are not admissible in a court of law. The reason is called "*chain of custody*". What this means is that no one can be sure that you or someone else didn't tamper with the test or the results of the test. When the court orders the test it is conducted under a controlled environment and it is reasonably safe to assume that it has not been tampered with. You can use your imagination to discover the reasons why a mother, a father or a named father might want to do a private test before going to the authorities. If the named father is incarcerated, is in another state, or has left the country, Chapters 8, 14 and 18 on locating the *obligor*, interstate collection, and international collection, respectively, will provide information on how to find out where he is so that you can continue your paternity case. The same rules that apply for locating deadbeats that have skipped out on their children will apply for locating named fathers.

Quite often women are afraid to establish paternity for their child because they are afraid of him and would rather suffer when the children are really in need of the child support. Domestic violence cases can be tricky when petitions for paternity, custody and child support exists. A few helpful hints:

a) The named father or spouse or boyfriend does NOT need to have been convicted of domestic violence or assault for you to be a domestic violence victim.

b) You do not need to have sought medical care or have been admitted to a hospital to be a domestic violence victim.

c) **All** court documents will request your address and phone number.

d) If you are a victim of domestic violence and resides at a domestic violence shelter or do not want your address known in order to protect yourself or your children from further violence or are concerned about violence due to your paternity and/or child support filings, **you must** file for an Order of Protection and ask that your address **NOT** be disclosed in court papers.

e) With that Order, all your need to do is to write "protected" where asked for this information and update the Clerk of the Court with an address and phone number as soon as possible so that the Court can reach you.

I cannot tell you how many women that I have spoken to who are living in poverty but have not petitioned for child support because they are afraid of physical abuse from the named father. It's important for women to be told that they can file and still be kept safe.

HOT TIPS FOR PARENTS

If the named father has a brother or a father, a cousin or a friend who looks a lot like him (could pass for him if you didn't look closely enough) be wary about paternity testing. Proper identification must be shown when a named father appears for testing but you might want to ask the court to advise you of the appointment time and place so that you can show up and verify that it is indeed him providing his DNA and not someone else in his place. Believe me, it has happened.

HOT TIPS FOR CASEWORKERS

Ask your clients to provide several pictures of the named father and send them to the testing center in advance of the testing date.

HOT TIPS FOR ATTORNEYS

If the child's mother has taken her own legal action, such as allowing her current husband to petition for adoption of the child, has sworn she does not know where the child's father is or who he is. Your client can still bring a paternity lawsuit to request a DNA test and determine if he is the child's father.

STOP THE SPREAD OF FATHERLESS HOMES:
Recognize non-invasive prenatal fetal cell/DNA paternity testing

A Petition for the Admission of Non-Invasive Prenatal Paternity Testing in State Courts

"Let's admit to ourselves that there are a lot of men out there that need to stop acting like boys; who need to realize that responsibility does not end at conception; who need to know that what makes you a man is not the ability to have a child but the courage to raise a child."

- President Barack Obama, Father's Day, June 15, 2008

Today, the practice of responsible fatherhood is of critical importance – to our society, to the expectant mother, and most of all, to the unborn child about to enter the world. Children who grow up in fatherless homes have a much greater risk of major challenges in life than those who grow up with a father in the home. **According to the US Census Bureau, this epidemic is rampant and currently affects 27 million children in the United States. 1 out of every 3 households in America exists without a father in the home.** These children, who suffer the absence of a father, often have problems linked to higher rates of poverty, failure in school, teen pregnancy, substance abuse, violent crime and depression. These statistics should give anyone pause and give us all good reason to support legislation that puts an end to a contributing factor that leads directly to this epidemic - the refusal of courts to order and admit prenatal paternity testing.

For a mother facing a pregnancy during which the child's father has left or otherwise failed to acknowledge a parental role, the process of

61

fostering responsible fatherhood cannot begin until all parties determine and accept biological paternity. Sadly, current U.S. statutory and case law fails to protect a child from a father that consciously abandons it during the 9-month period of time between conception and birth. New York State Family Court Law §532, for example, states that a man's "pregnancy-related obligations" materialize only AFTER a child's birth. Until the pregnancy produces a child, ANY and ALL costs associated with the pregnancy are deemed the woman's responsibility. This delay is also responsible for allowing a father the ability to evade his parental responsibilities entirely, leaving the mother alone to shoulder the emotional and financial burden of not only the pregnancy, but subsequent parenthood as well.

Since the 1970's, it has been possible to genetically link a father and his baby through invasive prenatal testing that required obtaining amniotic fluid. These traditional methods – Amniocentesis and Chorionic Villus Sampling – pose health risks to the child which courts have typically considered too high to warrant court order.

Now, a **safe and non-invasive, prenatal paternity test** has been developed in which the pregnant woman's blood is used to gather a sample of fetal DNA. This new method has been reported by the New England Journal of Medicine, is widely available, and is a simple blood test between the man and woman. Given the greatly reduced health risks to the mother, father and unborn baby, and the potentially life-changing benefits of resolving paternity before the baby arrives, it makes sense for all U.S. family law courts to recognize the use of non-invasive prenatal paternity testing to legally identify the father during the pregnancy.

We, the undersigned, are asking our President to **recognize non-invasive, prenatal fetal cell/DNA paternity testing and amend the current statutes in place** in order to allow the courts to admit the results of such testing into evidence. The earlier that a paternity test can establish a child's father, the earlier parents can implement a successful parenting plan. By allowing the establishment of paternity prior to a child's birth, you will firmly set in place the obligations of shared parenthood in a safe, cost-effective and timelier manner, benefitting the best interests of children, families and our society.

Please join our efforts online:

```
https://www.change.org/petitions/president-of-the-
united-states-stop-the-abandonment-of-women-during-
pregnancy-and-paternity-fraud-call-on-the-courts-to-
recognize-non-invasive-prenatal-fetal-cell-dna-
paternity-testing#share
```

Or:

Click on the link on my website to take you to the petition directly.

chapter 4:

when a minor becomes a parent (and grandparents become parents)

Missy was a single mother and had raised her daughter, Tara alone for most of her life. While Missy was never able to provide any of the extras in life that she would have liked to provide for her daughter – things like the dance classes that she always asked for or the music lessons that she wanted her to have, she was always able to keep a roof over their heads and provide the basics. She was proud of this because Tara's father moved away with his family a month after she was born and Missy never saw him again. He had promised that they would get married and move into their own tiny apartment and raise their daughter together. They would start their own small family. She only knew him by his nickname, "DJ" and never knew much else about him. She didn't have his social security number, wasn't sure if she knew his actual birth date and had only ever met his mother in passing when she came out to the park to call DJ home for dinner. Missy tried to find DJ after he and his family moved but after a year of calling around, she just gave up. He had never even come to say goodbye. When Tara was sixteen she became pregnant.

When she found out about Tara's pregnancy, Missy was afraid for her. She didn't want Tara to raise her baby and struggle in the same ways that she had to in order to raise her. She wanted something more for her daughter and her grandchild. She knew that she couldn't force Tara's boyfriend to "stick around" and help with the baby even though she wanted him to. She also wanted him to participate financially in the support of the child. She wanted him to pay child support. Tara's boyfriend was also 16 and a high school student, like Tara, and he did not have a job. Missy wasn't quite sure what to do at first but when she learned that Rhode Island – the state where they lived, was one of the thirteen states in the country which have *grandparent liability* laws on the books, she was relieved. *"Grandparent liability"* was one of the results of the "Personal Responsibility & Work Opportunity Reconciliation Act" of 1996 (also known as the "welfare reform act"). When the Act was passed, each state had the option of enacting the law, or to choose not to. The intent is to teach abstinence, birth control and the dangers of pregnancy to young people by holding their parents (who would become grandparents) responsible for any grandchildren born to their underage children. By creating the Act, Congress stood on a wing and a prayer that parents would instill in their children with more meaning than before (and presumably force them to listen and obey somehow) the consequences of unintended pregnancy. If the parents "failed" or didn't do a "good-enough" job (arrogant, obstinate, defiant, know-it-all children notwithstanding) and a child is born, then the grandparents are punished by being forced to assume full financial responsibility until their children are able to.

Acting as *guardian ad litem* for her daughter Tara, Missy waited until the baby was born and then filed for child support on Tara's behalf due to her underage status. She named Tara's boyfriend and his parents as *co-defendants*. The parents countersued Missy as an additional *co-defendant*, because she too, is a grandparent of the child. Arguments ensued, feelings were hurt and an agreement simply could not be made between the different parties. The boyfriends' parents were outraged that they could be held responsible for the actions of their son. They had never heard of such a thing before. They felt that they had always given him proper guidance and did their best to instill values. They had talks about sex and discussed birth control. Most importantly they encouraged their son to abstain and save something as important as sex for a serious relationship, when he became older. They thought that they had done what responsible parents do and so to relieve themselves of some of the pressures, they began to question Missy's parenting of Tara. They were sure that Tara was more to blame for the pregnancy than their son and that possibly she planned the pregnancy and was reckless with birth control. They wanted Tara to bear the financial burdens of the baby on her own until their son completed high school and college and was able to get a job and help.

The judge did not agree. He ordered all three grandparents to be responsible for the child according to the child support calculations. Because Rhode Island is an *"income shares"* state, the incomes from the three parents were calculated together. Missy earned a low-average income and already had one dependent to support. The other grandparents were high-earning professionals. They were ordered to be responsible for most of the child's expenses. It was a 10% to 90% split with Missy being ordered to pay 10% towards the baby's care and the other grandparents ordered to pay 90%. They were ordered to pay child support to Missy for Tara's baby as well as add the baby to their health insurance policy.

Currently, thirteen states have adopted this law which puts grandparents on the hook for grandchildren when they are born to underage parents. These states are:

Arizona	Idaho	Illinois
Maryland	Missouri	New Hampshire
North Carolina	Ohio	Rhode Island
South Carolina	South Dakota	Wisconsin
	Wyoming	

Deadbeat vs. Deadbroke

The majority of children born out of wedlock are born to underage parents. When minors become parents they are confronted with special issues that others do not have. In most instances, underage parents are not married. As discussed in Chapter 3, the law assumes that the husband of the mother is the father of her child. If she is not married, as far as the law is concerned, the baby does not have a father. Paternity will have to be established before she is able to claim who the father of her child is and get child support from the baby's father. What I have experienced is that most pregnant moms who are minors live with the delusion that they will be together with their child's father forever. This prevents them from seeking court-ordered support on the basis that it might harm their relationship with the baby's father. If they are even around by the time that the child is born, the fathers often swear they will support and love the child forever. Here and now is replaced by promises of a wonderful future together. So, instead of filing a paternity action after the birth of their child, most underage mothers go through the process and the shock of discovering how much it costs to raise a baby on their own. A small percentage will eventually take the father to court once it becomes evident that promises for support will not be kept. The rest carry the load on their own forever, enlist help and support from family and/or when a new man enters the picture he becomes the father figure and assumes financially responsibility of the child – sometimes forever, sometimes until that relationship too, ends.

The difference between an underage unmarried mother and an adult unmarried mother is that for the most part, the adult mother has had the opportunity to finish school and hopefully get a decent job to support herself. That alone does not mean that the RP parent in this case will survive financially. Without child support, many women end up on *TANF* (Temporary Aid to Needy Families). Eighty-seven percent of the women on welfare are there because they do not get child support. An education will at least, hopefully, give the woman some type of head start. Most underage parents do not have this benefit. If you are an underage parent, the information that is outlined in this book for paternity actions and child support enforcement applies to you as well.

You should pursue your child support case in the same manner. Many underage parents feel that it is useless to petition for child support since the father of the child most likely does not have a job, or he has one that pays very little. Although this may be true, at some point he will become employed or his income will increase. It is best to file for support as soon as possible, because his debt begins to accrue as soon as your application is approved. When he finally does become employed he will be in arrears, which means he will owe you the money he previously couldn't pay.

For Example:

Let's say that your child's father is sixteen years old. He lives with his parents and they support him completely. He does not have a job. Your child is born and the father cannot contribute anything financially. You have one of two or maybe three options:

- **Option #1:** You decide that it does not make sense to take him to court for money because he does not have any to give to you. Besides, you know that you cannot get any child support unless you establish paternity first and that involves testing. You have been through enough already with the pregnancy and the birth of your child and you do not want to be bothered. You decide to wait until he finishes high school, gets a real job, and makes some real money. He has promised to take care of you and your baby then. Two years later, your boyfriend graduates from high school and gets a job, but he still does not give you any money to help support your child. After a considerable amount of thought, you finally decide to take the difficult steps of filing a paternity action to establish parentage and to get child support. Months later, after you have had your day in court, your boyfriend has been ordered to pay $100 (or whatever dollar amount the court decides) a week, and you have just received your first $100 check. You will get $100 a week, every week. That's $400 a month.

- **Option #2:** You take your boyfriend to court immediately for paternity and financial support of your child. Months later, after you have had your day in court, your boyfriend has been ordered to pay $100 (or whatever amount the court orders) a week. You do not get any money now because your boyfriend does not have an income. Two years later, your boyfriend graduates from high school and gets a job. You inform your caseworker of where your boyfriend is working, or if you are representing yourself, you file a wage withholding with the employer, directly. A few weeks later you receive your first check of $600. You will get $600 a month, two hundred dollars more than your child support order states he must pay until he pays off the past-due child support. You can also file a writ of garnishment to receive a lump-sum payment from your ex's paycheck.

- **Option #3:** You live in one of the thirteen states which have grandparent liability laws and decide to file a petition against the grandparents. You appear in court, win your case, and the grandparents are obligated to provide weekly child support of $150 a week (or whatever the court orders) and it is *retroactive* to the date of your court filing. It took six weeks for you to receive your day in court so the grandparents already owe $900.

The day you file for child support is the day that your child's father begins to owe. If it is found that he is not the father, then of course he will owe nothing. If he is the father, then the debt continues to accumulate. When he begins to make payments, he will then owe his regular child support amount, plus an additional amount to pay for the two years that he did not pay anything.

Either way, you must go two years without getting any money while your boyfriend finishes school, but the outcomes are completely different. In the first example, you are starting from scratch when he gets his job because he doesn't owe you anything at that point. In the second example he already owes you money when he gets his job. He can begin to repay you. You decide which choice makes more sense for you.

Unless the teenage parent has been declared independent by a court of law, those who are underage are minors. In most states, your parent or guardian will have to petition the court as *guardian ad litem* for child support for your child. This means that they are standing up for you in court since you have no legal voice. Your boyfriend's parent or guardian may have to stand up for him as well. It's an interesting fact that according to Studies by the *Population Reference Bureau* and the *National Center for Health Statistics*, about two-thirds of children born to teenage girls in the United States are fathered by adult men age 20 or older and not by teenage boys at all. A review of California's 2010 vital statistics found that men older than high school age fathered 77% of all births to high school-aged girls (ages 16–18), and 51% of births to junior high school-aged girls (under 16). Men over age 25 fathered twice as many children of teenage mothers than boys under age 18, and men over age 20 fathered five times as many children of junior high school-aged girls as did junior high school-aged boys. An older father changes things substantially, so act accordingly.

Who has custody of a minor child's child?

When a parent or guardian steps up as *guardian ad litem* on behalf of their underage child in order to file a petition for paternity or child support, the payments will come in name of the adult. The money will be child support and it is for the benefit of the grandchild but must come in the name of the adult. That however has nothing to do with custody of the child. Some people assume that because the child support is in the name of the adult that must mean that custody of the grandchild goes to the grandparent as well. That is not true. The minor child has legal custody of their baby and can legally make any and all decisions for his/her benefit.

Consider the case of Katy whose mother constantly threatened to take her baby 3,000 miles away and said that she could do it because she received the child support money in her name and that made her the legal guardian. Katy's mother is wrong. If she left with the baby without having Katy's permission, it would be a case of kidnapping. Sometimes, it is also referred to as a *"child grab"*. You would need to read a different book for that.

So you want to raise your grandchildren?

An increasing number of grandparents have been stepping up to the plate to raise their grandchildren. Typically, these children are abandoned by their parents, who often are abusing drugs, incarcerated, or otherwise unable to care for them. If this is your case, you will not be able to get child support unless you have some type of legal guardianship over the child. Simply taking the child off his parents' hands for a while is not enough. If you want child support, you must get a child support award. You can get child support from one or both parents if the child is in your care. Once you get guardianship, your child support documents will be filed against both parents, instead of just one. You will follow the same procedures as everyone else, with the only difference being that you get double the trouble!

Truth be told, there is a lot that should go into the decision to raise a grandchild, aside from the emotional health of the young person under your care. Take Todd, for example: Todd took his granddaughter in when his own daughter, the girl's mother, became too sick to care for her. Battling a disease, she asked her father to take her daughter into his care until she became well enough to bring her back home. Todd's daughter gave him *"temporary physical custody"*. She hand-wrote a letter giving her father permission to take temporary custody of her daughter until she was able to return for her. Unfortunately, things turned for the worse and Todd's daughter lapsed into a coma. Because the transference of *physical custody* was done without a court order the *"temporary physical custody"* document Todd had was not enough to make medical decisions for his granddaughter or even enroll her in school. With his daughter now medically incapacitated, and unable to give her father the proper consent to raise her daughter as she had intended, Todd had to figure out how he could get proper guardianship of his granddaughter which would allow him to care for her as needed and as per her mother's wishes, without going to court. They had wanted a more informal arrangement and wanted to keep family business out of the court system. Todd found that there are two options for people who do not wish to go through the court system for custody:

Power of Attorney

If Todd's daughter was willing and he was in agreement they could have created a *"power of attorney"* document (*POA*) that would have given him temporary authority to make specific decisions for the child. If a *POA* had been signed, Todd would have had whatever legal rights were specified in the document. For example, he could have been given legal authority to seek medical care for his grandchild or register her in school. A generalized *POA* would have provided him with rights to all decisions without being specific. For the most part, POA's can only be created when the parent has become incarcerated, physically or mentally ill, homeless, being treated for substance abuse; or when the parent believes that the POA is otherwise in the best interest of the child. A POA does not remove a parent's legal rights and it can be revoked at any time.

Medical and Educational Consent

If Todd's daughter only wanted him to be able to make decisions for his granddaughter's medical care or only for her education, in some states there are *"consent laws"* which allow for grandparents to just make medical or just make school decisions for their grandchildren without going to court. In most states it's called a *"caretaker authorization affidavit"* ("CAA").

- **Educational consent**, or "open enrollment law", allows grandparents or other adults who are raising a child without legal custody to enroll that child in school.

- **Medical consent** allows a parent to authorize another adult to provide medical, dental, and mental health care for their children and obtain access to health records.

Unfortunately for Todd, those options didn't work for him because being in a coma, his daughter was unable to consent and sign for either the *POA* or the *CAA's*. He didn't want to but he had to take his case to court. Todd now had to decide whether he wanted to make an application for "*legal custody*" or "*guardianship*" of his granddaughter.

Legal Custody

Since Todd already had physical custody of his granddaughter, it would make it easier for him, as her grandfather, to obtain legal custody. A paper trail already existed as to why she was under his care and he was not petitioning the court in order to fight his daughter for custody as an unfit parent, which may have complicated matters somewhat. Legal custody may not be permanent; it can always be changed but it would allow Todd to make all decisions necessary for his grandchild. The only two decisions he could not make, as a person with legal custody, is the decision to emancipate the little one or to place her up for adoption. Todd's daughter could always petition to have custodial rights returned. Todd also learned that with the legal custody option, he could legally receive the child support that his granddaughters' father sends every month.

Guardianship

Another option Todd had was to apply for *guardianship* of his granddaughter. *Guardianship* is similar to *legal custody*, in that it is a legal relationship between you and your grandchild that is ordered by a court. In other ways, it is a longer and much more complex process. The department of social services is involved and may visit the family, conduct investigations and report to the judge with recommendations. In some states guardianships are more permanent than legal custody –

remaining in effect until the child is 18. In addition, similar to legal custody, Todd could receive the child support payments for his granddaughter.

Adoption

There was a third option available, but Todd knew that it was not the right option for his family. Adoption is a permanent option where the grandparent receives all parental rights and the biological parents rights are severed permanently. Todd's daughter was a great mother; he only needed to care for his granddaughter until she had overcome her illness. Adopting his granddaughter was not a desirable option.

HOT TIPS FOR UNDERAGE PARENTS

Keep in mind that if the grandparents of your child have been required by law to provide financial support, they will be required to do so until you are emancipated. The age of *emancipation* is a state by state issue and so the age of your *emancipation* will depend on the state in which you live. At times there are other matters which can delay *emancipation* as well as matters which can speed it up. Consider checking my website `www.dontgetmadgetpaid.com` for a listing of emancipation ages by state.

HOT TIPS FOR GRANDPARENTS

There are certain legal issues which grandparents should consider as they take custody of a grandchild:

- **Safety:** If the grandchild was removed from the home because the parents were unfit or otherwise unstable, you may need to consider getting Child Protective Services and/or the police involved if there is a safety risk.
- **Visitation:** Are the parents interested in visiting their child? Would visitation be in his/her best interest? Is there a visitation order in place?
- **Cost and time:** Which option requires more time in court or is more involved? How much can you handle at the moment and how much can you pay in legal fees if it comes to that?
- **Finances and health:** Make sure you understand how the choice would affect a grandchild's health insurance coverage (or the option to be covered under a grandparents health insurance plan), cash benefits if they receive them and child support payments. Only with legal custody or guardianship can a grandparent receive current child support or apply for it on behalf of their grandchild. A grandparent with legal custody or guardianship can make an application to the court for child support from one or both parents of the child.

HOT TIPS FOR ATTORNEYS

If your client wants to provide authorization for medical or educational consent, be sure that the statement contains the following information:

- Identity of the caregiver
- The names and dates of birth of the child at issue
- If appropriate, a description of the medical treatments for which authorization is given
- If appropriate, a statement that the parent is allowing the caregiver to enroll the child in school. Name the specific school, if possible.
- A statement that there are no court orders in effect which would prohibit the authorizations being made
- The signatures of the parent, legal guardian, or custodian, in the presence of two witnesses. The caregiver receiving the consent cannot be one of the witnesses signing.

chapter 5:
modification of your child support order

there may be a time when the amount of child support you receive does not seem as if it's enough. You may be taking money out of your pocket to cover costs that are not basic living necessities and therefore were not accounted for when you applied for child support. Items like birthday party gifts, school functions, school supplies, school trips and haircuts are often forgotten when calculating child support. When you deviate from the child support calculations and include "*add-ons*" such as child care and medical bills not covered by health insurance (to use two examples), the amount of a child support award can change significantly. This is what happened to me. Not yet divorced, my ex and I originally had a *kitchen table conversation* and silly me, without having an understanding of child support guidelines in my state, projections of what it might cost to raise our child, or anyone to help me through the process and provide some guidance along the way, I agreed to $50.00 a week. Our child was still in diapers, I lived alone with my daughter, and I was a working mother which meant that I needed child care. Do some quick math and you will figure out how far that $50 got me. I was busting my hump selling management consultant services in my sales position at work. Despite my degree in broadcast communications, I took the sales job because it paid well. To improve our economic resources, I was also writing a column for a newspaper and was on-air on Sunday mornings at a local radio station. Day care is expensive, especially when you have an infant or a child in nursery school. I was lucky enough to be able to bring my child with me to the radio station on the weekend but during the week at my sales job, I had no such luck. Then…the $50 a week abruptly stopped coming. Just stopped. There was no warning, no "heads-up", nothing. The lousy $50 a week that I belittled and scoffed - but which I had also come to depend on to help me pay my rent, work-related day care, food and everything else, was gone. I went through a few months of "the check is in the mail" type of nonsense with my ex before I realized that I had to do something. The next step after realizing that something needed to be done was to figure out what that something was.

After a bit of research – in between my three jobs and being a parent – I learned that there was an office that I could go to (the child support office) and that there were people there to help me get my child support from my child's father. I took a day off from work to go to the office and file the paperwork. On the day that my ex and I appeared in court, the hearing officer had already read my application. She knew that I had been receiving $50 a week from my ex, until the day that he stopped paying. She asked him if he still had a job and he told her that he did. BAM! The gavel went down and he was ordered to pay $50 a week, no questions asked. I was numb. I thought that I would have been given the opportunity to speak. I wanted to ask for more money. I wanted to tell the hearing officer that the day care costs alone were in excess of $400 a month (this was more than twenty years ago), and that the months that I had gone without the $50 a week that he had promised had put a strain on my budget. I was numb and I was angry and while I was slightly relieved that I would soon begin to receive the court-ordered $50 weekly again, I was not happy about it. By that time, I had sat down and run the numbers and I knew that the award was unfair and inappropriate. If we split our daughter's expenses down the line – 50% - 50%, he should have been paying me closer to $700 a month. I realized then, just how much of a joke and an insult $200 a month was and at that time, I knew how much he earned and knew that he could have paid more.

I went back to my research. A lawyer-friend taught me how to do some research at the local law school. He told me that I could go there and find out if I could *appeal* my case. Even though I had already been awarded child support, by doing my research I had reason to believe that the amount ordered was not fair or sufficient to raise my child. I learned that I had an option to *appeal* the court's decision. Please note that when I refer to "the court" I am referring to the person at the court who made the decision about your child support. The phrase "the court" is frequently used by attorneys and other court personnel so it's a good idea for you to become used to hearing it and reading about it. Throughout this chapter, I will either use the terms "the court" or the decision-maker. They are the ones who decide what happens with your child support. It is up to them to decide who owes, who pays, and how much. Decision-makers can differ from state to state. Filing an *appeal* means that you do not agree with the decision made by the court and that you want your case heard again so that another decision can possibly be made. It also means that you believe that the judge or hearing officer also made a mistake in rendering their decision. It cannot simply be that you just don't like it. Appeals can be tricky. You should only file for an appeal if you are certain that the amount of child support that has been ordered falls below the child support guidelines for your state or if there is a considerable amount of information that would benefit you that was not considered when the original decision was made. This is true whether you are appealing your case or if your child support award was OK when you first received it but it's been a while and you feel that it is time for your award to be increased. It also can be because financial circumstances have changed. In the end, I did successfully appeal my case and received a child support award of twice the amount that had been previously ordered. My weekly child support award was *upwardly modified* from $50 per week to $100 per week. The $400 was a far cry from the $700 which would have divided our child-related expenses equally. Because of where we lived, which was a *"percentage of income"* state, and my ex did not earn as much money as I did; at that moment, the writing on the wall became clear to me. I would always be the parent to provide the most financial support for our daughter – unless her father decided to bust his behind out there with three jobs – just as I was doing. Of course my case did not end there. We went on to have more "interesting" times in child support court but let's continue on with our discussion about modification.

You may be interested in appealing your case, as I did. A word of caution before you set out to file an appeal on your case. If you have already been heard in child support court, use caution when preparing your case because of the rule of *estoppel*, which says that you cannot bring something up at a later time in order to change a decision if you knew about the information beforehand, but did not reveal it. For example, a divorced couple agrees to an amount of child support. This agreed-upon amount is written into their divorce decree, and it is now permanent. The ex-husband later decides that he is paying too much and files papers to have the child support lowered. His reasoning is that his ex-wife's second job income was not considered when they calculated income and expenses to arrive at a child support amount comfortable for the two of them. This is where the law of estoppel is used. Since the husband knew about the second job income when the decision for child support was made, he will not be able to get his child support payment lowered. Although I said that the couple's child support award was made permanent in their divorce decree, nothing is ever permanent in the child support world; it is only temporarily permanent. Permanent, that is, until something changes to make the current child support award not fair or sufficient anymore, and until someone makes a move to do something about it. The Federal Child

Support Act of 1988 says that your local child support enforcement agency will review your child support case every two years. If a sufficient number of financial considerations have changed, your case will be reviewed and the child support amount may be increased. But, as they say, don't hold your breath. Many of the child support agencies are so backlogged that it is difficult enough for them to handle a regular caseload. So, in order to keep up with your child support case, it's up to you to understand how the courts determine whether there has been a *change in circumstances* significant enough to warrant going to court. That is not to say that the automatic increases never happen and that all child support agencies are slow to provide them. That simply isn't true. I know many agencies where their cases always receive on-time *COLA's* (cost of living increases) but I also know some whose clients wait and wait. My philosophy is to be familiar with your case so that if you are due for an increase, you are the first to know about it and can take action by contacting your caseworker if you don't hear from them first. If you are a pro sé parent, you need to be on top of your game even more so because you have only yourself to rely upon. You will need to know when you are due for an increase, where to get the proper paperwork, how to complete the paperwork so that you get what you need, and how to file the paperwork properly.

A *change in circumstances* occurs when financial circumstances have changed considerably, rendering the original child support order unfair or insufficient. A change might result in one of two decisions:

- An *upward modification* of the child support order, or a
- A *downward modification* of the child support order

An *upward modification* is an increase in child support and a *downward modification* is a decrease. Following are some incidents that can be considered a *change in circumstances*:

Deadbeat vs. Deadbroke

The NRP gets a new job, or increases his income through a higher salary or a bonus.

The standards for how much of an increase in salary is sufficient to grant an *upward modification* varies from state to state. In many states, the rule of thumb is that the income must be increased by at least 10 percent in order for the court to consider an increase in child support. If the NRP receives only a 3.3 percent cost-of-living increase per year, in two or three years, depending on your state (and every two or three years) you will be able to petition the court for an increase in child support. If the NRP gets a new job and is making 10 percent more than he was before, your child may be entitled to more support now. Do remember that along with the absent parent's ability to pay, an increased amount of support comes only if the additional money is needed. You must prove to the court that the money you are asking for on behalf of your children is something that they need. If you are simply asking for a "cost of living" increase every two years, that's one thing, but if you are seeking a modification due to changed circumstances, be prepared to prove your case in court.

The NRP receives an inheritance.

If you know of an inheritance that the absent parent has received or will be receiving, you may be able to seek an upward modification based on the absent parent's new ability to pay. For example, let's say that your child's doctor has recommended speech therapy, but neither you nor the absent parent has been able to afford it. Your child's speech is getting worse and you are despairing. Then, you find that your child's other parent has inherited a nice sum of money. You can then petition the court to have the absent parent pay the bill for the speech therapy since he can now afford it.

The cost of caring for your children increases as they grow up.

Children eat more, grow out of their clothes faster, and are involved in more activities as they grow older. All of this requires more money.

If it is a significant amount more, your circumstances may have changed and you should consider petitioning for an upward modification.

A new medical, mental, or emotional diagnosis is made, or your child becomes ill or disabled.

If you have increased expenses due to your child becoming temporarily or permanently ill or disabled in some way, you should consider petitioning the court for more financial support from the absent parent.

These are just a few reasons that an *upward modification* can be granted. Use your discretion.

You should always ask yourself two questions:

1. Is the absent parent in a better paying position than he was when the child support award was granted?
2. Is there a good reason for you to ask for more money on your child's behalf?

Some *changes in circumstances* do not fit into any specific category so do not rule out situations that may seem unusual. For example, lottery winnings, a substantial change in either parent's tax liabilities, recommended private school for your child, would all create the circumstances needed for upward modification consideration. Also, be sure of your reasons for asking for additional child support. If you are still unsure about what a change in income is, or what can be considered income, there is more information in Chapter 8. Before you get there, however, there is a lot more that you need to know about modifications.

The saying, "Be careful of what you wish for—because you just may get it," holds true when it comes to child support modifications. You may go to court expecting to get an upward or a downward modification only to have the decision-maker look over your paperwork, decide that either you are getting too much money as it is, and lower your child support award or that you are not paying enough and increase it! If that happens, you will end up with a modification, just not the type you expected.

Allow me to share with you one of my favorite cases. A mom walked into my office one day about 5 or 6 years ago. She explained that she had been passing by, saw my company's sign in the window – "Child Support Solutions" with our tag line "Don't Get Mad Get Paid" and wondered if we could help her. It was a Tuesday evening and the sky had opened up; it was pouring down rain. I had touched base with all of my clients that evening and was just about to call it a night when she walked in. Instead, I put on a new pot of coffee as she told me about her ex and the tug of war power struggle that she and her ex were engaged in over child support payments for their daughter. Lana had a child support order for several years. She received a meager amount of $300 per month and she begrudgingly settled for it because she didn't want to invite the stress and drama that a court appearance would bring into her life. Unfortunately for Lana, the stress and drama came without an invitation, and in the form of a petition that her ex had filed with the court, seeking a downward modification of her child support award. Her ex claimed that he was no longer working the same hours that he had been and could no longer afford the same amount of child support. Lana was in disbelief. He wanted to pay less than $300! Sipping her coffee and peering at me over her horned rimmed glasses, she told me that not only did she believe that her ex did not need a downward modification due to fewer working hours which he reported, but she also believed that he could pay a whole lot more.

Lana told me about the blue collar job where her ex had worked for over 20 years on which the child support order had been based. She then told me about the other job he had. Her ex also had a part-time job as a medical assistant in a hospital that she found out about a few years ago but which he had not told her about, nor had he informed the court that that he had taken on an additional job, which meant additional income and most likely additional child support for their daughter. I had heard stories like this before; they are a dime a dozen. Then Lana's story began to become really interesting. She told me that she had reason to believe that her ex was the owner of 3 or 4 apartment rental buildings in the state and that he had tenants in each of his apartments. If we were able to verify this for Lana and if her ex's properties were income producing, Lana would be able to not only successfully contest the downward modification that her ex filed, but depending on how much additional income was found, she would be able to petition for an upward modification of the order instead. My evening had suddenly become very interesting.

Lana returned to my office the next day with everything in hand which we needed to sign her as a client. Using the information and the documents that Lana supplied to us, we were able to conduct a proper and legal asset location discovery upon Lana's ex. When the results came in about a week later, I called Lana and asked her to come straight to my office after work. It was a Wednesday night and we normally were not open on Wednesday nights but we stayed open for Lana. I asked my assistant to stay late that evening and dismissed the rest of my staff, but no one left. They all wanted to be there when we shared the good news with Lana. By the time Lana arrived, we had ordered food from a local restaurant and picked up a bottle of Prosecco champagne (my favorite) from the liquor store across town. After we sat Lana down and prepared a rather large plate of food for her and poured a glass of bubbly, I could barely contain myself. We had located 14 income-producing properties throughout the country – mostly concentrated within 4 states. We worked very closely with Lana as she prepared her answer to the court in response to the petition for the downward modification and as she prepared a petition of her own – for an upward modification based on the new financial information she had acquired about her ex. The rest of Lana's story is just as interesting and exciting. At the conclusion of her case, Lana's ex was denied his motion for a downward modification and Lana received an increase of a few hundred dollars! It more than doubled her $300 monthly payment. Truth be told, she could have received a whole lot more but it would have involved that stress and drama that she was not interested in having. She was happy to walk away.

Deadbeat vs. Deadbroke

Lana's story would have been a good one to use as an example of a downward modification if her ex was being truthful about having lost some of his income. There are some times when a downward modification is reasonable and necessary. As always, whether you are requesting an increase or a decrease, you must be properly prepared when petitioning for a modification. You must also have good and significant reasons for receiving the amount that your child receives now, as well as any additional monies you are requesting. Likewise, requests to decrease the amount you currently contribute to your child's care must be substantiated as well. It is not uncommon for the NRP to petition the court for a downward modification. Some of the situations that might call for a downward modification are:

- The NRP goes on disability.
- The NRP retires.
- The NRP loses his or her job or has their salary greatly reduced.

There are few reasons for a judge to grant a downward modification. The main one would be that the current child support order is too high to begin with or that there has been a change of circumstances and the children do not need as much money. For example, additional child support may have been written into the agreement so that your child could have orthodontic care. Now that the braces are off, the additional money is not needed. An absent parent cannot get a downward modification simply because he lost his job. While it may be difficult for him for a while, the law sees the change as a temporary condition. The child support payment must still be paid in full. A downward modification can only be made under permanently changed circumstances, in most cases. Occasionally, a judge may order a temporary modification due to changed circumstances, but it is not the norm. These situations are difficult to discuss since they can vary greatly.

Changes in circumstances for the purpose of a downward modification cannot be voluntary. They must be circumstances that are out of the absent parent's control. For example, an absent parent cannot quit his job and then claim change of circumstances and request that the child support amount be lowered. Quitting a job is a voluntary action. An absent parent cannot decide to take a lesser position where he will be making less money and request that child support be lowered. Again, taking a lesser position is a voluntary action. Absent parents cannot go back to school, sell their businesses, or take time off to "find themselves" if it means that they will request that child support be lowered. These are all voluntary actions. Absent parents cannot voluntarily reduce their income and pay less child support.

If an absent parent loses his job (which is considered by the courts to be a temporary situation and therefore not immediately qualified for a reduction in child support because the child support payments can be taken from unemployment benefits), and finds another job making 25 percent less than he did at the last job, he may now be eligible for a downward modification. An involuntary 25 percent reduction in salary is substantial enough for a decrease in child support. Now let's assume that the absent parent found another job making 5 percent less than he did at the last job. He would not be eligible for a reduction in child support because most people are able to absorb a 5 percent reduction in salary. If the NRP remains unemployed for an extended period of time, a modification would be appropriate, however this would not be the case for "voluntary impoverishment" which means that the NRP has purposely placed themselves in a position of unemployment. If a NRP has found themselves unemployed for an extended period of time, care should be taken to keep records of job searches. The courts reserve the right to "impute" income upon a NRP if they think that they are purposely remaining unemployed or not trying hard enough to become employed.

There are other things besides child support that should be written into your child support order that may not be. If they are— congratulations, apparently you were on top of your self-representation child support case management, or had a caseworker or attorney who knew what he or she was doing. If not, don't despair. Lucky for you, you are reading a chapter on how to change your child support order to get what your child needs.

The first item that should be included in your order is health insurance. If the absent parent has health insurance available to him through his job, the law requires that parent to cover his children. If health insurance is not available to the absent parent, but is available to the custodial parent for a fee, then an upward modification is in order for health benefits for the children.

Life insurance is another item that should be included in your child support order. If the absent parent should unexpectedly pass away, your children would be left in the lurch for financial support. Sure they would be entitled to payments through the Social Security Administration but social security benefits are not a replacement for a life insurance payout. Have both so that your children are well provided for. Life insurance can be purchased inexpensively in any state. Have it written into your child support order that the absent parent is required to maintain life insurance in whatever amount is right for your particular circumstances. Either the absent parent can maintain the insurance, or you can have the child support order adjusted upward so that you can purchase and maintain the insurance on his behalf.

If you believe that your children will be attending college, you will want the absent parent to contribute to the financing of their education. At the very least, the absent parent should be required to foot 50 percent of the bill minus whatever contribution your children will be making themselves (if any) by working or taking out loans, etc. If your children choose an expensive school and the absent parent cannot afford it, he may not be required to pay. Take all of this into consideration. If you live in one of the following states: Alabama, Connecticut, the District of Columbia (Washington DC), Hawaii, Illinois, Indiana, Iowa, Massachusetts, Mississippi, Missouri, New Hampshire, New Jersey, New York, North Dakota, Oregon, South Carolina, Utah or Washington, parents with child support orders have a legal responsibility (in whole or in part) to make college tuition payments and cover expenses. This responsibility is in addition to child support payments for as long as the child may be in college. Expenses can include everything from tuition, fees for room and board, food not covered by a mean plan, clothing allowances, computer, printer and other related technology, cell phone expenses, and transportation costs (whether it's public or personal car along with insurance, gas, maintenance, etc.). Some states have absolutely no requirement for parents to help children with their college expenses and other states allow it only when the child has "special needs" and/or "require additional parental responsibility".

You may be wondering if you have a child support award that needs modification. The chart below will help you to determine your change in expenses from the initial entry, or the most recent change of your child support order, to now. It is similar to the chart that you used in Chapter 1. As with any chart or checklist in this book, you may want to photocopy it so that it can be used as needed.

Deadbeat vs. Deadbroke

Comparative income and expenses

	PRIOR	CURRENT	NET CHANGE
Rent/Mortgage	_____	_____	_____
Repairs	_____	_____	_____
Insurance	_____	_____	_____
Taxes	_____	_____	_____
Water/Sewer	_____	_____	_____
Electricity/Gas	_____	_____	_____
Telephone	_____	_____	_____
Garbage	_____	_____	_____
School lunches	_____	_____	_____
Meals eaten out	_____	_____	_____
Clothing	_____	_____	_____
Laundry/	_____	_____	_____
Dry cleaning	_____	_____	_____
Medical insurance	_____	_____	_____
Other medical costs	_____	_____	_____
Dental/Vision	_____	_____	_____
Prescriptions	_____	_____	_____
Other drugs	_____	_____	_____
Car payment	_____	_____	_____
Car insurance	_____	_____	_____
Car repair	_____	_____	_____
Bus/Train/Cab	_____	_____	_____
Baby-sitter	_____	_____	_____

	PRIOR	CURRENT	NET CHANGE
Other child care			
School tuition			
School supplies			
Extra activities			
Religious affiliation			
Newspapers			
Magazines			
Books			
Barber/Salon			
Union dues			
Retirement fund			
Recreation			
Vacation			
Pets			
Gifts for others			
Parties			
Birthday			
Holiday gifts			
Other_____			
Other_____			
Other_____			
Other_____			

Deadbeat vs. Deadbroke

	PRIOR	CURRENT	NET CHANGE
Subtotal (this page)	_____	_____	_____
Subtotal (last page)	_____	_____	_____
TOTAL	_____	_____	_____

TOTAL NET CHANGE;
CUSTODIAL PARENT _____

TOTAL NET CHANGE;
NON-CUSTODIAL PARENT _____

TOTAL NET CHANGE
OF EARNINGS _____

TOTAL NET CHANGE
OF EXPENSES _____

TOTAL CHILD SUPPORT
CHANGE NECESSARY _____

In order to complete this chart you may have to go through your checkbook, bank statements, credit card statements, and receipts for the past year and see where you have been spending your money. Your appointment book, smart phone, online calendars or PDA (personal data assistant), if you use one, may also contain a wealth of information. If you are anything like me, in addition to my smart phone and online calendar, because I am a highly visual person, I also list events that my children or I have to attend, and appointments that we must keep, on a large master calendar. For example, birthday parties, school fairs, doctor visits, etc. Make a habit of writing down everything that you do, and keep your date books and calendars for five years. They are good reference materials.

Now that you have checked your facts, you are ready to file your petition to modify your child support order. Pass the information along to your caseworker if you are working with the child support office and he or she will take it from there. Otherwise, if you are pro sé, visit the clerk of the court that handled your divorce/paternity suit or child support order and ask for a *Motion and Order to Show Cause*, for the purpose of a child support modification. The court clerk should have papers to give to you. If not, you can use the example Item #1 in this book. Simply create one yourself using a computer. Just be sure to follow it precisely and have someone check it over for you for accuracy. Once the form has been completed, either you or your attorney, if you have one, must sign it and file it with (give it to) the clerk of the court. The clerk will then set a date for a *hearing*. This means that she will tell you the date on which you must appear in court. You must arrange for a copy of your motion to be *served* (given to) the NRP. Generally, this must be done by either a private process server or by the sheriff. There is a fee for this and the cost should be in the neighborhood of $30 (if your income is below the poverty level, inquire about a waiver of the fee). Call your local sheriff's office and ask about their procedures. If you choose to use a private process server you can easily find one by Googling "process server" with the town or city and state where the NRP will need to be served. There is usually no fee to file your motion with the court. In some areas you can even serve the NRP yourself if you both live in the same general area, it is convenient for you and you will remain safe. Safety is paramount so if there is any chance that the NRP may harm you, it is always better to err on the side of caution and use another method. Any adult over the age of 18 can *serve* documents. Consider asking a friend or a relative to do the favor for you. One client of mine was having some trouble serving her ex. She knew where he lived but because he was always dodging bill collectors, he never answered the door for anyone unless he was expecting a visitor. We got around that by waiting until his birthday which was a little less than a month away and ordering three dozen helium "Happy Birthday"! balloons to be delivered to his house. My client had a friend of hers to pose as a delivery man and he brought the balloons to her ex's house. Of course, the ex, having peeked through the window blinds and seen the balloons thought that someone had a gift delivered for his birthday and he opened the door. Instead of the balloon delivery, much to the ex's surprise, the 'delivery man' handed him a subpoena to appear in court, informed him that he had been "served", and then turned and walked away. He kept the balloons of course.

Depending on where your quest for child support takes you, you may need to use and to file many motions. If it makes it easier on you, you can check out my website for a Forms and sample language. Instead of typing everything out yourself, it is much simpler to use the forms available on my website and just add your personal information where it is needed. You will be using the same case number that you were originally assigned when you opened your child support case. That case number will follow you all the way through until your children reach legal age and are no longer receiving child support or until you have been paid in full. Child support arrears do not ever expire. This means that you can continue to collect from the NRP until the obligation has been dissolved. You can even assign the right to continue to collect this debt on your behalf to anyone you wish. It can become part of your estate. Depending on where you live in the country, this might mean that you have to 'renew' your child support judgment with the court every so often. In most areas, child support judgments must be renewed every 10 or 15 years. Check with your local family court clerk about the regulations for your area. The process is very simple and it is just a matter of paperwork. Why walk away from a lot of money just because the NRP didn't pay on time as he or she was ordered to?

Collecting your child support is merely being reimbursed for what you have paid out already. If it comes down to it – just consider it part of your retirement fund or money that you will give to your child someday for a down payment on a house. It's your money. Your ex was unable to pay you along the way for whatever reason but now you have been able to collect it. It's *your* money. Another way to look at it: If someone came to you and said, "I am going to give you $30,000 but I am not going to give it to you today. I am going to give it to you in 15 years". Would you turn the person down? Would you say "no thanks"? It's the same thing. Consider it money that you cannot touch today but in 15 years, it's yours. If you move out of state, however, your case number will then change. If you have moved out of state, you must arrange for a certified copy of your divorce decree paternity action/child support order to he filed in the court of the county where you are now living. Call the clerk's office in the new county and ask whether your copies need to be certified or "authenticated" before you send them in, or if they need to be transferred directly from the court of the previous state to the new state. Procedures can differ from state to state and from county to county so be sure to call and ask for the proper procedures in your jurisdiction.

Once your decree/action/order has been transferred, you will receive a new case number. You can then file your motion and have the non-custodial parent served. Be sure to serve any public assistance agency that you may be receiving benefits from as well. Those should be sent to the administrator. If you do not know who the administrator is, simply call and ask. There is more information on how public assistance works with child support in Chapter 13.

Item #2 is an Affidavit in Support of Motion and Order to Modify Judgment. An *affidavit* is a written statement that you are telling the truth under oath about whatever it is you have to say. In this particular case, your affidavit (your written statement—Item #2), is supporting (backing up) your motion (request) to modify (change) your support order. In other words, you have filed your request to change your child support order and get more money. Item #2 will prove to the decision-maker why the extra money is needed and that the NRP can afford to pay it. You will want the decision-maker to be aware of all your expenses before your court date so that he or she can be better prepared for your particular case. By submitting Item #2, you will show that you are well-prepared, well-informed, and to be taken seriously.

Since child support awards are based largely upon the income of the NRP as well as your own, you will want to have up-to-date information on his income and assets to present to the decision-maker for consideration. Depending on your energy level, commitment to the modification of your child support and your relationship with the NRP, there are a couple of different routes that you can take to determine his income and assets.

Choice #1: You can ask. Some NRP's will be honest about what they have and what they earn. If the court determines that they should pay more, they will. This eliminates the need for you to take any further steps to get information. On the other hand, some NRP's will not be honest about what they have and what they earn. They may fear that the child support order will be increased and they do not want that to happen. Either they really are having trouble making ends meet and are not just "crying wolf," or they are just being a less than wonderful parent and provider, or maybe both. In this case, it is up to you to decide what to do. You can go ahead and ask, or you can move on to Choice #2. However, do realize that it is not the friendliest of choices to make. If you move on to Choice #2, you are possibly setting the scene for animosity between the two of you and maybe your children as well. These are personal choices that will affect your life, so make your decisions carefully. If you are really struggling and need your child support money and the NRP doesn't seem to be budging and providing ample support, you just may not have another choice. Additionally, keep in mind that due to their past behaviors (and only you would know what they are, if they exist) there are some NRP's who do not deserve the consideration of Choice #1. If that is the case, I encourage you to move straight to Choice #2.

Choice #2: *Subpoena* the information that you need from the NRP, his attorney, employer, or whoever else might have it. In this case, do not waste your time asking in person for information that you most likely will not get anyway. Go for the gusto and haul out the big guns. Item #3 is a Request for Production. In this document you are asking for records of any and all monetary involvement that the absent parent has had for the past three years. This will reveal anything and everything that you need to know. It may be helpful to serve this document along with a subpoena for him to appear at a certain location so that you may ask him questions as well. Yes! It's all legal, you do not need an attorney to do it, and the NRP must appear with the documents you request or face penalties. There is more information on how to properly file a subpoena and get the NRP to show his face in Chapter 11. For now, the Request for Production can be done by mail—requesting that the NRP submit the documents you request by a certain date to a certain place. You can have them sent to your home, office, attorney's office, grandma's house— wherever you choose.

When your court date comes, the NRP or his attorney will most likely object to a modification. Because you will have already done a "discovery" (a "sneak preview" look at the documents that will be shown in court—your Request for Production) there will not be too much information that he can dispute. After all, you asked for information concerning all of his money matters, and that's what you got. He cannot possibly dispute information that he gave you. The most that can be said is that your expenses are too high or that there has not been a significant enough change to warrant an upward increase in child support. This is why it is important for you to be able to prove your case.

At this point, it is up to the decision-maker to decide whether to increase your support or not. If you have gone over the expenses versus income chart with a fine-tooth comb and it shows that you are due for an increase, then you have a good chance of getting one. Although most of these procedures are typically done through attorneys, as I mentioned before, you do not have to have an attorney to get your modification. Just follow the simple directions that have been outlined for you and you should do just fine.

If you are considering hiring an attorney, however, the following two chapters should help you in your search. Attorneys are fine to work with if you can afford them and if they really know the ins and outs of child support enforcement. Sometimes they do and sometimes they do not. But, I love a good lawyer and they do have their good points. Decide for yourself if hiring one is right for you.

HOT TIPS FOR UNDERAGE PARENTS

Consider a "kitchen table conversation"

HOT TIPS FOR CASEWORKERS, ATTORNEYS AND PARENTS ALIKE

Encourage clients to keep a calendar/journal of expenses. An excel balance sheet would work well. This will help to determine actual expenses as opposed to perceived expenses – higher or lower.

Deadbeat vs. Deadbroke

**MOTION AND ORDER TO SHOW CAUSE,
RE: MODIFICATION**

IN THE CIRCUIT COURT OF THE STATE OF [INSERT YOUR STATE NAME]
FOR THE COUNTY OF [INSERT YOUR COUNTY / PARISH NAME]

In the Matter of the Child Support Order of:

[INSERT YOUR NAME],	MOTION AND ORDER TO
Petitioner,	SHOW CAUSE RE: MODIFICATION
	(Ex Parte)
And	
[INSERT OBLIGOR'S NAME],	
Respondent	

TO: [Insert Obligor's Name
                Obligor's Street Address
                Obligor's City, State, Zip]

        YOU ARE HEREBY ORDERED to file a written appearance by Affidavit in answer to the Motion and Affidavit filed by the Petitioner within thirty (30) days of the date of service of certified copies of this Motion and Order and Affidavit upon you, to SHOW CAUSE, if any there be:

        1. Why the Child Support Order entered in the above-entitled Court should not be modified to increase the amount of child support to the Uniform Guidelines amount.

        2. If this matter is contested, why judgment should not be entered in favor of Petitioner for Petitioner's reasonable attorney fees and court costs incurred in connection herewith pursuant to ORS 107.135.

        IT IS FURTHER ORDERED that should Petitioner fail to file such a written appearance by Affidavit within the time specified herein-above, a DEFAULT ORDER shall be applied for by the moving party.

        DATED this _____ day of _____, 20___

                                         _____
                                         CIRCUIT COURT JUDGE

IT IS SO MOVED:

[Your Name
Your Street Address
Your City, State, Zip
Your Phone]

Item # 1: Motion and Order to Show Cause, RE: Modification

AFFIDAVIT IN SUPPORT OF MOTION
AND ORDER TO MODIFY JUDGMENT

IN THE CIRCUIT COURT OF THE STATE OF [INSERT YOUR STATE NAME]
FOR THE COUNTY OF [INSERT YOUR COUNTY / PARISH NAME]

In the Matter of the Marriage of: [DOCKET NUMBER]
                                                          Docket Number

[INSERT YOUR NAME],
    Petitioner,

                  AFFIDAVIT IN SUPPORT
And   OF MOTION AND ORDER
                  TO MODIFY JUDGMENT

[INSERT OBLIGOR'S NAME],
    Respondent
    OF ANY STATE
    of Any County

       I, [Insert Your Name], being first duly sworn on oath, do hereby depose and say that:
       1. I am the Petitioner in the above-entitled matter.
       2. A substantial change in circumstances has occurred since the date of entry of the Child Support Order between the two parties. The change in circumstances include, but are not limited to, the following:

       [THIS IS WHERE YOU WILL DETAIL THE CHANGES IN CIRCUMSTANCES. LIST ALL OF THE CHANGES AND THE AMOUNT OF MONEY FOR EACH THAT YOU WILL NEED TO COVER THEM. AT THE END OF YOUR LIST, YOU WILL TOTAL YOUR CHANGED EXPENSES AND LIST THE ADDITIONAL AMOUNT OF CHILD SUPPORT THAT YOU WILL NEED FROM THE NRP. USE AS MUCH SPACE AS YOU NEED.]

                  _____
                  [Sign your name here]

SUBSCRIBED AND SWORN to before me this _____ day of _____, 20___.

_____
NOTARY PUBLIC FOR [STATE NAME]   My Commission expires: _____

Item # 2: Affidavit in Support of Motion and Order to Modify Judgment

Deadbeat vs. Deadbroke

REQUEST FOR PRODUCTION

IN THE CIRCUIT COURT OF THE STATE OF [INSERT YOUR STATE NAME]
FOR THE COUNTY OF [INSERT YOUR COUNTY / PARISH NAME]

In the Matter of the Marriage of:

[INSERT YOUR NAME],
    Petitioner,

And

[INSERT OBLIGOR'S NAME],
    Respondent

REQUEST FOR PRODUCTION

TO: [Insert Obligor's Name], Respondent

    Pursuant to ORCP 43, Petitioner hereby requests that Respondent produce and permit the party making this request to inspect and copy all documents described in this request by _____, on the _____ day of 20____.

    As used in this request, the term "Documents" means and includes, without limitation, the following whether printed or recorded or reproduced by hand, and draft, duplicates, carbon copies, or any other copies thereof: agreements, communications, correspondence, telegrams, memoranda, summaries or records of telephone conversations, summaries or records of personal conversations or interviews, diaries, graphs, reports, notebooks, statements, plans, drawings, sketches, maps, photographs, contracts, licenses, ledgers, books of account, vouchers, bank checks, charge slips, credit memoranda, receipts, audit papers, working papers, statistical records, cost sheets, loan files, drafts, letters, any marginal comments appearing on any documents, and all other writings or papers similar to any of the foregoing, including information maintained on computer media.

    Documents requested are all those in your possession or in the possession of your attorney, or under your control or available to you, specifically the following:

    1. All federal and state income tax returns for the tax years ____ through _____, inclusive, and documents showing any estimated taxes paid for tax years for which tax returns have not yet been filed, for you, together with copies of all partnership information returns prepared by or on behalf of any partnership co which you belonged during the same period.
    2. All federal and state income tax returns for the tax years through , inclusive, filed by any closely held corporation, limited partnership, or other entity in which you have, or had, an interest.
    3. Any list of personal property prepared by either party.
    4. All documents reflecting your income from all sources from to date, including, but not limited to, W-2s, 1099s, wage statements, and paycheck stubs.

Item # 3: Request for Production

5. All documents showing any interest you have in real or personal property, including deeds, contracts, vehicle registration, titles, bills of sale, and any other documents concerning any assets in which you have claim or may claim any interest.

6. All documents showing any existence and nature of any security interest in any asset owned by you or any asset in which you claim an interest, including, but not limited to, mortgages, trust deeds, and security agreements.

7. All documents relating to the purchase of any real or personal property in which you have an interest, together along with any closing statements prepared in connection with the purchase by you of any interest in real property.

8. All tax statements on any real property, business interest, or personal property owned by either party.

9. All financial statements prepared by or for you during the preceding five (5) years and loan applications submitted by you or any entity in which you have an interest to any bank or other lending institution or insurance company in connection with any application for a loan from to date.

10. All documents evidencing your ownership or interest in any general partnership, limited partnership, or closely held corporation in which you owned an interest at any time from to the present, or in which you now own an interest, including any buy and sell agreements, stock purchase agreements, and partnership agreements.

11. All documents which reflect the amount, location, and value of any stocks or bonds owned either jointly or individually by you.

12. All documents which reflect the amount and location of any checking accounts, savings accounts, money markets, stock brokerage, or other financial institution accounts or similar accounts on which your name appears, or has appeared, on which you are or were a signer, or on which you have had funds or securities on deposit, including periodic statements, canceled checks, check registers (and/or stubs), deposit records, passbooks, and certificates of deposit for the period ___ to date.

13. Records of all charge accounts, credit accounts, and lines of credit, including copies of all statements reflecting charges made and payments received on said accounts from the period _____ to date.

14. All policies of insurance on the life of either party, together with all records related thereto.

15. All receipts reflecting cash purchases to you from ____ to date.

16. List of all safe deposit boxes to which you have access, and a list of all the contents of any such safe deposit boxes.

17. All records of all trusts, estates, life estates, or other property in which you have any beneficial interest whatsoever, including a remainder interest or contingent remainder interest.

18. All appraisals prepared by anyone for any real property in which either party has any interest.

19. Any and all stock options or stock benefits between you and your employer, and any information concerning receipt of such stock for the past five (5) years.

20. All documents concerning any pension, profit sharing, retirement, vacation, savings, PERS, IRA, SEP, KEOGH, 401k, Social Security, veteran's benefits, deferred compensation, or other similar plans, programs, or accounts (past or present), including any and all statements reflecting your interest therein, any summary description of the plan, a copy of the plan, the name and address of the trustee, custodial and/or plan administrator, or other officer in charge of each account or plan.

21. All records reflecting all income received by (husband, wife, girlfriend, boyfriend) from all sources, from to date.

22. All records relating to any expenses or sums paid by you for which you have

received reimbursement from your private practice, or your_____ association/ employment with _____

23. All records of all trusts, estates, life estates, or any other property in which you have any beneficial interest whatsoever, including a remainder interest or a contingent remainder interest, including, hut not limited to, any Last Will and Testament, Codicil, or other instrument or bequest which names you as a beneficiary or contingent beneficiary.

24. Your current last Will and Testament, together with any Codicils related thereto.

25. All stock certificates, bonds, indentures, or any other security in which you claim an interest of any kind.

26. All health, medical, accident, hospital, and dental insurance policies covering you or any member of your family.

27. All records reflecting any indebtedness that you owe, including, but not limited to, notes and contracts.

28. Any records reflecting any guarantee made by either party.

29. All documents or correspondence concerning any credit extended by you or any debt owed to you by anyone.

30. All documents concerning any benefits available to you under any programs, Social Security, veteran's benefits, or any other program, private or public, under which you may have a claim for future payments of any kind or nature.

31. All documents listing, describing, or showing the existence of personal property, jewelry, gold, silver, precious metals, gems, artwork, antiques, coins, stamp collections, or other similar assets in which you claim an interest.

32. Copies of all documents showing the existence of any lawsuit or claim against you or your spouse or by you or your spouse against any person or entity.

33. All documents showing any gifts, transfers, or sales made by you of any asset with a value in excess of S500 during the preceding thirty-six (36) months.

34. All documents showing the existence or describing any furniture, fixtures, office equipment, or other similar assets owned by you.

35. All documents showing any farm implements, farm or logging equipment, tools, or other equipment or machinery owned by you or in which you claim an interest.

36. All records showing any interest held by you in any livestock, horses, or any animal and all documentation showing the value thereof.

37. All documents showing any interest you have in any patent, trademark, copyright, royalty, or other intangible asset.

38. All powers of attorney executed by you during the preceding three (3) years.

39. All documents of any kind or nature showing the existence or value of any asset of any kind or nature in which you claim any interest whatsoever.

■━━━━━━━━━━━━━━━━━━━━━━━━━━━━━━━━━━

This request is a continuing request. If the documents requested above come into the possession or control of you or your attorneys after the date requested for the production herein, Petitioner requests that they be produced at the time of their availability.

DATED this_____ day of_____, 20_____.

[Insert Your Name
Insert Your Street Address
Insert Your City, State, Zip Code
Your Phone #]

finding, hiring and firing an attorney

the first thing that most people wonder when they are trying to collect child support is whether they will have to hire an attorney. Having an attorney can make your life a lot easier since he or she can negotiate the legal system on your behalf. On the other hand, an attorney can also make your life a living hell if he or she does not know how to handle child support enforcement cases swiftly, coherently and with an emphasis on minimizing billable hours and maximizing results. You need to get the biggest bang for your buck. You can pay an attorney to work for you if you can afford it, you can find an attorney to work for you for free under certain circumstances or you can pursue your child support case pro sé (without an attorney). My company was built on helping parents collect their child support through our self-representation methods, but this chapter will deal with hiring an attorney whom you must pay, and how to creatively pay an attorney's fee. Before I continue let me also point out that it has been my experience as a child support expert for over 18 years that hiring an attorney is not always the best thing to do. It is not a cure all. Do not convince yourself that if you spend thousands of dollars to hire an attorney that you are guaranteed to collect. Do not beat yourself up or feel as if your situation is a lost cause because you cannot afford the benefit of an attorney. It is not always what it is cracked up to be. Sometimes they are successful with collecting child support for parents and sometimes they are not. Sometimes you pay them money and you get results and sometimes you do not. Sometimes…it is simply better to find another way. Don't get me wrong, as I have said before – I love a good attorney and in high conflict and/or high net worth situations, you almost have to have one. If you are considering hiring a lawyer, there are some things that you should know first.

<u>**Fact #1: You are the boss.**</u> Your lawyer may know how to work the legal system, he or she may have taken a course in "The Art of Arrogance 101,"and may be able to muddle through the paperwork more easily than you can. The key word, however, is, "hire." You are hiring the lawyer, you are paying the lawyer. You are the boss. Your boss may have hired you for your expertise in the job that you do, but he or she is your boss. Your boss sees to it that you are paid. If they are not happy with the job that you are doing he or she is sure to let you know. Your boss may even fire you, if necessary. You need to take the same attitude with the lawyer you hire. You are the boss. If you do not like the services that you are receiving, be sure to let the person whom you have hired know this. If worse comes to worst, you can fire your lawyer and get another one. We will get back to that later. Now this is not the same as being boss-y. Be sure to be assertive and to command the respect of your hired gun. Also be sure to give them their proper respect and to be clear of your expectations. They are professionals and you have sought him or her out for a reason.

<u>**Fact #2: Your "expert" may not be an expert at all.**</u> Just because someone has attended law school does not mean that he or she is a good lawyer; it also does not mean that they can effectively practice any particular type of law. If you were a pregnant woman, whom would you go to—an obstetrician or a cardiologist? If you had a choice, you would probably go to the obstetrician, because they are the ones who have been trained in medical school to help deliver healthy babies and

maintain healthy moms. A cardiologist could probably deliver a baby too, if necessary—most doctors could. An obstetrician, however, has been specifically trained to help pregnant women. Heck, if I had to, I could probably deliver a baby myself. Cab drivers do it all of the time. 'Nuf said.

It's the same with lawyers. Most lawyers could practice any kind of law if they had to. All they would have to do is spend a few days peering into some law books doing some research or pick the brain of one of their colleagues and most people would never know the difference. The majority of lawyers, however, do have some kind of specialty. There are real estate lawyers, criminal lawyers, malpractice lawyers, etc. Of course, you will want a lawyer who practices family law. For this reason, it is not always advisable to work with your cousin the real estate attorney, or your best friend's father, the criminal attorney; even though you know they have your best interests at heart. Law is a learned trade. The criminal attorney has spent his time learning criminal law, and the real estate attorney has spent his time learning real estate law. Family law attorneys have spent their time learning family law (under which child support falls), but they may not know how to get child support collected once it's due. That's an entirely different ball game. Remember, just because a lawyer is a family law specialist, it does not mean that he is good or that they know how to obtain the results that you need and want. On the other hand, someone who has your best interests at heart just may be the better person for the job if they are going to work tirelessly on your behalf. This is a case by case basis and one where if you know the lawyer personally, only you can decide to whom you should trust your financial welfare and well-being. Choose carefully.

You also should consider choosing an attorney who works in the same county, if not the same town, where your case will be heard. The reasons for this are simple. First, chances are that if your attorney works in the same town or county, he has what is known as the "home court advantage." (When sports teams play on their home court, they always feel more empowered and more of their fans are there to cheer them on to victory, and frequently the umpires are persuaded by the home crowd to rule in the favor of the home team.) It's the same on the legal court. The home court attorney may know the other attorneys in the courtroom and may even know the judge. He may be able to talk to the judge and relate to him or her in a way that a stranger could not. When possible, and when it makes sense, always go with the home court advantage. Second, if your attorney has to travel distances to appear in court on your case, you are going to pay extra fees.

If you are going to hire an attorney to collect child support money that's past due, your best bet would be to find a small law firm that specializes in the collection of debts. Attorneys who work for large firms usually will want to take cases that can make them a lot of money or bring them a lot of prestige. Unless the amount of money owed to your children is in the mid-five to high-five figures, at least, chances are that a large firm will not want to work with you since it will not be beneficial to them. There are firms, however, that specifically hire collection attorneys—that is, attorneys who are trained to collect debts from people who owe money. Typically, these attorneys' clients are companies that are trying to collect past-due debts. After a few letters are sent requesting the money that is due, these companies send the bills to an attorney to collect the money for them. People who owe money will usually respond to a letter from an attorney because they are afraid of legal action. If they do not pay the bill immediately, the attorney can file a lawsuit against the person or company that owes the money. Disclaimer: these attorneys work in the same fashion that child support collection agencies work. They will take a large percentage of what they collect as their fee. Typically these fees range from 25% to 33%, or even up to 50% of what they collect. That means if you are owed $100,000, they will keep $25,000, $33,333, or even $50,000 of money collected that should be going to benefit your children. They also take their money off of the "top" which means that they get paid first, before you see a single penny. This is not an option that I would choose. However, I am not going to sit in judgment of anyone who thinks that this is the best option for them. If you are in a tight spot and need your child support money and believe that the attorney that you recently saw can come through and get the money for you, then you have to make the best decision for you and your family. Before you sign on the dotted line, it might make sense for you to check out the self-representation options that my company offers. You have the very same legal options available to you as any attorney does and the law says that you have the right to represent yourself.

Moving on…begin your search by locating your nearest bar association. A bar association is an organization of attorneys created to enforce standards of ethical conduct, continuing education and some act as a referral service to the public. To do this, visit your local library, call directory assistance or Google it on your computer or smart phone. Depending on where you live, you may have a city or county bar association available to you. If so, contact them first. If not, try calling your state bar association. Every state has a bar association, but they may refer you to a regional office. Once you have contacted your nearest bar association, use their referral line to locate attorneys who specialize in the area you have chosen, which you think will work best for your own case. Remember we discussed the benefits and drawbacks of attorneys who specialize in general law, child support cases, family law (divorce), and collections. If they do not have any attorneys with the specialty you seek, move on to the next specialty on your list. Remember that a child support attorney (or family law or divorce) may not know collections and a collections attorney may not know child support. You also want attorneys who are willing to collect their fee from the NRP, as opposed to obtaining any upfront payments. Be sure to have that conversation with them when you speak.

There may not be any information listed with the bar association other than what type of law each attorney practices, but it's worth a try. Some bar associations have more information than others. If they do not have the information that you need, you may have to call each attorney to whom you are referred and ask each one yourself. The bar association will usually refer you to three or four attorneys at a time. They also may charge a fee, so ask them up front if they do, then decide if you still wish to use their service.

If you don't have any luck with the bar associations, Google collection agencies on your computer or smart phone or check the Yellow Pages of your telephone directory under collection agencies. Call all of the collection agencies that are listed and tell them you would like the name of their collection attorney because you would like to hire him or her. When you have a list of at least ten attorneys, call them all. It's important to call more than just a few since some may not be willing to work with you, and those who will work with you will all charge different fees. Yes, it's a lot of work but it will be worth it.

If you are unable to find an attorney through either of the previous methods, try calling small firms in your area that specialize in "general law." General law means that they are a jack-of-all-trades and will generally consider any case. These small firms work well because they work hard, and it's cases like yours that are the meat and potatoes of their business. If they do not know something, generally they will persist until they get the information that they need to help you.

Once you've got an attorney on the phone, asking for references is a good way of judging whether or not he or she will be good for you. Ask for a list of three clients whom the attorney has already helped and be sure to speak with all three references. If you are not able to get into contact with them all, call the attorney back and ask for others. When you call the references that the attorney has given to you, do not bother to ask if he was a good attorney. Chances are the reference was satisfied with the work that was done, or the attorney would not have given you the name in the first place. What you are going to ask will be more specific. Inquire about the procedures the attorney used and if he was a pleasure to work with or not. If the attorney you are considering uses mostly standard procedures and is not very innovative, he will not be a good choice for you. Those who intend to avoid paying child support are pretty skilled with tactics to help them do that and they tend to find attorneys who are skilled in the same ways. Using standard child support enforcement practices play into their games. You have to go outside of the box in order to collect when you are dealing with people like this. Likewise, if he operates in many of the ways that typically cause clients to be discontented with their attorneys, then you may want to continue to look.

Ask if the attorney ever:

- Failed to return phone calls
- Failed to file documents on time
- Increased their fees or the amount of time needed to complete the task
- Was late for appointments or court dates
- Didn't follow through on what he or she had promised to do

The best way to be referred to an attorney is through someone who has hired him or her before. If you know someone who has been divorced or has had to hire an attorney for child support purposes, ask if he or she liked her attorney and why. Find out if the attorney had any of the detrimental characteristics listed above.

Before you choose an attorney, you should have spoken with at least ten of them and gotten references on at least five. When you have at least three attorneys you liked over the phone, have checked their references, and it seems that you will be able to work with them, make appointments to meet with them. Now you are ready to interview. This is the last step before selecting the attorney that you will want to have work with you. Begin by writing down a list of questions that you will want to ask this attorney. When you meet with him or her be confident, professional, and relaxed. It may be helpful for you to bring a notebook with you, so you can jot down information that you want to remember. Here is a list of questions that you will want to ask any lawyer before you allow him to take your case:

1. Is he or she experienced with enforcing child support orders? You will want to know what methods he has used to get NRP's to pay. There are many methods that can be used, so basically you are trying to get him or her to regurgitate as many as he can

name and explain in about five to ten minutes. The next few chapters detail most of the methods. After you finish reading this book, you will know what to look for. Obviously, the attorney who is up to speed in terms of knowledge will be an attorney in whom you are interested.

2. Of course, you are still interested in financing your attorney. You will want to know: the hourly rate, is there a *consultation fee*, is there a *retainer* required, will he work on a *contingency fee*, will he take a payment plan? The attorneys in whom you will be interested are the ones who will agree to work with you in some way. We will talk more about financing options later in the chapter.

3. Is the attorney or the firm that they are with a subscriber to any *credit reporting agencies or utilize other methods of investigations?* The attorney you select may need to use the credit reporting agencies or other methods of investigations to gather information about the NRP. A subscriber to any of these agencies pays a monthly fee to have access to credit reports and investigative services, making it easier for the lawyer to get the information. A non-subscriber will have to pay another attorney or a private investigator a fee to get the information. Obviously, it will be easier and cheaper if he can get the information directly. There is more on how credit reports can be used to your advantage in Chapters 8 to 11. RP's are legally entitled to obtain a copy of the NRP's credit report under certain circumstances as well. That will also be discussed in Chapters 8 to 11. Additionally, there are other methods which can be used to obtain investigative information about the NRP if you are not using a lawyer or if your lawyer does not have capability. (Most lawyers do not have this capability. They purchase from other firms and then pass the cost onto their client. Not cheap at all). You can go directly to a private detective yourself. They will no doubt obtain the information for you but they are not the cheapest game in town. You can use online investigations – more about this in later chapters

and lastly (I have to toot our horns again), you can utilize the services of my company because we can help with investigations as well. With a no-hit, no-pay system, how can you lose? If we don't find the information sought there is no fee and we find the information quickly. Contact us directly for more information. There is more about using investigations to your advantage in Chapters 7 to 11.

4. Will he be willing to obtain liens and judgments against the NRP on your behalf? Is he familiar with how to have a wage *execution* implemented? Will he issue *subpoenas* and conduct *judgment debtor exams* for you? (Do not worry about what these things mean right now, you will find out in the upcoming chapters.) Chances are you will get a few raised eyebrows when you ask these questions. The lawyer you will be interviewing will probably be wondering where you got all of this information. Of course, you will be able to answer intelligently any questions that he asks of you, because you will have read this entire book. If you cannot remember everything, bring the book with you. The important thing is that you are investigating to select the right attorney to handle your case. That will earn you some respect.

After you have met with your three prospective choices, choose the one you feel will best represent you and with whom you feel the most comfortable. Remember that you should have a good relationship with your attorney. You should not feel as if someone is putting you down or doing you a favor by taking your case. You are paying good money to do a job. If you feel at any time during your interview that your chemistry is not right, or if you believe that this attorney is not capable of helping you, do not hire him or her.

Now that you know how to find and hire an attorney, you must be sure that you can pay the fees. Attorney fees vary from firm to firm and from state to state. Generally, you will be billed an hourly fee unless other arrangements are made in advance. If you do not have the money to pay an attorney up front for services, you can try a little bit of "creative financing." Not all attorneys will go for this so it is up to you to express your enthusiasm and confidence in your case and why the attorney should be willing to work unconventionally. The following questions should be asked:

Question #1: Ask the attorney if they are willing to take the case on a contingency basis. Contingency means that if he does not collect any money for you, then he is not paid. Usually personal injury cases work this way. The law firm pays all the expenses that are necessary to try the case or get a settlement. As in the examples earlier in the chapter, when the money is recovered, they take a percentage of the total amount. Do not be surprised if you find an attorney willing to take the case but at the higher fees that I quoted before. You may be asked for 40 or 50 percent of what is owed to you. Why? Because the attorney knows you are in a difficult position and may have nowhere else to turn. Another reason a lawyer may charge a lot is because child support cases can be difficult to work. Only you can decide if it's worth it to you. Also note that a contingency arrangement may be problematic if you choose to change attorney's midstream. Who gets what may be an area of contention between the two attorneys.

Question #2: Another option you have is to ask if the law firm is willing to put you on a payment plan to work off the debt you owe to them. Attorneys are often willing to make these types of arrangements. The key to whether either of these options may work for you is the amount of child support that is past due. Obviously, if you go to an attorney and ask for a contingency plan when your children are owed $3,000 in past-due child support, the plan would not work for you in most cases. The law firm in this case would only stand to make $1,000. While $1,000 may be a lot to some people, the average attorney would scoff at that amount considering the headaches that must be endured while attempting to collect the money. And, they only get paid if they are successful. After you have discussed contingency fees and payment plans and are making an appointment to see your potential attorney, there are a few more questions you should ask before you end your conversation. Find out if you will be charged a consultation fee for the time that it takes to meet with you. Some attorneys charge consultation fees and you need to know this before you make your appointment. If they do charge such a fee, you need to know how much. Most law firms also require a retainer. A retainer is a fee paid to an attorney when the client (that's you) hires him or her. It's a deposit that is applied toward the fees that you will be charged.

If you are really strapped for cash, as many residential parents are, especially when they are not getting child support, you may not be able to pay anything to an attorney. It is an option to consider if you have money to lay out. In the next chapter we will discuss whether it's possible for you to find an attorney to work for you for little or no money at all! But first, let's talk about what happens when you are not happy with the attorney you have already chosen and hired.

Firing Your Attorney

If you find yourself with a bad attorney, fire him. If you decide at any point that you would rather represent yourself instead of having an attorney work your case, or if you run out of attorney money (as many people do), fire him. One of the oldest relationship jokes around is that "the easiest way to get over a man is to get under a new one". Likewise, the easiest way to fire your lawyer is to get a new lawyer. The new lawyer will fire the old lawyer for you by contacting him to get your files and to take care of all of the necessary paperwork. If you haven't hired a new lawyer but instead will be representing yourself, it will be your responsibility to terminate your lawyer and take care of the paperwork. A word to the wise, most attorneys will not take kindly to being fired and surely will not take kindly to being fired by *you*. They will try every trick in the book to keep you hanging on, and then some will even refuse to promptly provide you with your case file – which happens to be your property. Here is an actual question written to me by a mom, and my answer to her. This mom soon became a client of mine.

Dear Simone: I have recently fired my attorney and have requested a copy of my file so that I can represent myself in my child support case but I have not received it yet. How long should it take?

-Shellie

Dear Shellie,

Thanks for your question. I happen to get this question a lot because parents frequently turn to me when they have decided to represent themselves. Often it takes a while for attorneys to comply and there is not much you can do about it unless you have the benefit of knowing your rights.

It is incumbent for the attorney to provide a full copy of the clients file upon request. The file belongs to the client and the attorney must act expeditiously so as to not jeopardize your case. Rule 3-700(D) (1) of the Rules of Professional Conduct requires that once employment has been terminated that the file is returned to the client "promptly". Promptly is not a specific time frame so it depends on the circumstances and that's where it can get tricky.

The attorney has to go through the files and remove personal notes, their work product and make copies of relevant documents. If the case is closed and there is no further work to be done, my personal opinion is that 30 days would not be unreasonable. If you are going to be continuing your case and it is going to court in one week, then my opinion would be that 1 day is more than reasonable.

In order to receive your case file sooner rather than later, I would coach a client of mine to have a reason to need your file asap. Example: My solution would be to make a decision on what direction your case is going in and then write a letter to your attorney based on that and send it certified mail, return receipt with a drop dead date of when you expect to receive your file. Providing a drop dead date is important because you want to leave as little room as possible for the attorney to decide when they think that you need your file as opposed to when you think that you need your file. If you expect your case to continue in any way, holding onto your file could cause you to suffer prejudice such as the inability to properly represent yourself or to meet court deadlines. The state bars have disciplined attorneys for failing to turn over files promptly, hence making your request in writing so you have a record of the timing. Cite the applicable authority above. You should also ask your attorney to inform you if any work product is being withheld (thoughts, legal research, and impressions of the attorney that were never communicated to you).

This information helped Shellie to collect the $100+ thousand dollars that she needed to collect from her ex. Upon receiving her letter, her attorney promptly returned her file (although she had previously been stonewalled) and she went on to properly complete the paperwork which was required to remove her attorney from the case, inform the court that she would be representing herself and successfully filing the motions to collect her child support arrears. Shelly went on to send me an email saying "you rock!" and to tell me that she had previously spent over $75,000 over the years with attorneys continuously battling child support with her ex-husband and that her consultation and 1 coaching session with me was all that she needed to collect all of her money at one time.

There may come a time when you wonder if your attorney has acted unethically. If you believe that this may be true in your case, consider contacting the registration agency in your state. The American Bar Association has a listing of all state registration agencies. You can find the list at:

`www.abanet.org/cpr/regulation/home.html`

chapter 7:
finding a free attorney

After reading Chapter 6, "Finding, Hiring and Firing your Attorney," you now know that there are some creative ways of paying your attorney once you decide to hire him or her. The attorney you choose has to be agreeable to it, of course. You will now learn ways of getting an attorney to work for you for absolutely nothing at all. Absolutely nothing out of your pocket, that is, and that's what we are concerned about, right?

Nothing is free. But, this does not mean that you have to be the one who pays. If you have decided to and have tried to hire a private attorney but cannot afford one the conventional way, and you have not found one who will work with you creatively concerning payment, you can try legal aid, government attorneys, and/or having the non-custodial parent pay the attorney fees.

Legal aid

There once was a time when across the country legal aid attorneys were available for residential parents who were trying to get child support from a non-residential parent. At that time, every county in every state had an office to serve you. The only qualifier was that you had to prove that you needed the help and that you could not afford services on your own. In short, these services were available to poor families - families whose income fell below the poverty line. There are very few states that still offer this assistance. Legal aid offices still exist and they still aid poor families with obtaining child support orders but they will not help you to collect the money. The only way to know for sure whether your state is one which will still help you to collect or if they have joined the rest of the offices that do not do this anymore, is to call and find out for yourself. I must say that I have been in this business for a long time and I have spoken with many parents and have not heard of a single office in years that still provides this service. That doesn't mean that one doesn't still exist somewhere. If a tree falls in the middle of the forest and no one is there to hear it fall, it *does* still make a noise. What I do know is that some of these aid offices have partnered with or can at least refer you to agencies that can help you, for free, if you are poor. Usually they are not law firms but they have an attorney or two on staff who will do some basic collection work. If you do not know where the legal aid office in your area is, try ones of these:

- Google it. Use your favorite search engine and type in keywords like: Legal Aid Office St. Louis Missouri (use your own city and state, of course). You should quickly be able to locate the office near you.
- Go old style and look it up in your telephone directory. In the White Pages, search for a listing under legal aid. In the Yellow Pages, look under both "attorneys" and "lawyers" and then search for any listing under legal aid. Be sure to look for advertisements as well. You can also check the Blue Pages under government agencies in your county. A telephone number for legal aid may be listed there.
- Call directory assistance (information) and ask for the legal aid office in your county. In most areas an information call will cost

you a few dollars even if you have an "unlimited" calling plan, so be aware of that. If you do not want to pay the extra money because you are on a tight budget, as many residential parents are and you can still find one, use a public pay phone to place the information call. Most pay phones will not charge you to call information. Then go home and place the local call from your home telephone. Looking for a public pay telephone has gone by the way of the record player – most kids these days have never even seen one. Here's a little tip: if you are looking for a public phone, stalk the gas stations in your area. They are the most likely places that you'd find such a dinosaur. Dinosaur or not, it can get you a free telephone number listing. Bring an alcohol wipe or some anti-bacterial spray with you on your quest; those things are loaded with germs.

- Similar to calling the information line on your home telephone, the directory assistance on your cell phone can find your listing for you. Also like your home telephone service, they will charge you for the service

- Call your local welfare department or child support enforcement agency. Tell them that you are searching for your county's legal aid office. Generally, they should be able to help you.

- Your local library has a wealth of information. Call or visit the reference desk and let the reference librarian know that you need to find the legal aid office for your area. If anyone can find the number and address in a flash, the reference librarian can.

- Finally, some law schools run legal aid clinics that serve the public. If there are any law schools in your area, find out if they provide these services. These may indeed be the last of the truly FREE lawyers.

In order to use the services of the legal aid office you must be either *indigent* or have an income that is considered to be at or below the poverty level for where you live. If you are on welfare, you will automatically qualify for services. If you have a job but make very little money, you need to find out what the poverty level is in your area to know whether or not you qualify. A quick search of the Federal Poverty Guidelines (not the Federal Poverty Threshold – that's a different formula) for your state will give you the information that you need. Try this link: http://aspe.hhs.gov/poverty/index.cfm. A large number of people fall into a gray area that is sometimes difficult to determine. There are some people who may be on welfare, or not have a job, they may not be getting child support for their five children, but because they own the house that they live in, they will not qualify for free legal services. Some people do not have any source of income, and are not receiving court-ordered child support or alimony, yet they have been forced to leave their homes with their children because they can no longer afford the upkeep. They still may not be qualified for legal aid because they are still married to their spouse who is a high earner. Therefore, it is thought that they do not need handouts. There are many situations such as these where residential parents are turned down for legal assistance even though they have no money of their own.

If this sounds like your situation, you must prepare your financial statement before your appointment with the legal aid office. Use the chart that is available to you in Chapter 1, "Establishing Your Child Support Order." It will help you to outline your expenses. You will also need to provide the legal aid office with information on all of your income, including child support and alimony, if you get any. You need to show that even though you may have a spouse who makes a great deal of money, he does not give any to you. Bring your overdue bills, eviction notices, and whatever else you have to plead your case. Although the legal aid office has guidelines that they follow when they accept clients, they have a little bit of leeway to make their own final decision.

If it is shown that you have no money to pay your bill, when you use the services of the legal aid office, as in the case of indigence, you will receive the services free of charge. If it is thought that you are not completely indigent, you may be asked to pay a reduced fee. Normally this is billed on a sliding scale according to your income. The more money you make, the more you will be charged, up to the normal fee that others pay. The less money you make, the less you will be charged. If the only reason you are not considered indigent is due to possession of property rather than income, and you are really desperate for help, ask if the legal aid office will place a lien on your property for the fees to guarantee their payment. I emphasize desperation here. Why would you want a lien on your property? However, as you will see I say many times throughout this book, that it is my job to inform you of your options. It is your job to make the decisions regarding your personal life.

A lien is a claim upon property that prevents its sale or transfer until a debt is satisfied. Legally, no one (not you, your husband, or any outside party) could sell your property until the debt to legal aid had been paid. In other words, you, or whoever received payment for the property, would have to subtract the amount of the debt from the payment, which would go to legal aid. If the sale somehow did go through without the debt being paid, the lien would still be attached to the property so that the debt now would be the responsibility of the new owner of the property. The idea is that legal aid is guaranteed its money when you actually have it on hand, and in the meantime you have the help you need. If you are planning to use the services of a legal aid office, keep in mind that they usually have a long waiting list. If you qualify for free or reduced rate services, put your name on the waiting list anyway. If something else comes up in the meantime, and you are able to get an attorney by other means, then it's just gravy for you. You need to have as many choices as you can. Do not worry about not needing their services when your time comes—it will be easy for them to go on to the next person on the list.

Government attorneys

Government child support attorneys are free to anyone and everyone who wants to use them—with a few catches, however. They are usually referred to as Title IV-D attorneys because they work for the *Title IVD agencies*. Title IV-D agencies are the child support enforcement agencies in every county that are bound by law to help you enforce your child support order. This is the office that you visit when you open your child support case…if you use "the child support office". Remember, many people have attorneys who file their child support petitions for them and many people file their own petitions and represent themselves. If you have a case that is easy to manage, the caseworker to whom you have been assigned may be the only person with whom you have contact. If your case is more of a nightmare and in need of more legwork—if the non-residential parent needs to be located, or if you need to file a motion for *federal child support evasion* etc.—a government attorney will have to be the one to handle these matters for you. The attorney will only become involved if certain services need to be implemented. The attorney is free and is available to anyone who has a case in a *Title IV-D agency*. This is not an attorney whom you can call up and hire as you would any other. They are sheltered and protected by the agency because there are not many of them. They have an overwhelming caseload and have a difficult time keeping up with the many cases that they are assigned. Frankly, publicizing their existence is sure to cause problems for them and a longer waiting list for you. The reason I am willing to cause such a ruckus is because no one at the agency will tell you about them unless they are forced to do so. This does not help you in the least bit. What does help you is knowing that there are things that these attorneys can do that can make a world of difference with your child support case. They will be covered in more detail in Chapter 12, "What the Government Can Do for You".

As with any other attorney or other goods or services that you can get for free, it will not be made easy for you. First, you must again put yourself on the waiting list, or at least let it be known that you want and need the services of these attorneys. You will be fully prepared after reading this entire book to inform the attorney of what services you feel will work well with your case. You can then ask if they have any further suggestions. You will be attempting to build a relationship with this attorney so that the two of you can work together to enforce your child support order. One bit of caution: since these are government attorneys, they work for the government and they do not work for you. Uncle Sam hires them to help collect on cases in which the government is particularly interested. If you are on welfare, the government is supporting you so it has a direct interest in whether you get your child support or not. Every child support case of those who are on welfare is handled by the state collection agencies—the Title IV-D child support enforcement offices to which I have been referring. If you read the introduction to this book, you know that when these agencies were opened in 1974 the government decided to give the same services to anyone who had a child support case. So even though these attorneys' primary interest is not in helping the non-welfare cases, they will. Just remember that they do not work directly for you so that means you can be even less bossy. It will be awfully difficult to fire them and you may not want to since they have the means to help you. They may not want to take your advice or even hear you out with how you would like your case to be handled. One client of mine recently complained that not only did she not get a chance to speak with or meet her attorney before her case was called but that she never got a chance to meet him at all! No introduction. No hand shake. Nothing. Her case was called and he proceeded to the front of the courtroom to plead her case. When all was said and done, he turned and walked out of the courtroom and that was that. One more final word—anything you share with them will be shared with the government as well. There will not be any client confidentiality in your relationship as far as the government is concerned. Also, you will be sharing your attorney with many others. If the non-residential parent of your child has another child with someone else, you may have to share your attorney with her as well. Can you imagine that? If you contact your local office for assistance from a government attorney, you are likely to get one or more of these responses:

Deadbeat vs. Deadbroke

- You may be told to retain a private attorney.
- You may be discouraged from seeking assistance from a government attorney due to a long waiting list.
- You may be told that you cannot contact the government attorney—he or she will contact you when they are ready.
- You may be told that there aren't any government attorneys.
- People may be rude to you and not help you at all.

If you get any of these responses, and chances are very good that you will, do not let them confuse or anger you. Read on—in Chapter 21, "Effective Complaining," you will learn how to deal with these issues.

Non-residential parent pays attorney fees

If you must take the non-residential parent to court to collect your child support, you can normally collect attorney fees from him. If, after reading this entire book, you decide that it may be in your best interest to go to court, you will possibly be in a better position to hire an attorney without any payment from you. Most judges will award attorney fees to the *plaintiff* (that's you) and attorneys know this. The drawback is that the amount awarded to you may be significantly lower than the fee you will be charged. This is where some more creative financing may have to come into play. Your attorney may not ask you for the remainder of the bill, but if he does you will be responsible for it. The non-residential parent may scoff at your attorney bill. If you are not able to collect child support, chances are that you will not be able to get this bill paid either. On the other hand, after appearing in court the non-residential parent may come to his senses. Maybe, or maybe not. These suggestions may not help all residential parents but it will give some of you another option, and for others it will actually work. If it does not help you, just press on. At the very least, you have just added more money onto the bill that the non-residential parent cannot run away from forever. For now— maybe. Forever—never.

<u>HOT TIPS FOR ATTORNEYS</u>

Consider taking child support cases on contingency. Align yourself with great supports, to provide the assistance that you will need. Consider my company's Leto initiative which is designed to streamline child support collections for attorneys.

chapter 8:

locating the non-residential parent

When I was a girl of about ten, I read mystery novels in which a teenage sleuth would solve problems in her town. I was fascinated with how the young detective would have the smallest clues and yet was able to solve her mysteries. This chapter reminds me of my childhood with that young detective. Most RP's with child support orders will find that, at some point, they may need to search for either the NRP or his/her assets, or sometimes both. The least of offenders may move to a different town or county or maybe take a new job, second job, or start a side business and not advise you and/or the courts. This may make it difficult for you to get child support payments from him/her or to receive an amount which is fair and in accordance with the child support guidelines. The greater offenders will go through a lot more trouble to remain hidden. It is not uncommon for those who owe child support (obligors) and who have learned the weaknesses and loopholes of the child support system to move to a new state for the sole purpose of avoiding child support payments. They may also put all of their assets into someone else's name - a new spouse, girlfriend/boyfriend/, friend, business partner, or even a complete stranger hired to conceal the information. They may lie and cheat on tax documents, work in cash-only businesses and more, all in order to avoid paying child support. That is the focus of the next three chapters. One will address how an ordinary parent with no formal investigative training and very little free time on their hands can find the NRP if they are MIA (missing in action), the next will address how this same parent can locate the NRP's assets which have so deftly been hidden away and the third will address managing the complexities of interstate cases, especially if you are going through the court system with all its back and forth red tape. A gazillion child support cases (only a modest exaggeration) are left untouched in the child support agencies and in the court system simply because the caseworkers, the lawyers and the parents involved do not have enough information. They cannot find the *obligors* (the NRP's that owe them money) or they mistakenly believe that they do not have jobs or income. If it is known that they do have a job or income, it may be mistakenly believed that they earn far less than they actually do. Of course there are those obligors out there who really are unemployed and who are really having a hard time. The problem is that most of the time, you can't tell the difference by being on the outside and looking in. You need to determine that information for yourself so you can decide whether to stick with what you've got or to strap on your battle gear and go out there and defend your children. Until your caseworker or your lawyer, or even you - if you are pro sé (representing yourself), are able to obtain more information, everyone's hands are tied. Unless you are ready, willing and able to hire a P.I., and have deep P.I. pockets at your disposal, if you want your child support, you may have to put on your own detective cap and get to work. Information that can be used to track someone down is abundant; you just have to know where to look and what to look for.

When I was in college and had my first apartment, I worked at a bank collecting on loans that were past due. Frequently, I had accounts where the customer skipped town without paying the bill. These accounts are called "skips." Part of my job was to perform preliminary "skip tracing" on these accounts before they were sent to our legal department. During my employment at that bank, I was honored for being "Collector of the Month" in my department every month that I was there. I will now share some of my secrets with you.

The first thing you want to do is gather as much information about the obligor as you can. If you lived with him/her you may have more information at your disposal than someone who did not. If you are still living with the obligor, or have access to his/her personal financial information, you are ahead of the game. Photocopy whatever paperwork you can, especially income tax records for the past three to five years and the obligor's Social Security Number. Brainstorm for any information that you can come up with. When you are done, get paper and a pen to list the following data:

1. What is the obligor's full name? Has he/she ever used any alternate names or other surnames? Does he/she have any nicknames?
2. What is the obligor's birth date? Where was he/she born?
3. What is the obligor's Social Security Number?
4. What is the most recent address that you have for the obligor?
5. List the addresses at which the obligor has lived for the past three years.
6. What are the most recent telephone numbers (landline, job and cell phone) that you have for the obligor?
7. Where does the obligor work? Write down the name of the company as well as the address. Do you know his/her supervisor's name? What does the obligor do for a living? What is his/her title at work?
8. List the obligor's employers for the past three years, as well as their addresses and phone numbers. Also list the supervisors or managers. Was he/she employed in the same capacity as they are now?
9. If the obligor is self-employed, list the clients that he/she has had for the past three years. If you have their addresses and or telephone numbers, list those as well.

10. What is the obligor's driver's license number, and which state issued it? What are the makes models, and the years of the vehicles that he/she drives? What are the plate numbers and the vehicle identification numbers?

11. Has the obligor been formerly married? If so, list all former marriages including the dates of the marriages and dissolution. List the former spouse's' names.

12. List the names and addresses of the obligor's parents, including the obligor's mother's maiden name. If they still work, what are their occupations and where are they employed?

13. List the obligor's siblings and friends along with their addresses, telephone numbers, and employment information.

14. List the obligor's creditors.

15. List the obligor's banks and insurance companies.

16. List any real estate that the obligor owns.

17. Does the obligor belong to any clubs or organizations? List them.

18. What hobbies does the obligor have?

19. Does the obligor vote? If so, where is he/she registered and for which party?

20. Does the obligor receive, or will the obligor receive in the future, any military, government, or private pension or other benefits?

21. List any military service of the obligor. Include the branch of service, dates and locations of assignment, rank, service number, date, and status of discharge.

22. If the obligor has ever been in prison, list the conviction(s), including the date and location of conviction, the offenses, and the locations of incarceration.

23. If the obligor is or has ever been on probation, list the state and county and the name of the probation officers.

24. Is the obligor presently married? If so, assemble all of the aforementioned information on his spouse as well.

Along the way you will undoubtedly uncover other information that you could not put your hands on or did not know about the obligor from the start. Add what you discover to the document that you are creating. The more that you know about your obligor, the better your chances are of locating him/her. It's like a game of hide and seek. Your obligor is hiding and you're going to find them. Now that you have your completed list, I will tell you how to use it. Ready?

Come out, come out, wherever you are!

When I wrote my first book "1-800-Deadbeat: How to Collect your Child Support" and my second book, "Deadbeats, What Responsible Parents Need to know about Collecting Child Support", the simplest way to locate anyone was through a telephone directory. Although it may seem silly at first thought — why on earth would anyone who is trying to hide have a listed telephone number, it was not uncommon. It was also very likely that if you used your telephone to call directory assistance that the telephone operator might say something like "I have so and so listed at that address but the telephone number is unlisted". When you have been placed into the position of needing to locate the NRP, every little bit of information which you can gather leads you closer to your goal. If you keep on digging, eventually you will hit pay dirt. When that happened, those unsuspecting telephone operators gave away the NRP's location. I am sure that they had no idea what they had just done.

You are about to move into the mind-set of finding someone who doesn't want to be found. How difficult or easy it may be can be determined by identifying the hiding level, (as described earlier in the preface of this book) as well as in the section of the 4-room support-matrix he/she generally tends to stay. The support matrix is explained below. I create these levels and matrices to make it easier for you to determine how much work it is going to take on your part to locate the person and identify the assets and also to keep your melt-downs at bay. He or she may be much easier to find than you think. We all have different work schedules, energy levels and BS thresholds. If you are ready to find him/her, if he/she owes you and your children tons of money and you want to assess whether they can really pay you or not right now or whether you need to ride it out a bit longer...I will tell you this - as I have said before, anyone can be found in 3 months or less, depending on how quickly you can move through the material provided. You can locate them *and* their assets. The only exception is if they are in hiding under <u>Level 4</u>. Otherwise, you can collect your child support from anyone. The question that you have to ask yourself is: "Does my child deserve to have this money". Whether you are capable of raising your children on your own or not – with or without the other parents financial contribution is beside the point. Keeping in mind that child support is a "right" that your child has – and not a privilege and not a handout. Does your child deserve this money, even if you were to simply deposit it into an account and save it for his/her eighteenth birthday? If you are an attorney or a child support caseworker, the question is – does my client deserve this money for their children? Am I willing to let no stone go unturned to service my client?

A word of caution to parents and attorneys alike: This is going to be an extremely intense chapter. I am going to give you <u>over 60 methods</u> to track down a NRP. Most of them will be no charge methods, some of them will charge small fees but I tell you how to get those service providers to give you their information for free as well. These companies have been vetted by me so you can be sure that you will get a healthy dose of information on the NRP if you use them...probably much more than you need to know. I will tell you how to use all of these services to your advantage and give you the heads up on when it may be time for you to step up your game and actually pay for a service.

Allow me to refresh your memory about the Levels of Disappearance. These levels will give you a good idea of how difficult it may be to find the person that you are looking for and the types of tricks that they may be up to. Combine it with the Support Matrix which follows and you should know what you will need to invest (time, energy, and on few occasions – very small [as in I'm buying a cup of coffee small] amounts of money) in order to find this person, get him/her served and into court, if necessary, garnishing wages, placing liens on accounts, seizing property, etc.

LEVELS OF DISAPPEARANCE

- **Level One:** Very basic. 98% of deadbeats can be found within days when they disappear under a level one. Yet, they have disappeared to the extent that it would take a private investigator (PI) several hundred dollars of your money to track him/her down. When they move they won't leave a forwarding address, they change cell phone companies from the one you knew them to have, they work off of the books. . .

- **Level Two:** It's getting warmer. This is a deadbeat that means business. They have done their homework and they know that it would cost you several thousand dollars to find him/her if you hire a PI and they are banking that you are not going to spend that money. Considering that not all PI's are good PI's and that the only thing that drives them is M-O-N -E-Y, you could go to one or two or three before you find the one that will put out for you. At this point, the deadbeat is shredding their trash; they do not have utilities and telephone bills in their name. Their vehicles and home may be in someone else's name or the name of their business.

- **Level Three:** It's downright HOT in here. I am not going to lie to you. If you have a deadbeat in level three, you are not going to find him/her through any traditional measures. In addition to hiding from you, he/she also keeps his/her information private from his/her bankers, his/her lawyers, his/her doctors and the IRS. At this level, not even Santa Claus would be able to find him/her on Christmas Eve to deliver a puppy. You would have to pay a PI a considerable amount of money to find this cat. If he/she already owes you a considerable amount of money, you might consider it a wash. You might – or you might want to consider some of the other tips/tools and points of leverage that

I have learned, taught and have used with success along the way…and none of them involve hiring an expensive PI.

- **Level Four:** If your deadbeat is at this level then he/she is in the Federal Witness Security Program (which some people incorrectly call the Witness Protection Program thanks to TV and the movies), or might as well be. He/she has burned all of his/her bridges, he/she has no contact whatsoever with family and friends. He/she receives no magazines, or newsletters, belongs to no clubs or hobby stores. He is dead to the world. This might work in your favor though. He/she is dead to the world, then that means that the time is ripe for you to go to court and have them declared legally dead. Then file the life-insurance claim that you have on him/her and collect your child support arrears that way. Dead is dead, right?

Every non-paying NRP will fall into one of the four areas of the following matrix. Find out where your NRP falls, combine it with his/her level of disappearance from above and you will have a snapshot of how much trouble you really have on your hands.

SUPPORT MATRIX

Willing to Pay / Capable of Paying	Willing to Pay / Not Capable of Paying
Not Willing to Pay / Capable of Paying	Not Willing to Pay / Not Capable of Paying

Telephone Directories

Let's start with the old fashioned telephone just to be certain that you are covering all of your bases. Hey – you never know. Call directory assistance and ask for the obligor by name in the city in which you last knew him/her to live. Be sure also to check under any other names that the obligor may be using. Every name that the obligor has ever used is a possibility. If you are able to get a telephone number, ask if there is an address listed as well. Some information directories will give you an address if they have one, some will not. Ask the telephone information bureau in your area (or in the area of the person you need to track down) if there is such a service that you can use. Most likely you will get one of these three responses:

1. You may find that there is a listing for your obligor, but that the telephone number is not available to the public. If this is the response that you are given, it is a win. You now know the general location of the NRP. Press on by using the lists of locator services below.

2. There is also the possibility that you will get a listed number and call it only to find that the number you have been given has been reassigned to someone else and that it is not a correct number after all. The smallest possibility remains that you could actually get a real working number for the obligor, but let's not bet the bank on it. This book would only have been three pages long if it really were that easy. Furthermore, many people use cell phones now as their main phone and so they no longer have land lines.

3. The last response would be that there is no listing at all.

Backward directories

When I was working in collections, there were times when we were able to find a current telephone number for an obligor, but no address. Conversely, maybe we had an address, but no telephone number. When this situation occurred we had special directories to help us out. There are several companies that publish or print these directories. In our office we used "Coles" directories and "backward" directories. They are backward listings of telephone numbers and addresses. In these directories you can look up a person's telephone number and find his or her address. Likewise, you can use an address to find a telephone number. These directories can be found at your local library, and the reference librarian should be able to show you how to use them. If your library doesn't have them because it is too small to stock such items, go to the largest library in your area-it will be sure to carry at least one brand. Also available are city directories at the local Chamber of Commerce. These city directories give the same information, with one additional plus: it may also state the found person's occupation and place of employment. City directories are mainly used to obtain current addresses for the service of legal documents. Since that is what you need it for — or something similar — it should work perfectly for you. These directories will also provide names, addresses, and telephone numbers of neighbors or former neighbors of the obligor. Continue on with this chapter and you will find out why and how this information can be helpful to you. These are some very old methods of "skip tracing". They may bear fruit for you or they may not. You may have to search high and low for a Coles directory these days because they have moved most of their research online and they now target their services towards certain industries as opposed to listing anyone and everyone. Even though that is the case I still suggest to leave no stone unturned. It is true that online is where you can find most of your information these days, so get yourself a hot cup of tea or a nice glass of wine and settle in for this next section. The ride is going to get bumpy and your eyes are going to get blurry.

The first thing to remember is that you are mining for information. If you expect to get all of the information that you are looking for in one shot, you are setting yourself up for disappointment. If you do get all of your information in one shot, email me personally at: simone@dontgetmadgetpaid.com because this is something that I want to know. Chances are that you need to uncover a lot of information about the NRP and it may take a few different sites to find everything that you need. This is especially true since I will be directing you to sites which can provide information to you for free or on a "trial membership" basis. I will also introduce you to some paid sites but I save those for last because most people can find what they are looking for before they have to resort to actually paying a fee.

What are you looking for? You are looking for any "hit" on the NRP's name, address, phone number (landline or cell), city or state where they live, employment, family members, neighbors, personal and real property, accounts (hint – record everything that you find – it may or may not be accurate but you will be able to determine that later), don't discount anything unless you absolutely can determine that it is false. Don't worry about anything else yet. Make organized lists. What I am about to provide to you is going to be lists upon lists of data storage houses. Some of them you will be familiar with and some of them you have never heard of before. You will be amazed at how many companies are actually out there storing your information…and then providing it to anyone who asks for it or even selling your information for a price. Then the people that they give it to or sell it to turn around and give it or sell it to others. Your name, your address, your phone number, your occupation – they are all whores to be given to any pimp who wants it and you didn't even know. I will say it again, unless you are in the Federal Witness Protection program – you can be found by anyone who puts in enough effort. If you can be found…the NRP can be found. We will start with the easy ones, by group, whether they are the popular and well-known ones or not and then move on to the more complex sites:

Social Network Search Sites

Don't let a single one fool you. Not a single one. ALL social networking sites are aggregators. An aggregator is a web-based application which gathers your information and content from various internet sources and compiles it in one place for viewing. They maintain a copy for themselves and they also sell your information and content of your social media sites to other companies.

Nearly everyone under the age of 70 has one social networking site or the other. Most people have several. For some, Facebook and Twitter are the preferred sites used to engage and interact online socially. Others choose accounts such as LinkedIn because it is perceived to be a site for professionals and if it's professional then some people think that it must be safer to include your personal information on their site. I have heard some people say that they like LinkedIn better because they didn't think that they would disclose their personal information and content or sell their demographics to third parties. If that's your train of thought – you are wrong. In fact, you may never have opened a social networking site at all and the data miners still have social networking information about you which may be very detailed and confidential. Not just about you but about your family too. Once it has been put out there in infospace – it's there forever and can never be deleted. Even when information has been deleted from the live site itself, the information remains. If your daughter posted something about her mom or your sister…and you are that mom or that aunt, there is information about you on a social networking site and you may not have put it there at all. The following is a list of social network miners. Even if the NRP deleted his/her account when they went on the run so that you wouldn't be able to find them, their information is out there in some social networking database. Did he/she list where they live? Did he/she say where they work? Check and see…

infospace.com – Type in the NRP's name and infospace will list everyone they have with that name. Simply click onto the link provided and it will take you directly to the source where they do their data mining. If they have mined data for Penelope Pitstop, you may have to click onto all of the Penelope Pitstops that they have listed until hopefully you find the one that you are looking for. It's free. I like free.

peekyou.com – Will not only list the name, but also the recorded age, email address if they have it, recorded city and state, known cities and possible relatives, making it easier for you to determine if you have the John or Jane C Smith that you are seeking. Listing relatives may be helpful because maybe Aunt Jenny knows where they have been hiding out. Peekyou.com will at first tell you that they have found the files you are searching for. Then they will tell you that they are loading them, and qualifying you for the files and on and on until you have waited with bated breath for what seems like an hour before they finally say: okay now pay. I have never found anyone on peekyou.com because I usually just give up mid-way. I don't know if they offer a free trial or anything of the sort. Try them if you like. Maybe you can send an email and let me know if you found your NRP and how much it cost.

mylife.com – Claims to manage and monitor your *entire* life online. They advertise that not only can you find your lost connections but that you can follow them as well (on social media) – all in one neat little place. They "say" that they offer the ability for you to monitor your identity and "share what matters". Mylife.com may not be one of the most popular sites but they have over 700 Million profiles for you to search. What's really interesting about mylife.com is that they also offer a feature where you can track *who's searching for you.*

STOP

This is important information. If the NRP is indeed trying to hide out and evade you and their child support responsibilities and learns that you are snooping on his/her trail, you stand to lose any ground which you may have gained. They will pick up their tent and run, stamp out any fires which may have been burning, cover them with dirt and your trail will be lost.

So what's a RP tracking down their child support supposed to do?

Whenever you are doing any kind of searching, for Pete's sake, NEVER use any email address that you use on a regular basis and which can be traced back to you in any shape or form. Remember, that all of your emails are tracked by all of the email companies out there and just as there are tons of ways to find someone who is hiding from you, likewise, there are tons of ways to find out who is trying to track you down. For someone on the run, this is something that they are looking out for all of the time. You need to go into stealth mode. One good turn deserves another, I say.

Step 1: Create a new account with a free provider such as Gmail. It doesn't matter which provider that you use – Gmail, Hotmail, Yahoo – as long as it's free because you don't want to pay for anything right now. Provide any name that you want and a password to go along with it. Again – you are in stealth mode. Do not use your real name. If you are Patricia, also do not use Patty or Pat. For gender and date of birth, you can also provide any data that you want, including using false information. Google will not verify this and it is not illegal. If you are planning to also use this account for the purpose of fraud or to otherwise commit a crime, then it would become illegal. Don't do that. Simply creating an alternate name in of itself is no more of a crime than a man named William choosing to go by an alternate name like Bill, or Bud or Mac or Buddy. A William could also use Bill or Bud or Mac or Buddy on their legal paperwork such as driver's license or insurance cards and it's still not illegal. Gmail will ask you to pick an email address. It doesn't matter what you choose, just as long as it can't be pinned on you. If you hate horses, it could be `ILOVEMYHORSE54321@gmail.com` Whatever.

Step 2: Navigate over to `www.notsharingmy.info` and type in your new email address, `ILOVEMYHORSE54321@gmail.com` then click onto "Get an obscure email". The site will give you a permanent forwarding email address.

This is what it will look like:

```
Your regular email:  ILOVEMYHORSE54321@gmail.com
Get an obscure email
```

You will see that your new email address is:

```
Your anonymous email is

11vhc@notsharingmy.info

Enjoy your privacy!
```

What's the purpose of all of this cloak and dagger? If the NRP is looking over his/her shoulder constantly wondering if someone is trying to track him/her down, they will now have the email address which was provided to the search engine that provided the data on him/her. If you use an obscure email address, that's all that they will be able to obtain. In my case, it would be 11vhc@notsharingmy.info. If he/she is a sneaky little devil (which undoubtedly they are because they are in hiding), they will probably try to find out who is looking for them and for what purpose. Maybe he/she is dodging bills all over all the country, several child support cases or maybe even the law. If they search 11vhc@notsharingmy.info it will only lead them to ilovemyhorse54321@gmail.com, and that will only lead them to the alternate name you created in your Gmail account.
***

<u>spoke.com</u> – Is a great resource because they take what they learn from a person's online presence and then they combine it with public records information. They claim it is to help you keep your connections in a centralized place and create a "supercharged" address book. Regardless of why they do what they do, if any of your NRP's info has

made it into the spoke list, it is possible for you to hit pay dirt with this free site. Oh – but you must register with spoke first in order for them to give you any info. They must continue to build their list, right? No worries – use your obscure email address and they won't get anything on you.

A word for your conscience

As I was writing this chapter, I had a conversation with someone about alternate names (such as Bill, or Bud or Mac or Buddy), obscure email addresses and other tools which I will teach you later on in the chapter. This person mentioned to me that some people might not feel good about creating and taking on false personas in order to chase down the non-paying NRP, even if there is absolutely nothing illegal about it.

I can't speak for everyone and if it doesn't make you feel good – then don't do it. Move on to other tools that I will give you. However, I don't see it any differently than when a woman tells the seamstress at the bridal salon that her wedding is 4 weeks earlier than it actually is in order to get her wedding gown completed in a several-weeks-ahead-of-schedule stress-free amount of time before the wedding. Women do that all of the time and it's a common practice. Is that wrong too? Conscience all better now?

emailfinder.com – This service culls email addresses from social network data provided by its users. It doesn't matter if the person has already deleted the email address after once having it listed or if the account itself has been deleted. If it had at some point been provided and emailfinder.com got its hands on it, it's there. You may find that you go to emailfinder.com and locate the person for whom you are looking and find that there are several email addresses listed for him/her. That's because once it is in their system, it will never go away. How does emailfinder.com get your and everyone else's email address? Why – when you register for a social networking site, you give them your email of course! I don't need to tell you at this point that you will be providing your obscure email address to emailfinder.com when you do your searching. This way nothing will link back to you at all.

Emailfinder.com, like a lot of these services, have small fees associated with the usage of their service and the retrieval of their mined data. You will want to always ask for the "free" trial memberships. Emailfinder.com has a 7 day trial which you can use to locate your NRP. Then you log-on and end your trial on the 6th day so that they don't stand a chance of charging your credit or debit card for the $7.95.

A word about your credit and debits cards

You weren't actually thinking that you would use your real credit or bank card, were you? Emailfinder.com or any (and all) of the services available to track down the NRP (and anytime – and I mean *anytime* – that you use your credit and debit cards online with *any* and *all* merchants) will capture your information – your name, your address, your credit card number and what you purchase – and compile it in a database for future usage. Your internet privacy aside – there is always that possibility that the NRP can be tipped off that you are searching for him/her and that would mess up your strategy. How can they be tipped off you ask – when all you are doing is a search within a paid service that you are using on the internet? More about that later. Right now let's discuss how to avoid the problem to begin with.

Head over to your neighborhood drug store or supermarket and buy a prepaid debit card. Any one will do. Hand over about $25 (or whatever you can afford to spend at the time) to activate the card, and the card is yours to be used without any trace of ownership. Some of these cards expire after 30 days unless you "register" them and allow the company to send a permanent card to you. You can either plan around this so that you do not use any card for more than 30 days or you can "register" your card with your alternate name and obscure email address. Have the card sent to a PO Box as well – don't use your actual home address. If you are strategic about it, you can get away with using these free trials and rarely pay a thing for the searches you conduct. There are pay services which we will talk about later but at this level, there should be no need to pay for anything. Just keep recycling the pre-paid card system.

Deadbeat vs. Deadbroke

People Search Directories

A people search directory is an online directory which can provide you with personal information which many years ago would appear in a printed yellow or white page book or a city directory. For those who remember using these books, if you looked someone up in the yellow and white pages, you would commonly find their full name, home address and phone number. If you used a city directory, commonly only found at your local library, you could also learn who their neighbors are, what their occupation is and where they currently were employed. People Search Directories are the Yellow Pages, White Pages and city directories of our times.

spokeo.com – People searches are different from social network searches in that they focus on searching for data on people in general, as opposed to what might be offered on a social networking site. In these sites, you are more likely to find addresses, work places, dates of birth, etc. Spokeo.com is one of those sites. Navigate to spokeo.com and type in your own name. If you are in spokeo's database you are likely to feel shocked by the results – and probably a little unsafe at the same time. Be aware that at any time, anyone can learn tons of personal information about you. Scary and bad on one hand – juicy and good on the other hand – because you can use this information to gain the upper hand in your child support case.

Spokeo.com will provide you with full name, email address, telephone number, age, current and previous home addresses, information on family members, relatives and spouse, photos, videos, social network profiles, neighbors, education, and occupation. The freakiest of all is that they will not only show where your house is located on a map but the site will zoom in so that you can have a good look at it and provide the full property records of your home including beds, bath, square footage, lot size and estimated home value. If you were to write to me and tell me that your spokeo.com lookup also showed a picture of you at home in your shower, with a bar of soap in your hand, I wouldn't be surprised. Needless to say, this information could prove to be invaluable when you are mining for information on the NRP. Invaluable. Keep your curtains closed.

pipl.com – I have been told that pipl.com is a favorite site for private investigators. It is also one of my favorite sites. What I like about pipl.com is that in addition to home addresses, email addresses, social networks, family members and the like, it also includes a photo taken from a social networking site, next to the data provided and asks…"is this the one"? Because there could be another person with the same name of the person you are looking for, it allows you to confirm that you are getting information on the correct person. You might have to click around a bit to find who and what you are looking for but I have never been disappointed. That doesn't mean that I find all of the information that I am looking for in one shot, but it does mean that I have always been able to find information on a NRP when I have used pipl.com. Another good thing to know is that while it is a subscription site, just like most of the others, if you click around enough and then threaten to leave the site by trying to close the browser, I have always received a pop-up offering a special deal for $1 instead of the subscription prices that they tried to previously push on me. Always. They will try to get you to pay later by withholding certain information until you do, but you can find a lot of information for a $1 – and when it's a trial membership, what can be better than that?

123people.com – This site, like pipl.com mines public information from the internet and combines it into one neat report for you to buy. This is one of those services where it will be difficult to obtain information from them unless you pay a fee. To pay a fee or not to pay a fee is entirely up to you. Before you decide to pay a fee to a site like 123people.com, I would encourage you to wait until you have learned about all of the companies that can offer information to you and then decide where and if you should spend any money at all.

zoominfo.com – Unlike the other sites, zoominfo.com focuses their information mining on professional work history and careers. Zoom advertises that they offer "extreme targeting and lead generation". This means two things: 1. That their information is fresh and updated because…2. They have bought your information from third party sources who recently sold it to them and they intend to resell *your* information to buyers who are targeting people like you in order to market their products. If your NRP has made their list, congratulations. He/she is fresh meat and you can count on more than half of their information being current. This is a great site if you expect that the person for whom you are searching is or at some point would have been a professional of some type, a business owner, searching for a job or even if he/she has a profile on a site like LinkedIn.

peoplefinders.com – Is another site which can offer address history, date of birth information, employment history, family members, associations, memberships, etc. They also offer a reverse cell phone look-up. I have not found peoplefinders.com to have the most current information but they do compile a large amount of information. You can benefit by simply having more leads to follow if you are in a dead-end situation or close to it. They are a fee-based site but like most fee-based sites, they offer a trial period.

peoplefinder.com – You might be doing a double-take right now but people*finders*.com and people*finder*.com are two different sites. They are owned by Intellius (which we will talk about later), which presumably may mean that their information is current and substantive. They also are very expensive. Obtaining a "report" on a person will cost somewhere in the neighborhood of $39-$49 and I have never seen the free trials offered which I see on many other sites. I refuse to pay them that kind of money, so I cannot comment on the quality or substance of their data.

radaris.com – One of the best sites available for gathering information. Radaris.com claims (and I believe this is to be true – at least to a great extent) that they can provide you with data for the past 40 years on the person you are searching for. They also claim to have data on over 97% of all adults in the country. (This is getting scarier by the moment) As if that isn't enough – they are so confident in their data that they offer a 100% satisfaction guarantee. Well – Good Golly! Are you ready to sign-up yet? Wait – there's more…radaris.com reports will provide you with every name which has been reported and recorded of the obligor (remember Jon, Jonathan or John?), every combination of names – John M Jones, Jon M Jones..., every name change (if any), age, residences for the past 40 years, the names and ages of former spouses and more. They offer a 2 day trial system where you can get your reports for a discount (otherwise pay full price if you are not a member) and remember, if at any time you are not happy with the service or the data that you have received, you can receive a full refund. Now go. Stop reading this book and hit the internet already! Just kidding. Believe me, you want to continue reading. I haven't quite blown your mind yet...but it's coming.

yasni.com – Once you go to yasni.com, and type in the name of the person for whom you are searching, you must then scroll down through various categories to find what you are looking for as opposed to having all of the information in a succinct report, the way that some other sites provide it. Some of the categories yasni.com offers are: images, telephone and addresses, Yellow Page listings, network profiles, interests, business profiles, private homepages, videos, documents, publications, etc...They have decent information but I find their site to be frustrating because of the way that it is organized.

zabasearch.com – Specializes in identifying the unlisted home address and phone number of a person. Their information is okay but not always new, fresh and updated. It always helps to have as many resources as possible because you never know where you will find the gems you are seeking.

peoplelookup.com – This site is like many others. You may end up finding information on the person you are looking for and then again, you may not. It can't hurt to try any resource. The only catch with this site is that I wasn't able to navigate a free trial offer and their reports were a little on the costly side.

peoplesearchnow.com – Do not confuse this site with the one before it – peoplelookup.com. Peoplesearchnow.com is a much different site. They can offer you tons of information. The only downside that I have found so far is that you may have to sift through very old information and the fresh current information. You will get both. The good news is that they do offer a trial. The bad news is that it's not free. (And you should know by now that I like free). If you combine a report with the 3 day trial period that they offer, you can get the report for less than $3.00. Less than your daily cup of coffee - if you buy your coffee where I like to buy my coffee. What's more is that even though it's only $3.00, I cannot imagine that they would not refund your money if you did not get what you intended to pay for – and that's the dirt on the obligor. I just *can't imagine*...

peoplesmart.com – Collects billions of records bought from many different companies and compiles the information into a single record so that they can turn around and resell that information in a concise format. They can provide personal details such as home address, phone number and email addresses. What's more is that they offer a reverse service which can be used to locate a person if you only have a phone number or an email address.

lookup.com – Lookup.com says that they are a real time (which means <u>live</u> and <u>instant</u> – the moment that it happens) search engine which enables People Searches, Reverse Phone Lookups, Social Lookups, Property Reports, Public Records and more. They say that you can find comprehensive and centralized people-related information consisting of people search records, public records, reverse phone data, street addresses, images, videos, email addresses and more. Lookup advertises that you can search Facebook and other social networking sites like Twitter, MySpace, LinkedIn, Wikipedia profiles and many more. The problem that I have is that I have never tried it. I have never tried it because I like when sites show you data that they have which they can offer to you. Lookup .com just tells you that they have it. To that I say – "I'm from Missouri – you have to show me" – especially if you are asking me to spend my money, even if it's only $.99. There are a lot of people-search sites out there. Multiply $.99 times 100, that's $100.00 of my money.

Okay, I am not really from Missouri but if anyone decides to try lookup.com, please email me at: simone@dontgetmadgetpaid.com and let me know if it worked for you or if it didn't.

lookupanyone.com – Lookupanyone.com should not be confused with lookup.com. They seem to offer similar information as other companies and they seem to be on the expensive side with no opportunities for a trial membership. The only reason that they made my list is because they are owned by Intellius and because of that I am assuming that they have something to offer. Lookupanyone.com rode into this list on the coattails of Intellius. I am not sure why Intellius (which I will tell you about soon) owns more than half a dozen search engine people finders when they themselves are a major people finder, but I am sure that they have their reasons.

usidentify.com – Another site which offers name, address, phone number, etc. They do offer a 3 day trial period in which you can obtain reports for less than a dollar – but then that number jumps up to nearly $60 once the trial period is over.

ussearch.com – Ussearch.com is perhaps one of the oldest people search engines around. They have been in existence on the internet since 1994 and I remember television commercials from years ago claiming that you could "find anyone"! The reports are rather inexpensive so there is no need to offer trial periods but then many times I find that you get what you pay for. I personally have not had much success with them.

toppeoplefinder.com – This site used to be a great site to find people. Regrettably, I have learned that it has been sold to another company and so it is now in transition. As of this writing, although the site remains, I have not been able to get into the database for any searches. Perhaps by the time this book goes to print and hits the shelves they will have worked out their bugs and their data will be fresh and online again.

dobsearch.com – This company focuses on identifying a person's date of birth. It will also provide you with the other common and usual data but use this search for DOB purposes only, if you have not found it already through another site. Reports are $3.99.

archives.com – Archives.com is an online genealogy company which helps people to trace their ancestry and build their family trees. However, because much of genealogy involves locating public records and piecing puzzles together, it can still be used to search public records and locate people for your purposes. Membership is free for 7 days and then it costs $7.95 per month.

ancestry.com – Ancestry.com is another genealogy company and in fact it's the largest and the most popular. Ancestry requires you to enter your basic information first (name, age, email address, etc) and then it will populate anyone in their system who may be related to you based on the information you provided. That's a great tactic because now they have your information to add to their database whether they have data to share with you or not. Since your purpose in this instance is not actually to build your family tree but instead to search for data on the obligor or find the obligor himself/herself and any related assets, you will want to do a work-around. Instead of entering your own data, enter the basic data of the obligor along with your new and private email address and see what populates. Ancestry.com offers a 14 day free trial.

whitepages.com – Just as the white page telephone book at one time held one of the largest paper databases of telephone numbers, the online version – whitepages.com does the same on the internet.

yellowpages.com – Intellius.com owns yellowpages.com. If you run a search on yellowpages.com it will retrieve the same information that inlellius.com would provide. Same information. Same pricing structure. Same look/same feel…heck I think that it's the same website but with a different name.

Public Data Brokers

Data brokers are companies that collect all of the same data which people finders collect about you. This information includes but is not limited to names and alternate names which you may have had; address history for many years, landline and cell telephone numbers, email addresses, social media sites where you have accounts, etc. What makes them interesting and perhaps what will make you more interested in them, what they do and what they have to offer, is that they also collect purchase histories, credit card activity (geo-coded of course, so that your exact location is gathered when the information is presented) and loads of public data. Data brokers actually build a profile on each and every person. Their databases include your DMV records, voter records, property records, weapons permits, internet search history, email messaging history (your browsing and your emails are monitored 24 hours a day), online blog and social media comments, shopping history, and court history – shall I continue? Their purpose is to gather your information and to sell it to companies who will target a person like you in order to sell you goods and services. Data brokers sell their slick packaged personal information about you to large companies with money to spend...but like most vampires, they won't discriminate too much. They will sell their golden egg information to you too if you are willing to pay for it. Imagine what you would be able to dig up on the other parent if you chose to pay one of the following companies for their data files...game OVER.

acxiom.com – The international Acxiom makes its home in Little Rock Arkansas with additional locations throughout the US. The quiet giant has over a billion dollars in annual sales and over 23,000 servers collecting your most intimate thoughts and movements online as well as in your every movement of your daily lives. The next time that you move the mouse on your computer and click, the next time that you vote, get a speeding ticket, buy concert tickets or have dinner at that private little restaurant, remember that Acxiom is watching. Contact them directly to inquire about access to their database.

lexisnexis.com – Lexisnexis.com is perhaps the largest data broker in the country. They collect both pubic data (DMV reports, traffic violations, etc.) as well as non-public data which in most instances is not available to the public. They too will give their data to you for a price. Because their main markets are attorneys, government officials and those in business and academia they offer both a subscription service as well as a one-time pay per search service. They will take your payment by credit card, allowing prospective employers, landlords and

Deadbeat vs. Deadbroke

those hunting deadbeats to take advantage of the service, simply and swiftly.

intellius.com – As mentioned a few times earlier, intellius.com is a compilation of many much smaller sites. Chances are that Intellius has some of your information because no matter how hard you try to conceal your private life, they have swallowed so many other companies that it is pretty difficult to hide from them. Not that it can't be done. Since that is the case, chances are good that you can find some information on the obligor you are seeking.

rapleaf.com – One of the biggest contributors to rapleaf.com is amazon.com but they will collect information from any large online store. For a mere .10 per email address (that's right – they sell you cheap), rapleaf.com will regurgitate all of the household, purchase and interest data that they have on a person. For starters they can supply you with a person's net worth, home value, income range, occupation and marital status, all of which can be invaluable information to someone looking to collect on a child support debt. They also gather information on any interests you have shown. If you are a boating enthusiast they may know that because you may have a subscription to boating magazines. Why is this important information to have? If you subscribe to boating magazines, you are likely to own a boat, want to own a boat or belong to boating clubs. Again, possibly very important information for someone running asset searches and looking to collect on a child support debt.

tlo.com – Tlo.com (TLO being an acronym for The Last One) is an online investigation company. They used to be called Merlin which offered subpar investigations to mostly debt collectors and has recently undergone a total transformation. They now offer some of the most powerful and unique investigations. In addition to the usual names, aliases, historical addresses mantra which most services claim to offer and some of them provide, tlo.com will also provide you with any license data which the obligor may hold – including but not limited to both driver's license numbers (which opens up many new search possibilities) and professional licenses. Not many companies can offer a social security number but tlo.com can. The real kicker, which demonstrates that they are now at the top of their field and that all of the other players need to catch up, is that they can also offer *vehicle sightings*.

Vehicle sightings can be useful if you are looking to seize a vehicle that the obligor owns and drives and/or if you have not been able to track down where he/she lives and/or works. The "sightings" will absolutely be able to place you in his/her area. This is how it works: You know that new License Plate Recognition that most states are using these days? Supporters of LPR say that it is used to crack down on crime by locating criminals and deter speeding by snapping plate shots and sending off tickets to offenders. Well, all of that may or may not be true but what I can tell you is that your plate information is also being sold – just like your credit card information and internet browsing history.

Tlo.com will allow you to instantly view current (within the last 30 days), recent (within the last 30-90 days) and historical (over the past 90 days) sightings of vehicles including date, time, and exact location stamps. Vehicle sighting reports are available to law enforcement, insurance companies, law firms and private investigators. What is that you say? You're not one of those but you would still like to get a report? Contact me by email for a work-around. You qualify. You just don't know that you do - yet. There's always more than one way to skin a cat.

What do I like about tlo.com most of all? They have a 15-day free trial period.

beenverified.com – I have heard that beenverified.com is a good site to use. It is advertised a great deal on dating websites and websites which provide referrals to care providers. They claim to provide full and complete public records reports so that the customer does not have to skip from site to site in order to gather the data that they need. I cannot provide any thoughts on beenverified.com though because they will not give any data to you until you pay – not even a teaser to provide you with some confidence that they can and will deliver what they promise. They also charge $19.62.

accutellus.com – In addition to the usual personal data, accutellus.com collects details from contest entries and giveaways which could possibly provide you with a different set of information. People who enter these contests usually provide their correct identifying information so that they could be reached should they win whatever prize is being offered. They may have nothing new and fresh to share with you and then again, they just may. One downside is that you must enter the state where you want to search for your obligor as opposed to simply using their name and searching across the country. The obligor could have moved and if part of your problem is that you do not know where he/she has moved to, this site will be time-consuming and frustrating to navigate. They also charge $9.95 whether you run one or 10 searches.

addresssearch.com – This service provides either a name and a mailing address or an email address. If you provide the name and address, it will identify an email address. Conversely, if you provide an email address, it will identify a name and a residential address. I have not had any such luck on either fronts, but you may.

instantcheckmate.com – Instantcheckmate.com provides the usual list of information and they include charitable contributions and their contributors. Their fee hovers at just under the ten dollar mark.

corelogic.com – If you are in need of a credit report on an obligor, corelogic.com may be the service to help. They cater to those in the automotive, insurance, government, legal and retail industries. A credit report can be a great tool to learn more about the obligor and his/her finances and possibly his/her employment as well. Most times we find that credit reports contain banking information, current address information and a whole lot more. If you have a judgment against the obligor for unpaid child support, you are entitled to a copy of his or her credit report from the three main credit reporting agencies, but you can also get one through corelogic.com.

(westlaw) west.thomson.com – You will find similar information with westlaw.com as you will with lexisnexis.com and tlo.com. In order to access westlaw.com, you will have to go through a library that has access to the database. Most likely, you will have to locate a law library near you because most public libraries will not subscribe to Westlaw.

They will allow you to conduct public searches through their "WestLawNext Patron Access" subscription.

Offline Resources

Post Office: It used to be very easy to get forwarding address information on an obligor from the post office if they had moved. Years ago, anyone could walk into a post office and obtain the forwarding address of anyone. In fact it was far too easy. Men who beat up, threatened, and stalked their former wives and girlfriends could easily get this information and follow an ex to a new address and continue the same patterns of abuse. Because of this, the "Domestic Violence Act" was put into place. You can no longer get information from the post office unless you have a valid legal reason for having it, and you must be able to prove that you need the new address to serve legal documents on the person you are seeking.

Your first step is to obtain a judgment against the obligor. If you have already been to court and have received a court order for child support but the obligor is not paying, that is enough. Proceed to the post office in the area where the obligor last received mail and inform the clerk that you would like to obtain the forwarding address on file for the obligor under the "Freedom of Information Garnishments Act". You may have to request a supervisor if the clerk that you encounter does not seem to know how to help you or is unfamiliar with your rights. If the supervisor is unfamiliar as well, be sure to seek out the Postmaster. Don't fall for the okey doke of "the postmaster is not here", "I do not know who that person is" or "I do not have a phone number to provide for you to reach that person". You should be provided with a name and a method of reaching the postmaster. If you are given any of the excuses above, I am sorry to say, but you are not being told the truth. Part of the job of the front-office staff is to serve as gatekeeper as the Postmaster goes about his/her performance of important Postmasterly duties. They are playing a good game of keep-away. Your job at that moment is to show that you know the game and meet game with game.

159

Deadbeat vs. Deadbroke

The Postmaster is the head honcho at the post office and every station has one. He or she will be more familiar than a postal clerk with what can or cannot be done legally. If you have a problem with the Postmaster as well or are not able to get through the gatekeepers, simply get his/her information and write a letter stating what you are asking for and why. Supply your proof of a need for legal service and ask for assistance. After receiving your letter, the Postmaster may realize that you mean business and that you are not going away. If he/she is unfamiliar with the law, most likely they will decide to take the time to find out the facts. A small suggestion that you may consider legal action for being denied your right to this information may cause him/her to think twice before again turning you down. I do caution you not to make threats which you do not wish to follow through. It's just not good form. If you intend to file the complaint, then do it. Otherwise, just move on to one of the next methods.

Having a judgment is the easiest and perhaps the only way for a person in your position to prove that you have a valid legal reason to have the obligor's new address. If you need the address to take the obligor to court for the first time, your task becomes a bit more difficult. There is almost no way to prove that you will be using the address within the realms of the law. You may have to serve him or her "by publication." This is described later in this chapter.

If the obligor did not move but instead just rents a post office box where he/she receives or received mail, the postal clerk will be able to get the physical address that the obligor provided from the application when the box was rented. If the post office box was rented under a business name the information contained on the application is considered to be public knowledge. You will not have to prove legal reasons for wanting the renter's address, so you can get this information by visiting the post office, by mail, and even over the telephone.

Often you will find that deadbeat obligors move around quite a bit. Even if you have received a new address, that doesn't guarantee the obligor still lives there. If you want to know up front whether the obligor still lives at the address that the post office is supplying to you, simply add to your form another line: addressee still receives mail at this address, with a check line for yes and a check line for no. The postal clerk will then check the appropriate line and you will have your answer. If the answer is no, you will have to continue sending forms to the post offices that serve each new address until you are provided with one that is current or until you reach a dead end on this circuit. Whichever comes first.

Voter Registration Records: If your obligor is civic-minded, he/she may be a registered voter. If you move from the area where you initially registered to become a voter, you must re-register in the new area. Most registration offices require that you submit valid current identification when you register. A person might be able to get away with going back to their old district to vote if they still live in the same area and thereby bypass the requirement to provide current address information. If they move to a new area entirely, that's not going to be possible. If you have located a town or a city but cannot find a street address for your obligor, this may be a good source for you. All voter registration information is open to the public and may also contain political party affiliation as well as a date of birth and occupation.

Utility Company Records: Utility companies can be a good source of information. If your obligor skipped town but is still in the state somewhere, this could be your gold mine. When most people move but stay within the same state, they transfer their utility service to their new location. Utility companies are not supposed to give out this information, but they do all the time. Many of my clients have reported that using pretext as described in Chapter 9 is one of the best ways to get information. My client Jolene assumed the identity of a more-than-helpful delivery person and apparently she played her part very well. Her premise was that she was calling the utility company because John Bitters ordered some merchandise which had been on back order. She explained that the merchandise had just come in and she attempted to deliver it but could not because he had moved. She went on to further explain that the contents were perishable and wondered if they would please supply the current address so that she could attempt redelivery.

Deadbeat vs. Deadbroke

For Jolene, it was as simple as that. I should mention that John Bitters lived in a small town and that probably helped Jolene because if she had tried that in any large city, I would bet the bank that she wouldn't have gotten anywhere with her story. I asked Jolene what she would have done if the customer service representative that answered the telephone had simply refused to help her. She laughed and told me the first representative that she spoke with did not give her the address, so she hung up and called back. She kept calling until she got someone who was willing to help her. One time she got the same representative twice, so she hung up again. I loved hearing Jolene's story. The student surpassed the master.

Motor Vehicle Commission Records: The Motor Vehicle Commission in all states used to provide information the same way that the post office did in the past. But that was prior to 9-11 and prior to the Domestic Violence Act. Now they too are limiting with whom they share information. Most states now prohibit the release of driver and registration record information. The exception to this rule is, of course, if you are an attorney or a member of law enforcement. Look up the number for the motor vehicle commission in the state where the absent parent is known to have last lived and call and ask about their policy. You may find that the state will still provide information as a matter of public record. In this case, you will need to write a letter requesting the information. Include the driver's full name, most recent address known, date of birth, and Social Security Number if you have it. There is a small fee involved as well, and you should inquire of the cost. The motor vehicle commission will respond to you in writing with the requested information. Be sure to call both the department of driver's records and the department of registration records. They are separate departments and may have different records on the obligor. If someone at the motor vehicle commission says that they will not supply the information to you, send the letter anyway. Who knows if the person that you spoke with is familiar with the policies? Also remember that if you have proof that you need a current address in order to serve legal documentation you will probably get more help. Once you receive an address from the commission, be sure to verify it through the post office to be sure that it is current. If the obligor's driving record indicates that he/she has received tickets or has had accidents, this may indicate the area where he/she spends a lot of time.

Neighbors: Former neighbors can be another good source of information. If the obligor is no longer living at the last address known to you, use the city directory to get telephone numbers of his former neighbors. As mentioned previously, the city directory can possibly provide you with the address and telephone number of the person for whom you are searching as well as the same information for the people that live nearby. If the obligor lived in an apartment building, you will find names, addresses, and telephone numbers of other people who live in the same building. If he/she lived in a house, you will find names, addresses, and telephone numbers for the people who lived next door, down the block, across the street, etc. You could take this as far as you want. You can consider calling them with the same delivery person technique that Jolene used. After seeing how well it worked for Jolene, I explained the technique to other clients and it has worked great with neighbors too. You might be surprised at the amount of information an unsuspecting neighbor will regurgitate if you ask for their help. Good neighbors are always willing to help other good neighbors. If you find that your obligor was not a good neighbor at all, then you could consider being completely upfront about who you are and your business with the obligor. You might find that your obligor's former neighbor is pleased to help you catch your bandit. Pump them for all of the information that you can.

Former Landlords: The best former landlords to find will be the ones where the obligor skipped out owing rent. They will be happy to help, especially if you tell them that you will relay to them information on the whereabouts of the obligor once he/she is found. If your obligor left on good terms with the landlord, then you may not be able to talk them into giving you private information on one of their former tenants. Subpoena any information that you might need from an unyielding former landlord. They may have details that the obligor listed on their rental application which will be helpful to you. If you are lucky enough to find the landlord before they refund a security deposit to the obligor, you can garnish the refund. Chapter 9 covers *garnishments*.

Former Employers: Many years ago former employers would have been able to share information with you and if the obligor was a horrible employee and caused nothing but problems, you may have received an earful. Nowadays, they have to be careful about what they share – even to prospective new employers and those otherwise calling for a reference. If the obligor left on good terms, you can forget about getting information either way. The exception of course – is with the subpoena. Wave that thing around and they are bound by law to assist.

Clients: If the obligor is self-employed, has some regular clientele and you know who some of them are, they too, will be able to provide information on the whereabouts of the obligor. Certainly clients know how to get in contact with someone who is providing a service to them! Not only that, but they will also be able to fill you in on how much money they have supplied to the obligor over the past year-or longer if they have an ongoing relationship. If they were provided with references before they did business with the obligor, the references will be able to help you as well. The biggest bonus, though, is the humiliation that the obligor will suffer when his clients confront him about the subpoenas they've received from someone who is trying to collect child support. The humiliation alone may be enough to cause the obligor to want to pay you so that it doesn't happen again. Whatever works is to your advantage, and causing your obligor some humiliation can be quite satisfying if you are dealing with someone who has made a skilled practice of dodging you, giving you the run-around and messing with your money.

Professional Licenses: What does the obligor do for a living? Is he/she a doctor, lawyer, Indian chief, or anything else which requires a license to practice? If so, check with the source of where he must be licensed and you may find current address information. Most licensing bureaus have detailed information that is available to the public. Even if the obligor holds a license which he/she doesn't use anymore, they may still keep it current. My husband for example, holds a series 7 (securities and exchange) license. He keeps it current although he has gone on to greener pastures and is no longer in the industry. The address that you find listed may be a business address, not a home address, but it's better than not finding anything at all. The obligor does not need to be at home to be served. An obligor can be served at a business address. Is he/she a plumber, massage therapist, trucker, or an insurance agent? All of these professions must be licensed. Maybe the obligor works for a supermarket and belongs to a union. Trade unions should have information as well. They will be less likely to want to give you any information at all but they cannot refuse a subpoena.

Obligors in the Military: Did your obligor join the military? While enlisted, did he get shipped off to some foreign country, and you now have no idea where he is? Collecting from military employees can be difficult, so there is an entire chapter focused on just that. For our purposes in this chapter, however, you should know that there are special military locators available. I also provide you with a few tips and tricks to help you to navigate the military system.

Alumni Associations: Alumni associations try to keep current addresses on graduates for informational purposes so they can send invitations to reunion parties and requests for alumni gifts and other donations. Dream up a really good pretext as explained in Chapter 9, and chances are that they, too, will tell you whatever they know.

Hobbies: Does the obligor ride a bike? If so, has he ever had a bike permit? If the answer is yes, he may have a permit in the town in which he lives. Does the obligor enjoy hunting or other similar sports? He may have filed a gun, fishing, or hunting license. These licenses are all a matter of public record in most areas.

Family and Friends: Surely you must know some of the obligor's family and friends. Contact them for information if you think that they will even entertain the idea of having a conversation with you. Start by trying to appeal to their good nature. Let them know that child support is something that your children need. They may not budge to help you one bit. Or they may want to help you but feel that they will be betraying a family member or friend if they do. Start by asking, but if they don't tell you anything, you can rely on the subpoena. It's like a magic wand. Wave it around in someone's face and-poof--like magic you get what you want! Of course, you will want to start your inquisitions with the family members or friends whom the obligor has stiffed in some way. They will be the ones most likely to spill the beans.

Other Government Records: If the obligor owns a business, it should be registered with the state somewhere. Check corporation records, partnership, and assumed business records (DBA) with the secretary of the state in which the obligor lives. An assumed business name is a business name that a company has chosen to operate under, even though their legal business name may be something else. An assumed business name must be registered with the state. This information can be given over the telephone. Does the business that the obligor operates collect any sales tax? If so, it must too be registered as a company which collects sales tax. This is public information as well. There are other licenses you should check out, such as: a dog license, a parking permit, a sign permit, a fire permit, or a vending permit.

Real Estate Tax Records: If the obligor owns any real property, he/she will be listed with the county, along with the property owned, the amount of taxes paid, and the most current address known. This information is all public knowledge and can be obtained over the telephone.

Criminal Records: If the obligor has been in trouble with the law, the county where the offense occurred will have a good deal of information on him/her. Contact the probation or parole officer, if there is one, and get information from that source. The more recent the violation, the more recent the information that you receive will be. If the violation is an old one, it will only be useful to make contact if you are searching for a Social Security Number or perhaps the name of family or friends. Any other information will most likely be outdated. Depending on the officer, he or she may not be willing to provide you with any information stating that they are not permitted to by law.

While this may be technically true, I have requested information from probation officers plenty of times and have received it plenty of times. If the one that you have to contact is not agreeable or simply wants to stick to the letter of the law, probation officers can be subpoenaed too.

Other Court Records: Has the obligor recently divorced, or is he/she divorcing? Has he/she recently been sued or is he suing anyone? All of these matters are public records and any information that you cannot get immediately, you can subpoena. All you have to do is ask (and maybe send a small fee for printing and postage) and the information is yours.

The Internet: The Internet is life itself these days. Most people hop on and navigate to their favorite browser first thing in the morning to check their emails, how much money they have made overnight, the weather, current news and events and much more while enjoying their first cup of coffee. As you read earlier in this chapter, the internet provides many ways for you to locate someone who has skipped out on you if only you know which sites to go to and how to make them work for you. It is not *completely* foolproof, but it can provide information that might have taken a lot of research for you to find on your own in the old brick and mortar kind of way.

At the same time, sometimes doing things the slow and steady way wins the race, since the internet does have its flaws. Also keep in mind that this is just data. If the information put into the system is flawed, the information coming out will also be flawed. Garbage in. Garbage out. And if you are a person like me who purposely works on cleaning up internet files that I don't wish strangers to know about – such as my home address, personal telephone numbers and the like, you may also find a great deal of misinformation and disinformation. Just as I can help you to find anyone, (absent of those under Federal Protection, as we discussed), I can also help you to virtually disappear on the internet in order to protect your privacy or safety or simply to keep your name of out the whoring masses of the data miners who want to make money off of you and track your every move electronically. But alas…that might be another book someday. I say all of this to say - don't rely <u>solely</u> on the internet; it is just one of many tools that you have at your disposal.

Deadbeat vs. Deadbroke

If you haven't figured it out already, the sites that I have provided to you can be a goldmine and if you haven't figured it out already, the downside to most of these sites is that they can take a lot of your time and they can become frustrating for those who do not appreciate the art of sitting at a computer for hours conducting research. I have had many clients who tend to go blind after more than an hour of research so you just may be one of those who decide to throw in the towel and let someone do it for you. I would be remiss in my responsibilities if I didn't clue you in that my company could help you in that regard. We find deadbeats; it's what we do. Keeping in mind the stress and the trauma that many residential parents face with their collections and pursuits of the other parent, most of our location services have been designed with a no-hit, no-pay policy. So if we don't find information, there is no fee. As my father used to say – you can't beat that with a baseball bat! To add icing to the cake, (because one of my hobbies is baking and I do love a good icing), another priceless service which we offer is coaching support to walk you through your options of what you can do with the information once you obtain it.

Tips to finding someone on the internet:

1. Experiment with variations and alternate spellings of names. For example, if you are looking for "John", also try Jonathan, Jonathan, and Jon.
2. Begin with just one initial and then add more letters to your search in the event that the person's name may be misspelled in the directory, intentionally or not. Try J. Smith instead of John Smith. Proceed to Jo, then Joh, etc.
3. Does John have a middle name? I have known people who chose to publically list their phone number using their middle name rather than their first name to save the monthly fees that the phone company charges for an unlisted number. What would stop anyone else from doing the same to avoid being easily found? Try J. Edward Smith or Edward Smith or J.E. Smith. Also, some people who have a common name, like Bob Peterson

for example, may choose to differentiate themselves from the other Bob Peterson's by using their middle initial. This is helpful for example, when Bob Peterson wants to have a credit check run. No doubt that a million Bob Petersons will pop up even when using a social security number. One fellow that I knew many years ago used both of his middle initials in order to separate himself from the common-name pack and called himself Bob T.K. Peterson.

4. The obligor may also be using an alternate name or a nickname. If you are looking for Bill, try Billy, William, or Will. Don't forget that you must also then try Billy, William, and Will with alternate spellings and middle names, as well.

5. My first name is Simone, but I can't count the times that I have received mail addressed to Simon. Names can be misspelled and can "sound like" something else. Consider all of the possibilities.

6. Also remember that the obligor can have phone records and all other records listed under his new partner's name, his mother's name, his best friend's name, or his business name, etc.

Credit Reports

Credit reports are one of the most valuable tools available to you. Although it has become easier and easier to operate in today's nearly cash-less society without some type of credit or without someone checking your creditworthiness for evaluation, we are not a credit-less society. Even if you operate without credit cards, service providers will still want to know your credit worthiness. Everyone from the cell phone company to the gas and light company will screen new clients to determine if they need to take a deposit against future charges. By obtaining a credit report on the obligor, you can get the most current address available on file, possibly employment and asset information, as well as details on the obligor's credit history and financial standing. In short, if you hit pay dirt, you can get everything you need. The one obstacle you have will be finding someone who will run a credit report on the obligor for you. (A small obstacle, mind you). As a judgment creditor you have a legal right to this information, but the credit bureaus will not give it to you willingly. There are far too many scammer and identity thieves out there lurking around to get someone's information so that they can steal it and do whatever identity thieves do. Unless you operate a company that extends credit to consumers or you are an attorney; you are plumb out of luck. That is, of course, unless you have friends in high places who will get a copy of the report for you, or unless you hire someone to obtain one for you. If you don't mind waiting forever, using a government attorney through the state child support agency is also another way to go. If you do mind waiting forever, contact several attorneys who specialize in collections until you find one who will be willing to run a report for you-for a fee, of course. If you have decided to hire an attorney, hopefully you have already found one who has this capability. Once you have the report, call the credit bureau and ask for help interpreting it, if you need to. Once again, I should inform you that credit reports are a part of the CSS services, should you require one and that you can also submit a subpoena to the credit agencies and to that they must comply.

Locator Services

The child support agencies have two locator services available to them. One is the *State Parent Locator Service* (SPLS) and the other is the *Federal Parent Locator Service* (FPLS). Parents with residential custody who are on TANF can use these services without charge, all others are customarily charged a fee of approximately $10, with a maximum fee set at $25, although the state often absorbs all or most of the cost. The state locator service is a computer network that will check all state records available in an effort to locate the obligor. If unsuccessful, the file will be sent to the federal service, which will conduct a search of federal records. If the federal locator is unable to locate the obligor, it is legally bound to try the search again every three months for three years.

Having the government conduct the search for you through all of its means sounds like a great idea. But all that glitters is not gold. The state locator has seventy-five days to complete the search and report back to you with a hit or miss. If the file is forwarded to a federal service, the time it takes to get back to you can vary. In the time it can take to complete all the government searches, you and your children may starve. This process often takes a year or longer. This is precisely why you may need to take matters into your own hands. When you visit your state agency to request a locator service, you will be asked to fill out a form called "registration of absent or punitive parents" and pay the fee requested. Ask at that time to have the state and the Federal locator service run concurrently to save you some time and headaches. It is a common practice to exhaust the resources of the state locator before running the federal, but it does not have to be done that way. You may be told that if you are not on welfare or if you are not receiving the services of the state agency (if you are representing yourself, for example) that you cannot apply for locator services, but that is untrue. Press on and insist that the caseworker check the guidelines. Anyone who requests this service is entitled to it as long as the fee is paid.

Private Investigators

If you are thinking of hiring a private investigator, there are some guidelines you should follow so that no one takes advantage of you.

1. Decide how much money you are willing to spend and don't let the investigator talk you into spending any more.
2. Include the investigator's expenses in this amount since they are not included in the fee quoted to you. You may decide that an investigator is too costly.
3. Get an agreement on what expenses you will be expected to pay for and get it in writing.
4. Get an agreement on what the hourly rates are and get it in writing.
5. Ask for an accounting of the investigator's time and expenses.

6. Ask how the investigation will be conducted. Fieldwork will be a lot less cost effective than telephone work.

7. Put the entire agreement in writing.

8. Ask for at least three references who can recommend him based on his skip tracing abilities.

9. Agree on written progress reports and ask that you receive them frequently.

10. In your agreement, be sure to have a clause where you can terminate the investigator at any time, with a full refund on any unused retainers, if you are not happy with the service.

11. If you do terminate your investigator, do not have any further contact with him until you receive your refund. He may charge you for whatever conversation you have and then tell you that you have no money left to refund.

I have been in a position where I have had to hire professionals whose service required a retainer. I know many would argue this point with me but it is my experience that retainers are generally positioned to never be refunded. If you pay out a retainer, do not expect to get any portion back, no matter what they tell you. Just my .2 cents.

Service by Publication

When all else fails and you are unable to locate the absent parent to serve them with legal papers, the law allows you to "serve by publication." This means that you must place an advertisement in the newspaper where the obligor is last known to have lived, announcing that he is being sued for child support. The advertisement must appear in the section where legal notices are posted and must include all of the pertinent information. This is a common practice and is allowable by law when you have not been able to serve the obligor in person, despite your best efforts. You must get the judge's permission to serve the other parent/obligor by publication. To do this you must file a motion with the court and ask the judge to sign it. If you cannot find the form on your own, it is available on my website. When filing your motion, you must attach an affidavit (a signed written statement) that states how you have attempted to otherwise serve the other parent/obligor and that you have been unsuccessful. You must also provide proof of your previous attempts of service. This is important because if it is not done "just right", the judge will deny your request.

Deadbeat vs. Deadbroke

MOTION AND ORDER TO ALLOW SERVICE BY PUBLICATION

IN THE CIRCUIT COURT OF THE STATE OF [INSERT YOUR STATE NAME]
FOR THE COUNTY OF [INSERT YOUR COUNTY / PARISH NAME]

In the Matter of: [DOCKET NUMBER]
                                                          Docket Number

[INSERT YOUR NAME],
  Petitioner,
                                                          MOTION AND ORDER
                                                          TO ALLOW SEVICE
  And   BY PUBLICATION

[INSERT OBLIGOR'S NAME],
  Respondent
  OF ANY STATE
  of Any County

    [Your Name Here], petitioner in the above-captioned matter, hereby moves the
Court for an order allowing Service by Publication.
    This motion is based upon the attached affidavit, which is incorporated herein by
reference.

_____
[YOUR NAME HERE]
Petitioner

IT IS SO ORDERED.
DATED this _____ day of _____ , 20____ .

_____
CIRCUIT COURT JUDGE

Item # 4: Motion and Order to Allow Service by Publication

I have saved possibly the best resource for last. What I am about to share with you is so sublime that I almost fashion myself as an evil genius at the moment. It involves the usage of perhaps the most powerful search engine ever – and their power continues to grow. I am talking about Google.

How completely amazing would it be if you could program Google – the most powerful search engine in the world – to work for you? Now that you know how social network aggregators, people search directories and data brokers operate – in that they are always scouring for information and always creating new profiles and updating their content whenever new information presents itself – would you like it if you could program Google to personally send you live-time updated information as it happens? If a new address for the obligor is located or a new telephone number or new employment…if he/she gets a speeding ticket or anything else which might take you or lead you in the direction of asset location, how beneficial would that be to you? And if it were *free*, would you love it even more?

Let me tell you how you can make this happen.

Step 1: Determine and record the searches that you want to conduct. Remember – garbage in – garbage out, so be specific about the information which you want Google to return to you after you program it to bend to your request. If you want all new live-time general information about your obligor, Baxter M. Blackdoodle, then write down "Baxter M Blackdoodle" with the quotation marks. That should be enough to return information on a person with that name because the name is rather unique. If you are searching for John Jones, you might want to include the last know state where John lived or a last known address, so you would write "John Jones Missouri" or "John Jones 366 State Street, Missouri", keeping the search criteria within quotation marks. Feel free to come up with as many configurations as you like on Baxter M. Blackdoodle, including searches on cell phone and/or landline numbers, writing them like this – "919-555-3333". The reason for the quotation marks is that after you program your Google-

Frankenstein, they mandate that Google-Frankenstein only return results when an exact match is made. This will virtually eliminate irrelevant information.

Step 2: Log into your new email account

Step 3: Go to google.com/alerts. One by one, work through all of the configuration data which you want Google-Frankenstein to alert you to as it happens. Type the first configuration alert into the field, select "everything" as the result type, "as-it-happens" as the frequency, results should be "all results" and delivery should be to your new email account.

You have now programmed Google-Frankenstein to email you personally and directly when any new information hits any of the aforementioned search engines.

Priceless

By now you may be feeling woozy and downright afraid to walk out of your very own front door. I should mention that just as I can teach you to find anyone with my methods mentioned above, I can also teach you how to protect your privacy on the internet and how not to fall prey to the data brokers. Knowing now how easy it is for people to use information such as this to violate others, you may be interested in internet privacy to protect yourself and your family from stalkers, identity thieves, data brokers and other crazy people. If you are feeling uneasy about all of this information and want to do something about it, contact me at: simone@dontgetmadgetpaid.com.

You can completely wash yourself from the "system" and all of the Big Brother eyes that watch you. Finding people and finding out what they are up to for child support purposes, is my business. Sometimes there are other reasons to follow people on the internet and to use searches.

Another note:

While some deadbeats and others think that they can hide by using some of these tips and tricks that I have shared with you (and I hate to think that I have provided any information to anyone who might use it for anything other than good), keep in mind that I have a work-around for them all. Obscure email addresses, pre-paid card ownership and purchases, deleting content which still exists on servers, etc. I can make all of this information available to you. The challenge is deciding when to use it and how to use it with integrity. As Kenny Rogers sang in "The Gambler", "you gotta know when to hold 'em and when to fold 'em". If you aren't familiar with the tune, look it up on YouTube…which coincidentally is also operated by Google.

HOT TIPS FOR PARENTS

Chew this chapter slowly and allow it to digest. Then go back, re-read it and mark off the first 10 websites that you want to try. Work them one at a time, otherwise you are sure to become overwhelmed. Determine how many you can carve out the time to do in one day. Consider setting aside one hour a day for your searches.

HOT TIPS FOR ATTORNEYS AND CASEWORKERS

You and your staff and use these search engines yourselves or suggest that your clients buy the book (or buy a stack and provide to your clients) so that they can run the searches themselves and then return the results back to you. Heck – it would be a great idea if you suggested that they read the entire book. It will go a long way towards helping them to help you to do your job.

chapter 9:

locating assets

If you have located the obligor, the next step is to find his or her income sources and assets so that you can seize them and cash them in. Using many of the same methods that you used to locate the obligor, you can locate their assets. The only difference is that the first time you were looking for a current address of the obligor so that you could serve them legal papers, and now you are looking for income streams, or assets that you can convert into income. Contrary to what many believe, income is not only what a person earns. Unearned income, or income that is not received via a paycheck, is considered to be income as well. Examples may include rental incomes, dividends and interest from stock ownership, etc. Virtually everything that belongs to the obligor can be construed as income or converted into income for your usage. You just have to know where to look and what to look for.

Deadbeat vs. Deadbroke

Credit reports

As you have found in Chapter 8, credit reports can reveal an enormous amount of information which can be helpful to you. They can help you to locate an obligor who has skipped out on you. They can also help you to discover what he owns and some places where he might be stashing his cash, whether they are banking institutions or systems of non-bank banking. If you do not have access to a credit reporting system, find someone who does and pay to have a report run on the obligor for you, as described in Chapter 8. You can also receive one through the credit agencies directly by serving a subpoena and providing your proof that you are entitled to such personal information. Your proof will be a certified copy of your judgment. This is what you will be looking for:

- If you haven't done so already, confirm the home address that's listed on the credit report with the post office. Next, find out if the obligor owns the home that he lives in. If he does, consider the option of placing a *judgment lien* (a lien that is enforced by a court order) on the property and threaten to force a foreclosure on the property unless you are paid in full. See Chapter 10 for more details.

- Does the obligor own any other real estate? Again, consider the option of forcing a foreclosure on the property.

- Does the obligor own cars, boats, motorcycles, or anything else that's valuable? If possible, drive by his house and assess the situation. Consider the option of filing a Writ of Execution with the court so that you can have the property seized and sold at auction. See Chapter 10 for more details.

- If the obligor does not own the property where he lives, find out who does. Call the landlord to see if he or she will cooperate by advising you if the obligor has a security deposit on file. If the landlord will not cooperate, of course you subpoena them. If you discover that there is a security deposit, file a Writ of Garnishment to have the money released to you. See Chapter

10 for details. A savvy landlord may decide to contest the garnishment contending that they are a lien holder on the account. Most people, including landlords, don't contest garnishments—they don't know that they can. If they do contest it, there is no guarantee that the judge will stop the garnishment from continuing. If the judge will not stop the garnishment, the money is yours and the obligor will have to come up with another security deposit. If the judge does stop it, at the very least you can file a judgment lien against the deposit. When the obligor moves from the apartment, the money will be refunded to you as long as he does not owe anything to the landlord. If he does move owing money and the deposit is awarded to the landlord, at least you tried. Better luck on the next attack.

- If the credit report reveals a current employer, you can have the obligor's wages withheld and/or garnished if you haven't done so already. See Chapter 10 for details.

- Most likely the employer will not be forthcoming with information over the telephone. They do not know who you are for one thing and for another this is very personal information that they would be delivering. We live in an identity-theft-era and they would be crazy to provide this information to you even if you prove to them that you are entitled to have it. The employee could sue. That being said, it can't hurt you to try. All they can say is NO. The encouraging news is that on my side of the fence, having made calls such as this numerous times of behalf of my clients, I have received this information over the telephone many times. If you don't have such luck, chances are high that you will have to provide a legal document – a subpoena – in order to have the employer to regurgitate this information to you. When you contact the employer whether it be by phone or by subpoena, you will want to ask these questions:

a) Does the obligor receive any bonuses or commissions?

b) Does the obligor participate in any company savings plans or deductions such as an IRA or a 401K.

c) Does he own any company stock?

d) Does he have a pension plan?

These items can all be considered income for the purposes of child support collection. If the obligor has any of these benefits, Chapter 10 will tell you how to tap into them for past-due child support.

- Subpoena the employer to send you a copy of the front and back of the last paycheck that the obligor cashed, if he or she is receiving paper checks. If he or she receives their pay by direct deposit, you will ask for the name of the banking (or non-banking) institution, the address on file for the institution, the routing number and the account number to where the deposit is wired. The back of the paycheck will reveal the same information.

- Once you are in receipt of the banking information, you will be able to garnish the obligor's checking account, savings account, non-banking debit card balance (wherever the money is being deposited) for past-due support money. Previous employers are good for this information as well.

- While you are at it, subpoena the bank for other accounts that it may be holding for the obligor. Usually, if a person is going to have more than one account for whatever purpose, they will hold them at the same institution. If you find other accounts, they can be garnished as well.

- If employers, or former employers, do not have any information to supply to you, try the trade union to which the obligor belongs. Trade unions should be able to supply "earned income" information as well as information on any benefits, bonuses, commissions, and union benefits received by the obligor.

- If the obligor is the owner of a business that requires a license that costs a lot of money to get—a liquor license, for example—file a judgment lien against it. Without a license, the restaurant or bar that the obligor operates cannot serve liquor, which can be damaging to a business of that sort. In a case like this, the license itself will most likely mean nothing to you. Most of the time ownership of the license cannot be transferred in this way, so you will not be able to convert it into money that way. However, if the obligor's business can go down the tubes without the license, he may be inclined to pay you the past-due child support to regain the usage of the license that now belongs to you. Who knows, you may be able to find a way to have the license legally transferred after all. The worst-case scenario would be that the obligor doesn't pay you one dime in past-due child support and you don't relinquish the control over the liquor license. Your position hasn't changed any because you weren't getting any support anyway, but the obligor's business will be damaged in some way, if not completely. It's not a bad deal since you still have other tactics to use.

- If you find any credit card accounts, loans, or any other means of credit listed on the obligor's credit report, subpoena the original application that the obligor completed from the creditor or lender. It may contain information on other assets that are not listed on the credit report. These may be assets that you can garnish or otherwise convert into income.

- If you are able to locate a CD owned by the obligor, you could either garnish the interest that the CD earns or, through a Writ of Execution, you can have the deposit turned over to you. Figure out what will bring you the greatest return before you make your decision.

- If you know the obligor to be a stockholder for publicly traded stock, you will need to subpoena information regarding his stock portfolio from his stock brokerage. It helps if you know who the brokerage is. If not, you will have to find out through one of your sleuthing techniques or go through a government attorney to have a 1099 401k search done. See Chapter 10 for more information. The government attorney will be able to use federal records to access the obligor's 1099 information (interest earned from banks or other financial institutions). The attorney will be able to find out where the earned interest has come from and what company is holding the money. This information will be reported back to you and you can then subpoena the broker for details on the stock that the obligor owns. A government attorney is the only person who can access 1099 information.

- Chapter 10 tells you how to seize personal property belonging to the obligor. This property can be sold and the profit applied to back child support. Follow the methods outlined when you find property on the credit report or through any of your other means.

- If the obligor owns or at some time owned an aircraft, boat, ATV or motocross bike, etc., check to see if it is still registered in his name. If it is, you have hit the jackpot—move to seize and sell it immediately. Aircraft registrations are listed with both the Federal Aviation Administration (call 405-954-3011), and with the state. A boat will be listed with the state, unless its size and tonnage (weight) are such that it must be listed with the federal government as well. To find out, call the state Marine Board and the U.S. Coast Guard.

- Those obligors who are in the military, and other federal employees from whom it may be difficult to collect, can have their incomes garnished. See the chapters that focus exclusively on this.

- If the obligor receives income from a trust fund, subpoena information about the fund from the trustee. Once you know the amount of income which the obligor receives from the fund, you can either place a wage withholding on the income or have the income garnished. You may be able to have the trust fund itself garnished as well. It depends on the language of the trust.

The trust document will reveal those answers. That being said, it is highly likely that unless you are a legal professional that you will need one to read the trust document and to decipher it. They can be very complicated. To have an attorney read and interpret it for you may be worth the few hundred bucks you will be charged. Don't forget that you can always seek out the services of a free attorney as outlined in Chapter 7 or maybe a friend of a friend has an attorney in the family who would be willing to help read and interpret the language.

- If you believe that the obligor will be receiving an inheritance through someone's will, contact the government office that handles wills in the county where it will eventually be probated and ask for a copy. If he is listed as a beneficiary, have a lien placed on any money due to the obligor.

- If an immediate family member of the obligor dies without a will, and you believe that the obligor may receive some inheritance, you may be able to place a lien on the obligor's share of the estate. Once they reach the probate department, wills become public information.

- A percentage of unemployment benefits can he withheld for child support payments. Subpoena information from the obligor's previous employer to find out when the obligor lost his job and any other details that may be important for you to know. Then contact the unemployment office to find out what information it needs from you to begin withholding some of the benefits that the obligor receives. Some states will not allow an *obligee* or private attorney to have unemployment benefits withheld. If the state in which the obligor lives will not allow you to withhold wages, you must work through the state child support agency. Government attorneys are given more leeway in this area and will be able to get a withholding in any state.

- Workers' compensation benefits can also be withheld for child support. If the obligor's employer will not tell you who its insurance carrier is, subpoena for the information. Contact the

185

carrier to request the address it is using to send checks to the obligor, the amount of the payment, and when the benefits will run out. Of course, you will need to provide information to get your process started. Ask about this in your first conversation.

- If the obligor is disabled in some way, you and/or your child may be entitled to disability payments. Pay a visit to the Social Security Administration Office in your area to find out. If you need to know whether the obligor is receiving Social Security benefits, without actually applying first, you will have to go through a government attorney.

- If the obligor has received, or is due to receive, a settlement from a lawsuit, you can have this income garnished. Visit the county courthouse in the area where the suit was filed and obtain the names of the attorneys who are representing both the obligor and the person or entity that he is suing. File a Writ of Garnishment against the funds that the obligor is due to receive. If the state in which the obligor lives will not allow you to do this, although most of them will, keep close tabs on the lawsuit and file your garnishment immediately following the settlement. Do not let the obligor know what you are doing. If you do, he will probably try to hide the money as quickly as it comes in. In some states before a law settlement can be released, the plaintiff (the one receiving the money) must sign a document swearing that he does not owe any past due child support. Further, a check is *supposed* to be done to confirm this.

- If you cannot find any assets that belong to the obligor and you become really desperate, you can search the obligor's trash for anything that might lead to asset information. Look for credit card receipts, bank deposit slips, statements, etc. Legally, once trash is put out on the curb it is public property, so don't worry—you won't be breaking any laws.

- You can also use pretext and conduct a survey. Before I got my job as a bill collector for the bank, I worked as a marketing research surveyor. I would call people at their homes to ask their opinions on a variety of topics. I have handled everything from political surveys to surveys about the newest brand of peanut butter. At the end of every survey that I was able to get completed before the consumer hung up on me, I was instructed to ask some personal questions. These questions included what they did for a living, their address, where they banked, and then, of course, would they like to receive a coupon for a free jar of peanut butter (or whatever else was being offered). The surveys that I was assigned to were almost always successful if the consumer knew that he was going to get something at the end. Search your mind for something that you think the obligor would like to have and that he would be willing to disclose certain information to get. Most people like free things. Just be certain that you make the survey sound believable. Once you have an idea of your "offering," decide what information you need to get from the obligor. Your list might include: where do you bank, what is your occupation, are you married, do you hold MasterCard/Visa accounts, what is your approximate income, etc. Then get to work and put together your "survey." It might go something like this:

Survey person:	Hello, may I speak with Mr. John Doe?
Obligor:	This is John Doe.
Survey person:	Mr. Doe, this is Mary Jackson from MMM Marketing in the Ohio Theatre Group and we would like to give you four free front row center tickets to our next production of *LesMiserables*, just for answering a few questions.
Obligor:	OK.
Survey person:	When did you last visit the theater?
Obligor:	Oh, about six months ago.

Deadbeat vs. Deadbroke

Survey person:	How often do you attend the theater?
Obligor:	About two or three times a year.
Survey person:	When you purchase tickets for the theater, do you pay for them on a MasterCard or Visa account? By answering this question please know that we will not place you on a mailing list of any type.
Obligor:	I usually pay by MasterCard.
Survey person:	And which bank is that under?
Obligor:	People's Bank of North America.
Survey person:	Do you bank with People's as well?
Obligor:	Yes.
Survey person:	About how many theater shows have you seen in your lifetime?
Obligor:	I don't know, maybe fifteen.
Survey person:	If you have children, do you take them with you to theater shows?
Obligor:	No, I don't take them.
Survey person:	Just a few more questions and then we are done. What is your approximate age? Under thirty or over thirty?
Obligor:	Over thirty.
Survey person:	What is your occupation?
Obligor:	I'm a licensed plumber.
Survey person:	And your income, is it over or under $50,000?
Obligor:	Over $50,000.
Survey person:	Thank you for your time, Mr. Doe. You will receive

a letter in the mail from the Ohio Theatre Group
within fourteen days. The letter will include a
number for you to call to claim your free tickets and
reserve seats for the show. Have a great day!

Obligor: Thank you.

Of course, you will want to customize your queries to the obligor with a survey that makes sense to you. It's better if you ask someone else to make the call for you so that there's no chance that the obligor will recognize your voice. Also, be sure not to use the names of companies that actually exist because that's illegal.   Last but not least, please…whatever you do, use one of those throw away phones so that the call cannot be traced back to you. Use your imagination and create names that sound real. The obligor will never know the difference. The key is in the presentation. Sound confident and sincere.

chapter 10:

enforcing your child support order

Statistics reveal that only 25 percent of the custodial parents who have child support orders ever receive all their money. Therefore, 75 percent of the child support orders entered aren't worth the paper they are printed on. Having a child support order means nothing, unless you get paid. Let's recount what you have learned so far: you have learned how to establish paternity and what to do if you are underage. You have learned how to get a child support order and how to have your order modified if your circumstances have changed or if the child support order you received was not sufficient. You can find your deadbeat if he skips town and you are able to effectively hire a private attorney (if you want to go that route) and maybe even get legal services for free. You now also know what is legally considered to be income—it's not just what one gets paid in his or her paycheck. Now, one way or the other, you will learn the steps that you can take yourself to get blood from an unyielding stone. Ready? One, two, three, SQUEEZE!

Truth be told, there are many options that you have to get your money. The problem is that most people don't know about them. The officials who are paid to help you either don't know about these options, don't have the time or fortitude to use them themselves or they simply don't want to tell you because most likely it will create more work. By now you have noticed that this book is about work. How much work are you willing to do to collect your money? Just how mad are you? Are you not going to take it anymore? If you are willing to do the work, then you will get your money. Most people know about wage withholding. That's when they take the money that is due to you directly from the obligor's paycheck. That's not all there is, but we will begin there because it is the simplest way to get what you want.

Wage withholding

A wage withholding (also called an order withholding earnings or a payroll deduction) is a court order requiring the obligor's employer to deduct money from his paycheck and forward it to you or to the state agency. It is the easiest way to collect your money and it has a lot of benefits.

- Once notified and presented with a court order, the employer cannot refuse to deduct and forward the money.
- The employer must forward the money no later than ten days after the deduction.
- If the obligor quits or is fired, the employer is required to inform you, and tell you where the new job is if they know.
- Under federal law, a wage withholding must be permitted for anyone who has a child support order where the payments are thirty days past due or if three consecutive payments have been missed. So as long as the obligor keeps his job, you will have a steady payment coming to you. Keep in mind that typically you can only get about 60 percent of the paycheck amount plus an additional 5 percent for arrearages over twelve weeks if the obligor has not remarried and has no dependents. If the obligor has remarried and has dependents, the amount that can be

deducted decreases to 50 percent and 5 percent for arrearages over twelve weeks.

- Although employers are required by law to withhold wages and forward them, I have heard of employers (in small closely-held companies, where they think that they can get away with it) ignoring a wage withholding order. You should know that the law is on your side. If the employer pulls this with you, they are legally liable to pay you what they should have withheld from the employee! One letter to the owner of the company should fix this small problem. If not, do not hesitate to contact small claims court and sue them. You will win your case for your past due child support from the employer and undoubtedly any fees you have occurred. If you need any help constructing your letter to the employer or your small claim petition for the court, contact me. That's why I'm here. You can also visit the document library section on my website.

- You can get a wage withholding through your local child support agency or by going to court yourself and filing an order to withhold earnings. Take a look at Item #5, the Ex Parte Order to Withhold Earnings. This is the motion you will use when you file for a wage withholding, so take a few moments to familiarize yourself with it. This form may be available at an office supply store. Simply fill it out, and submit it to the court clerk. The small fee involved will probably be about $5. Otherwise, it is also available on my website www.dontgetmadgetpaid.com.

Wage garnishment

Many people confuse wage withholdings with wage garnishments. They use the two terms interchangeably, as though they mean the same thing. Be aware: they don't have the same meaning nor do they work the same way. While a wage withholding is an order from the court to deduct a certain amount of money on a continuous basis and send it to you regularly; a wage garnishment is an order from the court to deduct one lump sum of money (usually a large sum) and send it to you. A wage garnishment is a one-time deal. You will not get regular payments and it does not permit for future child support that may become due. It does have its benefits, however. How would you like to go to court for past-due child support, get awarded a judgment for the amount past due, and then have that entire amount taken out of the obligor's check at once! It can be done. Just thinking of it gives me goose bumps. Remember that the only way you could lose your court case is if the money is not owed to you. If you have a court order in place, and the obligor is in arrears, the only defense he has is mistaken identity. If he does not show up in court, you automatically win.

Interstate wage withholding

If your obligor lives in another state, you can still get an *interstate wage withholding*. Simply visit the child support office in your area and they will handle the whole thing for you. If you are pursuing the case on your own, it's not much different than handling a case that's in-state. Prepare the forms and bring them to the family court in your county and give them to the clerk. You will then have to arrange to have the order served to the employer. If you have an obligor on your hands who is a real pain in the neck, prepare yourself to bulldoze him. This goes for the interstate obligors as well as the obligor who lives in-state. Reread Chapter 9 and withhold earnings or garnish anything and everything that the obligor receives as income. We are not just talking about paychecks here. The plan is to make his life so miserable that it would be easier to pay you than to have his funds constantly intercepted.

Writ of garnishment (personal property)

Paychecks are not the only things that can be garnished. Any liquid property (cash) that the obligor owns can be garnished for child support. This includes savings and checking accounts, CDs, etc. Personal property that is not money but can be seized and sold for money can also be garnished. In the event that you have found the obligor's liquid assets (cash) and you would like to seize them (take them away), you will need to file a Writ of Garnishment. A Writ of Garnishment is filed with a banking institution, employer, or some other third party that is holding money for the obligor. This is different from a wage garnishment because a wage garnishment takes money directly and only from earnings. A Writ of Garnishment takes money from a source where the money is just sitting. Some examples might be bank accounts, IRAs, etc. If your obligor has taken his liquid property (cash) from one of these sources and transferred it to a friend or relative to prevent you from getting your hands on it, you must obtain it in another way. In this instance, you must file what is called a creditor's bill. We will discuss how *creditor's bills* work later in the chapter.

A Writ of Garnishment is an order from the court demanding that the third party that is holding money for the obligor turn it over to the court. Similar to the wage garnishment, it is a one-time lump sum that does not provide for future child support, but it can pay you what's past due. If you have a child support order and the obligor owes you $3,000 in past-due support and you find an account with $3,500 in it, you can have the account "garnished" for $3,000. If the account you find has only $800, you can wipe out the $800 and the obligor will still owe the remaining $2,200. When you have located the funds in the bank or other banking institution, call them and ask what their specific procedures are for garnishing an account. Most institutions have several branches and you will need to know which branch needs to be served with your writ. Then find one online or use the one on my website. Complete the form and take it to the court clerk with whatever small fee is required and file the paperwork. You will also need to arrange to have the paperwork served. See Item #6, Writ of Garnishment. Writs must be answered in five days. Generally, you will not have a problem with a banking institution since they are accustomed to receiving documents of this type. Once the court receives the money, it is required to hold it for approximately ten days before releasing it to you. This gives anyone who denies owing the money a chance to request a hearing. Common objections are that the money belongs to someone other than the obligor or that the money is exempt from garnishment. If the obligor states that the money belongs to someone other than himself, he must be able to prove this. If he says that a portion of the funds is exempt, and can prove it, you will receive the remaining balance. An example of exemption would be: in most states you are only permitted to take a percentage of the obligor's paycheck during a garnishment—usually 25 percent. If the obligor can prove that the entire $3,000 that was taken from his bank account consisted of deposited paychecks, then you would be entitled to 25 percent of each paycheck. If the obligor deposited three weekly paychecks of $1,000 per week, you would get $750 and the rest would be returned. In the meantime, however, you would have certainly ticked him off and maybe shaken him up enough to decide to pay up and not to mess with your child support anymore. In addition, if this were a checking account from which the money was taken, checks could be bouncing all over town. If the money was obtained from a CD or stock that had to be sold, the interest would be lost and perhaps there would be penalties to pay. Now, doesn't that make you smile?

Writ of garnishment (personal property in the hands of a third party)

Personal property in the hands of a third party can be garnished as well. The only drawback is that most people don't understand it. Banks are used to getting garnishments that they must fulfill, the neighborhood mechanic is not. For example, the fancy car that you want to seize is at the dealership for its scheduled and predictable 40,000-mile checkup. You have the Writ of Garnishment served to the dealership and they have no choice but to hand the car over. In this instance, they would have to notify the sheriff's department that the car is in their possession. The sheriff would come and remove the vehicle and place it in storage in the same manner as if it was taken from the obligor's home. The same procedures would then follow. If you find yourself serving a garnishment to a mechanic or other entity that may not be accustomed to garnishment procedures, be sure to contact them (the owner or manager) and make them aware of their responsibility. Otherwise, an unknowing employee may release the vehicle and you will have to start from scratch.

Writ of execution (personal property)

Personal property that is in the hands of the obligor can also be taken away. It can then be sold and the profit turned over to you. This process is a bit more complicated and will cost you more to do, but the benefits can be great! Close your eyes for a moment and imagine the obligor leaving his workplace at the end of the day only to find that his car is gone. Better yet, he awakens early on a Saturday morning to a knock at the door. He opens the door and sees the sheriff standing there with an order in his hands to seize his household belongings. It can happen. But don't get your hopes up yet, the procedures that you must follow are enough to cause anyone to turn and walk away. So I ask you—how badly do you want your money? A Writ of Execution first begins at your family clerk court office. There you will ask the clerk to file a Writ of Execution, which will cost you about $5. Item # 7 is a Writ of Execution. You will see that it instructs the sheriff to seize the property. The Writ of Execution must be issued to the sheriff along with Item # 8, which is a Sheriff's Instruction. A Sheriff's Instruction tells the sheriff what items must be seized. You must provide the sheriff with specific details of the item or items on the list. If you are seizing a car, for example, you must include the year, make, model, color, vehicle identification number, and some type of proof that the car belongs to the obligor. You must also tell the sheriff where the property will be located and when it will be there. The sheriff will charge you a fee for seizing the property—usually about $100. You will also be required to post a bond in the event that the sheriff is sued for seizing property that should not have been taken. The amount of the bond will be based on the value of the property that is being seized. The sheriff may ask you to approximate the value of the property. If you are seizing a car, or any other personal property, and you estimate the value to be $10,000, you can expect to pay anywhere from $100 to $300 for the bond. As a rule of thumb, the bond will cost 1 to 3 percent of the total estimated value of the property. You can get a bond by contacting a bondsman, insurance agent, or attorney. You will also be required to pay for a tow truck or a moving van for the items being removed. The sheriff will take the seized personal belongings to a storage facility, where they will stay, until the sheriff holds a "sheriff's sale" and the items are sold. You must also pay the storage fee. All of these fees must be paid up front before any seizure of personal property can take place. This is why you must be committed to a "by any means necessary" policy to get your child support. You can see why many people do not go this route. Sure, you can add the fees that you had to pay out onto the judgment that the obligor owes to you, but if you are like many custodial parents, you don't have the money to do this. I am not by any dissuading you from using this option. I quite in fact like it very much. If I were owed a lot of money, it is an option which I personally would use.

There are some items that the government will not permit you to take from the obligor, because they may be essential to his or her basic living. A car or any furniture is exempt up to the value of $1,500. Books and tools are exempt up to $750, and a rifle up to $500. If the personal property you wish to seize is worth a lot of money, much more than would be required to satisfy your judgment and the additional fees entailed, including the cost of the sale, then you may consider enlisting help from someone in the form of a temporary loan. Keep in mind that you can only get the amount of money that the property sells for, minus the cost of the sale. If the car valued at $10,000 sells for $4,000 at the auction and the cost of the sale was $200, you will receive $3,800, less the exemption of $1,500. If you invested $1,000 to have the property seized, you net $1,300. So before you decide to seize personal property and have it sold to pay your past-due child support, check your numbers and make sure that you don't get caught behind the eight ball. Food for thought: you could always have the personal property seized and sold and willingly break even just for the fun of it.

You could also bid on the property yourself—up to the amount of your judgment—and own the property without any out-of-pocket costs. You can do this because you have a judgment for the amount of your unpaid child support, and you have a judgment lien on the property, so you will receive the proceeds of the sale, up to the amount of your judgment. If the bidding goes higher than the amount of your judgment, pay a little extra, if you can afford it. If the property is yours, you can then sell it privately for more money if it is worth it, or you can keep it.

Writ of execution (real property)

Writs of Execution can also be filed against real property (real estate) to prevent someone from selling property without paying you first, or to force a foreclosure in order to get your past-due child support. A Writ of Execution against real property is more complex than a Writ of Execution against personal property. In this circumstance, it is best that you seek help from an attorney, if you can, unless you are really good with numbers or know someone who is who can help you to run them. To begin, use your investigative techniques learned in Chapter 9 to discover the value of the house and how much equity the obligor has in it. Equity is the amount of money that has been invested in the property. For example, if a house was purchased for $100,000 and $50,000 has been paid between the down payment and mortgage payments, there is $50,000 of equity in the house (remember that a portion of every mortgage payment goes to interest). Since you will need to pay out a lot of fees to force the sale, and there are costs associated with the sale, you will need to know how much you can get out of the house before you proceed. Again, you need to keep yourself from getting caught behind the eight ball. The amount of money that is exempt will be between $12,000 and $15,000. Also confirm that his name is listed on the deed because you will need to prove that the house belongs to the obligor. In some states, a home cannot be foreclosed on at all because of the Homestead Act. Your trusty attorney should be able to tell you if your obligor is in one of those states. You can also Google it. Sounds like a headache, doesn't it? There is good news, however. When threatened with a foreclosure due to a judgment on their property, most people will find a way to pay the judgment rather than take the chance of losing their property. It's a game of "uncle."

Deadbeat vs. Deadbroke

Sometimes just showing him that you mean business will get you what you want.

Creditor's bill

There are countless cases where the obligor will go to any length to avoid paying child support. Obligors will lie about their assets and income. They will place assets into a corporate name to avoid ownership. They have also been known to transfer assets into someone else's name, usually a new spouse or significant other. In this case, you will need to file a motion that is called a creditor's bill. A creditor's bill is simply a lawsuit that you are filing against the person who is in possession of the property that you believe was transferred. Transferring property to avoid paying child support is illegal. By filing a lawsuit against the person or the company holding the property, you will be able to subject him to the scrutiny of subpoenas and interrogatories to discover how he obtained the property. Once you are able to prove that the property used to belong to the obligor, you will be able to get a judgment lien on the property and proceed with a sheriff seizure or foreclosure. Again, check your numbers to make sure that it's worth it. One word of caution: this is another one of those complicated cases where you *may* need to enlist the help of an attorney. I say may because many attorneys will not know what a creditor's bill is when you first mention it to them. They will most likely have to do their research. If you are bold enough and brave enough – and if you have the emotional fortitude, you can do it yourself. If you *choose* to seek out the assistance of an attorney, it will be your choice. At least you know what you need, and you know what to ask for. Additionally, in some jurisdictions if you sue a company you are required to have an attorney.

Till-tap

This is one of my personal favorites. If your obligor owns a store that is open to the public and that has a cash register, wait until the busiest time of year for that type of business and file a Sheriff's Instruction for a till-tap. During a till-tap, the sheriff will go to the obligor's place of business and empty out the cash register—lock, stock, and barrel. Since you will want to get all the cash that you possibly can, you will want to instruct the sheriff to go during the busiest time of day. Hopefully there will still be some customers in the store to witness this action. If you don't know when the busiest time of the year or of the day is, do some research and find out. Call stores similar to the one that your obligor owns and tell them that you are doing some research—most people would be happy to answer a few short questions. Better yet, have someone your obligor doesn't know call his store and get the exact information you need.

Credit report investigations

I know an obligor who left his wife and children and soon thereafter took up with another woman. He paid no child support to his family, though he was very wealthy. For five years, his first wife tried to track him down as he moved from state to state to avoid paying her. He placed money in overseas accounts and property in his new wife's name. They later adopted children and moved into a mansion. Because she was relentless, his first wife eventually caught up with him and he was jailed. There are obligors who will fight tooth and nail to avoid paying child support. This man was obviously one of them. What disturbs me is that state agencies aided him and his new wife with the lifestyle that they led. If child support arrearages were noted on this man's credit report, he never would have been able to adopt the children that he and his wife had, nor would they have been able to buy the mansion that they lived in. This is one of the reasons that I am a staunch supporter of reporting past-due child support to the credit agencies. It happens frequently. Obligors go on to live lavish lifestyles while leaving their children in the lurch. They purchase homes, new cars, take vacations, and adopt children. If past due support was listed on credit reports, they would not be able to accomplish such feats until the support was paid. If your obligor owes you six months or more of past-due child support, simply contact your local agency and insist that they do this. It is your legal right.

Payment guarantee

In some states, the court may require that the obligor post a bond, or a cash payment, to assure future child support. If the obligor fails to make a scheduled payment, the payment is taken from the bond, or cash payment, and forwarded to the custodial parent. In New York, for example, when you file your court documents requesting a hearing for this matter, cite 471 Family Court Act. In North Carolina, you must show that the obligor showed "intentional disregard for the financial obligation to the family." In other words, you must show that the obligor spent inordinate amounts of money on unnecessary goods. Instead of a bond or a cash payment, it is called a trust fund and it is set up for a period of three years. If your state does not have a provision for the guarantee of payment, a letter to your congressperson is in order. Write asking that she sponsor an act for the guarantee of child support. See Item 9 for a sample letter to your Congressperson. This sample and other sample letters are of course available on my website. I include such sample letters to make it easier for parents to contact their elected officials to let them know what they need and what they want. If you complete the form and send it directly to me at simone@dontgetmadgetpaid.com, I will compile them and represent you in your state to get such a bill passed. If you send one directly to your Congressperson, please send us a copy. It will help us to fight for your state when we know that you are writing. If your Congressperson gets enough of these letters, it would be nearly impossible for her to turn a deaf ear to the requests.

HOT TIPS FOR UNDERAGE PARENTS

Writs of Garnishment, Writs of Execution, Creditors Bills…it can all seem so daunting. Remember to take it all step by step. You can do this!

Deadbeat vs. Deadbroke

EX PARTE ORDER TO WITHHOLD EARNINGS

IN THE CIRCUIT COURT OF THE STATE OF [INSERT YOUR STATE NAME]
FOR THE COUNTY OF [INSERT YOUR COUNTY / PARISH NAME]

[DOCKET NUMBER]
Docket Number

[INSERT YOUR NAME],
    Petitioner,

And

[INSERT OBLIGOR'S NAME],
    Respondent

EX PART ORDER
TO WITHHOLD EARNINGS

TO: [Employer]   [Obligor's Name]
      [Employer Address]   [Social Security Number]

Based upon Petitioner's Motion,

YOU ARE	DELINQUENT
HEREBY	AMOUNT OWED $_____
ORDERED TO	CONTINUING MONTHLY
WITHHOLD &	SUPPORT
PAY OVER TO:	PAYMENTS: $_____

An amount equal to 25 percent (or the continuing monthly support payment amount, whichever is less) of the beneficiary's benefits for temporary total disability, or an amount equal to 25 percent of the beneficiary's benefits for permanent partial disability and permanent total disability due or becoming due for each month beneficiary becomes or is eligible for these benefits, whether the benefits are paid monthly or in a lump sum payment.
[INSERT PERSON'S NAME OR ENTITY CAUSING THE WITHHOLDING] will inform you when there is no longer a current monthly support obligation.

EVEN IF THERE IS MORE THAN ONE ORDER TO WITHHOLD, IN NO EVENT SHALL YOU WITHHOLD MORE THAN 25 PERCENT OF BENEFICIARY'S BENEFITS DUE OR BECOMING DUE FOR EACH MONTH BENEFICIARY BECOMES OR IS ELIGIBLE.

THIS ORDER supersedes any order to withhold previously entered and shall continue in effect as long as there is current support owed or until further order of this court.

DATED_____   _____
                                                      CIRCUIT COURT JUDGE

Item # 5: Ex Parte Order to Withhold Earnings

WRIT OF GARNISHMENT

IN THE_____ COURT OF THE STATE OF [STATE NAME]

For the county of _____

_____, Plaintiff   Case No. _____

_____, Defendant(s)   Writ of Garnishment

IN THE NAME OF THE STATE OF [INSERT STATE NAME], TO:

_____

You are now a garnishee.

AS A GARNISHEE, YOU NEED TO KNOW THE FOLLOWING (the following information is to be filled in by the creditor):

On [INSERT DATE], plaintiff/defendant (cross out one), named above and called "Creditor", has obtained a judgment (a court order for the payment of money) against the plaintiff/defendant (cross out one), named above and called "Debtor." The Debtor's Social Security Number or employee Identification number is_____ (insert if known).

The following amount is necessary to satisfy the Creditor's judgment:

+Judgment debt	$_____
+Prejudgment interest	$_____
+Attorney Fees	$_____
+Cost Bill	$_____
+Post-Judgment Interest	$_____
+Delivery Fee for this Writ	$_____
+Sheriff Fees other than Delivery Fees	$_____
+Other (Explain. Attach additional sheets if necessary.)	$_____
$Total other from additional sheet (if used)	$_____
+ Past Writ Issuance Fees	$_____
+ Past Delivery Fees	$_____
+ Transcript and Filing Fees	$_____
from other counties	$_____
= Subtotal	$_____
LESS Payments Made	($_____)
= TOTAL Amounts Required to Satisfy in Full this Judgment	$_____

THE CLERK OF THE COURT HAS NOT CALCULATED ANY AMOUNTS ON THE WRIT AND IS NOT LIABLE FOR ERRORS MADE IN THE WRIT BY THE CREDITOR.

I certify that I have read the Writ of Garnishment; and to the best of my knowledge, information, and belief, there is good ground to support it.

DATED , _____,20_____

Signature of Creditor's or Creditor's Attorney   _____

Type or Print Creditor or Creditor's Attorney   _____

Address _____Date _____

Item # 6: Writ of Garnishment

Deadbeat vs. Deadbroke

WRIT OF EXECUTION

In the _____ Court of the State of (INSERT STATE)
For the County of [INSERT COUNTY]

No. _____

_____, Plaintiff

Vs.   **EXECUTION**

_____, Defendant

To _____, County, _____ State

WHEREAS ON [DD/MM/YYYY] in the _____ Court of [INSERT COUNTY],
_____ Recovered a judgment from
_____

for the following sum(s): _

Which judgment, or a certified transcript thereof, was on [INSERT DATE], duly docketed in the judgment docket of the Court of [County Name], [State Name], where it remains in force and unsatisfied in whole or in part:

THEREFORE, IN THE NAME OF THE STATE OF [INSERT STATE NAME), you are commanded that out of the personal property of the said judgment debtor(s), or if sufficient personal property cannot be found, then out of the real property belonging to said judgment debtor(s) on or after the date said judgment was docketed in your county, excepting such as the law exempts, that you satisfy the amount of said judgment with interest and costs and disbursements that may have accrued, LESS the amount of which has been paid on said judgment, and also the costs of this writ, and make due return of this writ within sixty days after you receive this writ.

Witness my hand and the seal of this court on this _____ day of _____, 20_____.

Judgment Debt	$_____		
Interest	$_____	_____
Attorney Fee	$_____	Name and Title
Cost Bill	$_____	By_____, Deputy
Additional Costs	$_____	
Total	$_____	
Payments made	$_____	Issued at the request of: _____
Balance Due	$_____	
Accruing Costs	$_____	
Disbursements	$_____	_____
Keeper's Fees	$_____	_____
Mileage	$_____	_____
Total	$_____	_____

Item # 7: Writ of Execution

SHERIFF'S INSTRUCTIONS

IN THE CIRCUIT COURT OF THE STATE OF [INSERT YOUR STATE NAME]
FOR THE COUNTY OF [INSERT YOUR COUNTY / PARISH NAME]

In the matter of: [DOCKET NUMBER]
                                                          Docket Number

[INSERT YOUR NAME],
  Petitioner,

                                                      INSTRUCTIONS TO
And   SHERIFF

[INSERT OBLIGOR'S NAME],   ([County] County)
  Respondent

TO THE SHERIFF OF [INSERT YOUR COUNTY NAME]:

    YOU ARE HEREBY INSTRUCTED to execute the enclosed Writ of Execution for the following described personal property of the defendant, to-wit:

[INSERT DESCRIPTION OF PERSONAL PROPERTY IN COMPLETE DETAIL EX: Black 2008 BMW 550SL, NJ License Plate No. 115-GTW, VIN No 569875699P],

    by immediately proceeding to debtor's residence located at [INSERT OBLIGOR'S STREET ADDRESS, CITY, STATE, ZIP CODE], or to such other location as may be hereafter identified within your county and at such place or places to then and there take possession of the equipment described above from the respondent or his agents or employees or any other person who may be in possession thereof and deliver it to the petitioner.

    Enclosed is our check in the amount of $150 as a deposit to cover your fees and expenses. If you have any questions or problems, please contact the undersigned. Thank you for your assistance.

                Insert your name or your attorney's name
                Street address
                Town, State, Zip Code
                Telephone Number with Area Code
                Date

Item # 8: Sheriff's Instructions

Deadbeat vs. Deadbroke

LETTER TO CONGRESS TO SPONSOR BILL FOR PAYMENT GUARANTEE

Date

Your name
Your street address
City, State, Zip Code
222-444-4444

Congressperson Bill Brown
Street address

City, State, Zip Code

Dear [Insert Congressperson's Name],

    I am writing to request that you sponsor an Act for the guarantee of child support in your state. Many states such as New York, North Carolina and New Jersey have such laws. If the obligor repeatedly misses child support payments they may be required to post a surety bond or advance cash payment to provide for future child support payments in the event that they fall behind. If (insert your state) had such a law, it would aid in preventing my child support from lagging so far behind.

    Please respond to this letter. I can be reached at the address and telephone number above.

Sincerely,
[Insert Your Name]

Item # 9: Letter to Congress to Sponsor Bill for Payment Guarantee

chapter 11:

what the courts can do
(if you ask them to)

as you are working to get your child support, you will find that there are many people who will not be helpful to you. It may happen for a variety of reasons—sometimes it will simply be that they don't know how to help you. They may not know how to obtain the information that you are requesting to give it to you. It's easier to be rude to you than to admit that they don't have the slightest idea of what you are asking. Depending on the source you go to and to whom you speak, they may be consciously or unconsciously trying to protect the NRP parent. Sometimes, it will be a combination of ineptitude and sheer meanness. Whatever the case, you don't have to feel as though you must beg for the information that you seek or the action you request be taken on your case. If you have a legal and valid reason for digging into the personal financial life of someone, the law allows you to do it.

Deadbeat vs. Deadbroke

Subpoena

Let's say that you are certain that the obligor has accounts with an investment company, but you don't have any account numbers or any other means of proof. You call and/or write to the company and ask that they release the information to you on the basis that you have a judgment against their client. Not surprisingly, they refuse any information to you. If this happens, take comfort in the fact that you can subpoena any information that you wish to know from them, as long as your petition has been filed with the court and you have been given a case number. You can find out how many accounts the obligor has, how much money is in them, when they were opened, as well as any personal information that they may have on the obligor. They may have a current address, employment information, and other bank account or credit information, and it is all available to you through a subpoena.

A subpoena is a court order that demands that the entity being subpoenaed (the investment company, in this case) appear as a witness to answer questions. In this case, you would want to ask questions about the obligor's finances and other personal information that they may have. If you want them to bring supporting documentation (statements, deposit slips, etc.), you must file a subpoena duces tecum. This requires that they not only appear, but that they bring whatever paperwork you want them to bring. In most cases, you will only need to file a subpoena duces tecum as a scare tactic. Once served with a subpoena, the most uncooperative person will suddenly provide you with what you need rather than take the time to appear and answer your questions. Simply make contact after the subpoena has been properly served and ask if they would prefer to provide the information that you request or if they would rather appear in person. Nine times out of ten, they will comply if it will get them off the hook. Remember to have them send copies of all of the supporting documents. Use the subpoena liberally. It can provide a wealth of information.

If your obligor has moved out of town without leaving a trace, and you are certain that someone in their family must know where they are, though no one will say a word, you can subpoena them all to give you whatever information you need. A subpoena is issued under penalty of law, so they must comply or face the judge themselves. It's also a good way to get information from someone who would like to spill the beans but fears some type of reprisal. If subpoenaed, they would have no other choice but to talk. A subpoena can be a beautiful thing. Re-read the previous paragraphs and consider the possibilities.

To obtain a subpoena form, contact your court clerk. Some courts require it to be stamped or certified by the court, and you may have to pay a small fee. You must have a court case to use a subpoena, and you must put your case number on the subpoena. If the court clerk does not have a subpoena form, you can possibly get one online or of course, you can use one from my website. After completing the form, take it to the clerk's office to be signed. Bring a copy of your judgment with you. You may have to pay a small fee for this service (approximately $10-$20, fees vary depending on where you live). As I have mentioned in chapters before, if you are poor you can request a waiver of the fees. Requesting one doesn't always mean that you will get one. Depending on where you are in the country or the person who is helping you on the particular day you happen to ask for a waiver, or whether it's a full moon or not – you may just get the waiver you request. The courts have discretion in some areas. You must then have someone other than yourself, who is over the age of eighteen, serve (deliver) the subpoena upon your witness. The only catch is that it must be personally delivered. It cannot be mailed or given to a secretary, coworker, neighbor, etc. While that can be a nerve-racking proposition, I am sure that you can think of several creative ways to get the subpoena into their hands. Consider our "balloon delivery person" from before. Most people are suckers when they think that they are going to get something.

Aside from the balloon delivery person, I know of another great story when it comes to creative ways to serve a witness. This story is not my own, so I am not relaying first-hand information. It comes to me by way of a colleague who is also engaged in a business which frequently requires serving legal documents upon people who try to shield themselves from situations like uh, - being served legal documents.

Apparently there was a fellow who had gone down a path of personal self-destruction. Let's call him Bobby. Bobby owed bills up the wazoo, had a nasty drug habit that he was trying to kick but wasn't having much luck kicking it and I don't know everything about his personal financial information but he was also divorced with a gaggle of kids. If I had to take a guess I would say that under those conditions, he probably didn't pay any support to his ex-wife and children, either. His ex-wife was not a client of mine so I cannot say for sure. Anyway, the guy was in hiding for the most part – hiding from bill collectors, hiding from the drug pushers to whom he owed money, hiding from a string of women he had scorned along the way since his divorce. Meanwhile, there was someone who was trying to dig up information on a third party for some legal purpose or another and Bobby had information he wanted. He hired a process server to serve Bobby with a subpoena, but Bobby couldn't be found. Mr. Bobby Nothisrealname had done a great job of hiding himself but his parents were right out in broad daylight, and it was assumed that his parents surely knew where their son was taking cover. Word had it that they were financially supporting him. It was decided that the document server would subpoena Bobby's parents in order to get to Bobby. Problem was that they lived in a huge house on a hill, surrounded by 10' tall wrought iron gates, complete with snarling dogs and a Fort Knox security system.

After learning that Bobby's parents were art collectors and were not able to pass up a great piece of art for their collections (addiction must run in the family gene pool), the server contacted the family secretary and informed her that he had a set of photographs which might help them to complete their collection of a famous rock star that they loved. A deal was made and the next day the server found himself driving through the big iron gates, past the dogs and straight up to the front of the house where he was greeted by Bobby's parents. Rolling the window down, the server looked directly at Bobby's father and asked him "are you Mr. Bobby Nothisrealname Sr."? "Yes, I am" answered the gentleman. Handing him an envelope which contained the subpoena, the server says: "you have been served". Mr. Nothisrealname Sr. already had a firm grip on the envelope which he thought contained priceless photographs. The server jammed his car in reverse and backed all the way down the long driveway at full speed and took off. The server used a technique popular with PI's and other *skip tracers* called *"pretexting"*. *"Pretexting"* is a professional word for lying your face off. The person who is *prexting* will make up a story about who they are or why they need certain information from the person that they are talking to. They make up such stories because they know that otherwise they will not get their desired outcome. Hence, the best skip tracers and PI's are the best liars around. Some people may have a moral problem with *pretexting* and I am not suggesting that you do it. I will say it again – it is my job to provide you with your options and information, it is your job to make the decisions for your personal life.

In addition to finding creative ways of serving your witness - if you must do it creatively, you must also pay the witness for attending court and the travel involved. You can expect to pay no more than $100 for an appearance and 55 cents per mile for travel. After the clerk signs the subpoena, you will need to make two copies of it. Keep one of the copies for yourself. The other copy and the original will need to be given to your "process server" (the person you select to serve the subpoena) to serve to your witness along with the fees for the appearance and mileage (and balloons), if any. Keep in mind that a witness may only be legally required to make an appearance to answer your subpoena if it is in the same county in which he lives, works, or conducts business. Most people would be hesitant to snub a subpoena. If you can't get to the county in which he lives or works, have the subpoena served anyway. The witness may not know that he doesn't have to appear. If your witness would rather end up in a legal proceeding than deal with you directly, you will need to provide a place for the deposition to take place. A deposition is the legal term for the question and answer period that will take place between you and your witness. A deposition can take place at almost any location. It does not have to be at a court building. If you do wish to have it at the courthouse, you will have to arrange with the clerk to have a private room. Otherwise, it can take place at your home or office, the witness' home or office, or anywhere else you desire. You will need to provide a court reporter. A court reporter is someone who will record the questions and answers during the deposition. Expect to pay $50 to $75 an hour for a court reporter. You can get a *transcript* (written record) of the deposition for an additional fee. Be sure to ask what the fee is before you request one. By the end of your deposition you will have all the information that your witness can provide to you.

Judgment debtor exam

Sometimes the only person who can provide the information that you need is the obligor himself. If that is the case, you will need to file a judgment debtor exam. A judgment debtor exam is similar to a subpoena in that the court is requiring someone to appear and answer questions. The difference between the two is that the subpoena is served upon any person, other than the *obligor*, whom you would like to call as a witness, to come and answer questions about the *obligor*. A judgment debtor exam is served upon the *obligor* to answer questions about his or her personal financials or whatever else may be necessary. The most difficult task when planning a judgment debtor exam can be finding the obligor in order to have him or her served. In some cases, you know where they are and you suspect or know that they have cash or assets; you just can't get to them. If you don't know where the obligor is, or if they tend to be a bit elusive and only come out at night like a vampire and other blood suckers, then it makes your job more difficult. If your obligor is vampire-like, then you will need to re-read Chapter 8 and find more methods to flush them out. If you know where they are and they are doing a good job of hiding what they have, read on.

The first thing you should know is that rarely will a judge allow you to conduct a debtor exam until you have first attempted to execute on personal or real property, and failed, or until you have sent a *Notice of Demand to Pay Judgment* (Item #11) and it has been ignored. My personal strategy is to send the demand letter first. Most deadbeats ignore demand letters, especially when they are from someone to whom they owe child support. He or she will laugh it off and muse at the humor of it all. That's exactly what you want them to do. Of course, you also want your money, and if after receiving your demand letter your obligor pays you, then you have what you want, right? Right. But what you don't have is the abundance of knowledge that a judgment debtor exam can provide to you. During a debtor exam you can ask the obligor about cash he may have on hand, in an account, or invested. You may ask if anyone is holding any cash for him in any form. You may ask about any personal or real property that they may own or have transferred recently. In short, you can find out the value of everything that they have. This serves two purposes for you: first, you can begin to form a list of things that you may want to have seized by the sheriff. If you have never been inside of the obligor's home, how else would you know what he has? Second, it will do your soul good to have the deadbeat squirm a bit.

The obligor may lie during the exam, which is why you want to have him bring all of the supporting documents so that you may examine them. This includes, but is not limited to, tax returns, pay stubs, checkbooks, bank statements, etc. You can make the list as long as you like as long as it is relevant. The obligor can also decide not to show up at the exam. If he decides not to show, the judge can order (and you will ask that the judge order) a bench warrant for his arrest.

Chances are that if this is your first time appearing before the judge requesting a bench warrant because the obligor did not appear, the judge is likely instead to order a *show cause* hearing for *contempt*. This gives the obligor one last chance to appear and answer your questions. If he does not show a second time, a warrant may be issued.

It is important to understand that it is the judge's decision whether or not to order a bench warrant for the arrest of the obligor. There are no hard and fast rules here. A judge may order a warrant for the first failure to appear, or she may order it for the second failure to appear. She may not order it at all and you will have to persist to get one issued. For this reason, you want to be sure that you have all of your facts correct and you present them to the judge in such a way that it is practically impossible for her to turn you down. Explain the hardships that the obligor has put you through in your pursuit to collect child support from him. Outline the many times that the obligor has refused to appear in court or has finagled his way out of a court order somehow. Tell the judge everything and leave out nothing. Read your statement to the judge before asking for the bench warrant for contempt of court.

Once you have been able to sway the judge in your direction and the obligor is subsequently arrested, he will be held until you can get there to conduct your examination, or until he is able to post bail, if the judge sets a bail. The bail amount should be equal to the amount of past-due child support. If the obligor is able to post bail, you can garnish it.

If the obligor lives in another state, or if it would be too difficult for you to travel to conduct a judgment debtor exam, some states will allow you to do it by mail instead. This is called a *written interrogatory*. If you are interested in this method, call the clerk of the court in your county and ask if your state allows this type of debtor exam. You will be able to write down the list of questions that you want your obligor to answer. This list can be either personally delivered to the obligor or delivered by certified mail. The completed interrogatory must be returned to you within twenty days, along with any supporting documentation that you have requested. If it is not, the same procedure as above applies. Remember that each motion that you file will require small fees to be paid at the courthouse, as well as service fees if you hire a process server or the sheriff to serve the obligor. Only plan on conducting a debtor exam or interrogatory if you are dealing with high stakes and would bet your bottom dollar that the obligor is sitting on a gold mine that should belong to you and your children.

To conduct a judgment debtor exam, not only must you serve the obligor, but you must also file a motion with the court to conduct the exam (Item #12). The motion must state where, when, and at what time the obligor must appear in court. (The court clerk will provide you with this information when the judge signs your order—Item #13.) It must advise the obligor that he must answer questions under oath and, if you so desire, it may also provide a restraining order. The restraining order will advise the obligor that he may not sell, transfer, or dispose of any assets before the exam takes place. It may also state the supporting documentation that you are requiring the obligor to bring. During the same visit, you must file an affidavit stating that you either attempted to execute on property belonging to the obligor or that you sent a demand letter and did not receive full or partial payment (Item #14). The judge will then sign the order, and the clerk will give you a certified copy to serve upon the obligor. There are some states that will allow you to serve the obligor by certified letter, but check with the court clerk before doing this.

On the day that you and your obligor must appear in court, the judge will call every debtor who is there to be examined. One by one, like a herd of cattle, they will be sworn in. After your obligor has given his oath you can then proceed to a quiet place (any quiet place will do) to go ahead with your exam. If there are any documents or answers to your questions that need to be clarified, you can go into the courtroom and have the judge make the final determination. During your exam you may discover that the obligor has some *nonexempt assets*. If you do, go immediately to the judge when your exam is over and request that an order for the obligor to turn over the *non-exempt* items be issued. Item #15 is an example of some of the questions that you may want to ask your obligor.

Contempt of court

The person being charged with contempt of court faces jail time because he has not done what the court has ordered. In your case, if your obligor is being charged with contempt, he has not paid court-ordered child support. Everyone is urged to utilize this method of child support collection, though it is not a cure-all. In fact, it may not work at all. Basically, what contempt of court will do is to drag the obligor into court to explain why he hasn't paid child support. Rarely will a judge order jail time for an obligor for his first contempt of court charge.

Deadbeat vs. Deadbroke

Usually obligors get far too many chances to pay before a judge will order a warrant for their arrest. If the obligor is arrested, child support must be paid before the obligor is released. That's where the system gets weak. The obligor should be required to pay all back child support before being released. Anyone who has been through the process can tell you that is not the case. More often than not, the judge releases the obligor with a warning in the form of a "purge" and requires him to pay only a portion of the child support before being released. Purges can be $400, $900, $1200, whatever the judge (or whoever is hearing the case deems to be appropriate. Then the swinging door begins and the same process tends to repeat itself like it did from the movie, "Groundhog Day", where Bill Murray repeated the dog days of his life over and over again. Although the contempt of court proceeding leaves much to be desired, here are several reasons for suggesting that you use it:

- If you only get 50 percent of what the obligor owes you (or 20% or 1%), that's a loaf of bread more than you had before. While on a business trip not too long ago with my husband, by mistake, I nearly threw away a receipt which I should have saved for my taxes. Quickly, I retrieved it from the garbage can at the airport. My husband, amazed that I would stick my hand in a trash receptacle, asked me if it really meant that much to me. Nodding my head, I replied, yes. Based on the value of the receipt, I told him that I would get a credit from Uncle Sam of about $1.00. That $1.00 means about a pound and a half of bananas at my house on grocery shopping day. So yes, that receipt will keep my kids in bananas for another 2 days. He smiled because he thinks the same way that I do – but he didn't think that I would stick my hand in a garbage can!
- If you have to file repeated motions for contempt of court, eventually the judge will give the obligor jail time.
- If you get nothing else, you will get the satisfaction of seeing that the obligor was jailed.

- I suggest that you employ every method that you can legally, physically, emotionally and mentally handle at one time. As the saying goes, if you throw enough mud on the wall, something has to stick.

A contempt of court proceeding is filed the same way any other motion is filed. Visit the clerk's office for the appropriate forms, get one online or go to my website. You will need to simultaneously file a motion for an *Order to Show Cause* and an *affidavit* (Items #16 and #17). The motion for the *Order to Show Cause* states that the obligor must appear in court to explain the reasons why he should not be held in contempt for failing to pay child support. The *affidavit* will outline the reasons why he should be. You should attach a copy of your court order stating the amount of child support that was ordered, as well as a detailed account of missed payments and payments received, if any. Also provide a history of all your collection efforts. You want to demonstrate to the judge that you have given the obligor many opportunities to cooperate and that he blatantly refuses. These forms will need to be filed with the court clerk, who will tell you when to appear in court. You will receive a certified copy of the *Order to Show Cause* (Item #18), which must be served upon the obligor. Of course, you will keep a copy for yourself before you hand over the original.

At this point, the case is very clear-cut and, unless the obligor can come up with some proof of payment, he will be held in contempt. The only defense that he may have is that an illness or disability has prevented him from making the payments. Unemployment or underemployment is also often used as a defense, but it holds no legal grounds – with one caveat. I hesitate to put this information in writing in a book because I know that there are some who read my books, not to collect child support, but instead to get out of child support. If you want this information, email me directly. I will share it with you and if you have one of those absent parents who is declaring an inability to pay, you need to know this or you will forever be sunk.

Deadbeat vs. Deadbroke

What happens from this point is purely potluck. It depends upon the judge assigned to you, what her personal beliefs are, and maybe her mood that day. The law allows for jail time for an obligor on his first contempt hearing. It allows the obligor to stay in jail until he is able to come up with the entire amount of back child support that he owes. This rarely, if ever occurs. Generally, he will be let off on a warning with a small amount of support paid toward the arrears. Unpaid child support will be considered arrearages and will be ordered to be paid off slowly. But holding the contempt hearing is better than not holding it. The threat of jail will continually hang over his or her head and if you have the kind of obligor who keeps you running back and forth to court on contempt charges, eventually their luck will run out.

SUBPOENA

IN THE CIRCUIT COURT OF THE STATE OF [INSERT YOUR STATE]
FOR THE COUNTY OF [INSERT YOUR COUNTY NAME]

[DOCKET NUMBER]
Docket Number

[INSERT YOUR NAME],
Petitioner,

And   CIVIL SUBPOENA DUCES TECUM

[INSERT OBLIGOR'S NAME],
Respondent

TO: [Obligor's Name
      Address
      City, State Zip Code]

IN THE NAME OF THE STATE OF [INSERT YOUR STATE NAME]:

You are hereby required to appear on the _____day of_____ , 20_____ ,
commencing at A.M./P.M., at the home of [Your Name], Plaintiff, [Your Address], for
your deposition by the plaintiff. You are required to appear and remain in attendance
until the completion of your deposition. You are further required to bring with you any
and all documents which are set forth on Exhibit A attached hereto and by reference
incorporated herein.

ISSUED this _____day of_____, 20_____.

Item # 10: Subpoena

Deadbeat vs. Deadbroke

NOTICE OF DEMAND TO PAY JUDGMENT

IN THE CIRCUIT COURT OF THE STATE OF [INSERT YOUR STATE]
FOR THE COUNTY OF [INSERT YOUR COUNTY NAME]

[DOCKET NUMBER]
Docket Number

[INSERT YOUR NAME],
Petitioner,

And

NOTICE OF DEMAND TO
PAY JUDGMENT

[INSERT OBLIGOR'S NAME],
Respondent

TO: [Obligor's Name
     Address
     City, State Zip Code]

DEMAND IS HEREBY MADE upon you pursuant to State Statutes, for payment, within ten days of your receipt of this Notice, of that certain Judgment entered against you in the above court. Payment may be made through the court or to the undersigned.

PLEASE TAKE NOTICE THAT your failure to pay will result in further court proceedings. **TOTAL AMOUNT DUE: $**_____.
DATED this _____ day of _____, 20_____.

_____
                Plaintiff

Item # 11: Notice of Demand to Pay Judgment

**MOTION FOR EXAMINATION OF
JUDGMENT DEBTOR**

IN THE CIRCUIT COURT OF THE STATE OF [INSERT YOUR STATE]
FOR THE COUNTY OF [INSERT YOUR COUNTY NAME]

[DOCKET NUMBER]
Docket Number

[INSERT YOUR NAME],
Petitioner,

And

**MOTION FOR EXAMINATION
OF JUDGMENT DEBTOR**

[INSERT OBLIGOR'S NAME],
Respondent

Plaintiff moves for an order:

1. Requiring Defendant [Obligor's Name] to appear at a time and place to be fixed by the court and answer under oath questions concerning any property or interest in property that defendant may have or claim, and then and there to produce the following documents of the defendant:

2. Refraining defendant from selling, transferring, or in any manner disposing of his property liable to execution pending this proceeding.

3. This motion is based upon ORS 58.111, the records and the files herein, and (choose one) (either) the return service of an unsatisfied execution (or) proof of service on the attached affidavit of a notice of demand to pay the judgment within 10 days (or) proof of service on file herein of notice of demand to pay judgment within 10 days.

_____
Plaintiff

Item # 12: Motion for Examination of Judgment Debtor

Deadbeat vs. Deadbroke

ORDER FOR EXAMINATION OF
JUDGMENT DEBTOR

IN THE CIRCUIT COURT OF THE STATE OF [INSERT YOUR STATE]
FOR THE COUNTY OF [INSERT YOUR COUNTY NAME]

[DOCKET NUMBER]
Docket Number

[INSERT YOUR NAME],
  Petitioner,

And

[INSERT OBLIGOR'S NAME],
  Respondent

ORDER FOR
THE EXAMINATION
OF JUDGMENT DEBTOR

This matter coming on for hearing on plaintiff's motion for examination of judgment debtor, and it appearing from the records and files herein that the judgment in this matter is unsatisfied and (choose one) (either) an execution herein has been returned unsatisfied (or) a notice of demand to pay judgment within 10 days has been served upon defendant in a manner provided by law, it is hereby

ORDERED that [Obligor's Name] appear before the presiding judge of the above-entitled court in Room No. _____ of the [Insert Your County Courthouse], [Insert Your City], [Insert Your State], on the _____day of _____, 20__ at the hour of_____, A.M. /P.M., and answer under oath questions concerning any property or interest in property that defendant may have or claim, and it is further

ORDERED that Defendant be, and hereby is, restrained from selling, transferring, or in any manner disposing of any of his property liable to execution pending this proceeding.

DATED this _____day of _____, 20_____.

_____
CIRCUIT COURT JUDGE

Item # 13: Order for Examination of Judgment Debtor

224

AFFIDAVIT IN SUPPORT OF MOTION

IN THE CIRCUIT COURT OF THE STATE OF [INSERT YOUR STATE]
FOR THE COUNTY OF [INSERT YOUR COUNTY NAME]

[DOCKET NUMBER]
Docket Number

[INSERT YOUR NAME],
Petitioner,

And

AFFIDAVIT IN SUPPORT
OF MOTION

[INSERT OBLIGOR'S NAME],
Respondent

STATE OF [INSERT YOUR STATE]

County of [Insert Your County]

I, [Insert Your Name], being first duly sworn, depose and say that:

    1. I am the Plaintiff.

    2. On or about [Insert Date], I caused a notice of demand to pay judgment to be deposited in the U.S. Mail postage prepaid, in a sealed envelope addressed to [Obligor's Name], defendant, at [Obligor's Address. City, State], by certified mail, return receipt requested.

    3. The notice of demand was served upon the defendant on [Insert Date], as shown by the face of the receipt attached. [Attach a copy of the face of the receipt.]

    4. A true copy of the notice of demand is attached hereto, marked "Exhibit A," and by this reference made part hereof.

_____
Plaintiff

SUBSCRIBED AND SWORN to before me this_____ day of_____, 20____.

_____
NOTARY PUBLIC FOR STATE My Commission Expires:

Item # 14: Affidavit in Support of Motion

Deadbeat vs. Deadbroke

SAMPLE QUESTIONS FOR AN ORAL DEBTOR'S
EXAMINATION OR WRITTEN INTERROGATORY

DATE: [NAME OF COURT REPORTER, IF ANY]

1.   **Personal Information**
   A. Full Name:
   B. Residence address:
   C. Residence telephone number:
   D. Spouse's name, occupation, and employer:
   E. How many children under the age of 18?

2.   **Occupation**
   A. Employer or name of business:
   B. Type of business:
   C. Your occupation:
   D. Business address:
   E. Business telephone number:
   F. Business associates:
   G. Name of employer's bank, address:
   H. Employment history for the past three years:

3.   **Income**
   A. Income from occupation or business:
   B. Incomes from all other sources, including pensions,
        disability, unemployment, and other businesses:
   C. Commissions or renewals earned or anticipated:
   D. Pertinent information from state and federal tax returns and
        other books and records brought to the examination:

4.   **Interests in Real Property**
   A. Beneficial or fee interest:
   B. Amount of equity in home and who holds mortgage:
   C. Purchaser or seller on contract: With whom, how much is
        owed?
   D. Lessor or lessee:
   E. Remainder or contingent interest:
   F. Beneficial use of any use of any real property in the name
        of another, including spouse:
   G. Mortgage or beneficiary under deed of trust:
   H. Any other interest whatever in any property in your state or
        any other state or country:

5.   **Securities**
   A. Stock:
        1. If a shareholder in a close corporation, is the debtor an officer or
           director?

Item # 15: Sample Questions for an Oral Debtor's Examination or Written Interrogatory

2. Who are the other officers, directors, and major
    shareholders?

3. Any other stock?

4. Any accounts with brokerage houses:

B. Debt:

    I. Checks, drafts, or notes payable to the debtor:

    2. Bonds, dividends, certificates, certificates of deposit,
       deposits, or other interest-bearing instruments:

6.   **Cash Equivalent**

A. Cash on hand:

B. Safe deposit boxes:

C. Bank, savings and loan, and credit union accounts of any
    kind:

D. Deposits of money with any other institution or person:

E. Cash value on insurance policies:

F. IRS and state tax refunds due or expected:

7.   **Choses In Action**

A. Accounts receivable or debts on open account

B. Liquidated or unliquidated claims of any nature, including
    in contract and tort:

C. Claims against insurance companies:

D. Security interests and other liens or claims:

8.   **Other Personal Property**

A. Household goods:

B. Automobiles, trucks, motorcycles, and other vehicles:

C. Boat or other vessel: How much is owed on it?

D. Inventory, tools, machinery, and fixtures:

E. Farm equipment, animals, or crops:

F Jewelry or other valuable property including
    sculpture, paintings, antiques, stamps, coins, etc.:

G. Patents, copyrights, trademarks, trade names, royalties, etc.:

H. Any documents of title, including warehouse receipts, etc.:

I. Any interest in any other business, partnership, or joint
    venture:

J. Real estate listings:

K. Any licenses or permits from public authorities:

L. Any other property, tangible or intangible, which might
    have a potential value:

9.   **Trusts, Etc.**

A. Is any property held for you in trust, guardianship,
    conservatorship, or custodianship?

B. Are you a trustee, custodian, guardian or conservator?

C. Are you an heir of anyone who has passed away?

10.   **Legal Proceedings**

A. Do you now have a legal claim against any party or does any
    party now have a legal claim against you?

B. Have you been a party to any legal proceeding over the past
three years?
1. If so, have you satisfied any judgment against you?
2. Has there been a levy against any of your property?
3. Has any third party satisfied any judgment for you?
4. Have you collected any judgment?
C.   In the past three years has the IRS or any state or county agency
asserted a claim for unpaid taxes against you?

11.   **Other Indebtedness**
A. Names and addresses of secured creditors and amounts
claimed by each:
B. Names and addresses of unsecured creditors and amounts
claimed by each, including tax collectors:
C. Names and addresses of judgment creditors, amount of
each judgment:
D. Names and addresses of those to whom you have applied
for a loan in the past 3 years:

12.   **Transfers And Losses**
A. Transfers of property within the past 2 years to relatives,
charities, mists, or others:
B. Money deposited in accounts in the name of another over
the past 2 years:
C. Loans repaid over the past 2 years:
D. Assignments of payments, notes, contracts, insurance
policies, or wages over the past 2 years (Example: purchases of
property, including stock, for another over the past 2 years):
E. Transfers of any property over the past 2 years, not in the
usual course of business:
F. Does anyone else hold title to or possession of any property
in which you have any rights or interests?

13.   **Books And Records**
A. Name and address of accountant-bookkeeper:

MOTION AND AFFIDAVIT FOR ORDER
TO SHOW CAUSE, RE: CONTEMPT

IN THE CIRCUIT COURT OF THE STATE OF [INSERT YOUR STATE]
FOR THE COUNTY OF [INSERT YOUR COUNTY NAME]

[DOCKET NUMBER]
Docket Number

[INSERT YOUR NAME],
Petitioner,

And

[INSERT OBLIGOR'S NAME],
Respondent

MOTION AND AFFIDAVIT
FOR ORDER TO SHOW
CAUSE RE: CONTEMPT

Petitioner moves for an order requiring the respondent to appear and show cause, if any there be, why petitioner should not be held in contempt of court for failing to comply with the provisions of the Judgment previously entered herein on or about [Date], as specifically alleged in the affidavit set forth herein below.

Petitioner declares that:

1. The maximum sanction the Petitioner seeks is an order incarcerating respondent in the county jail until he complies with the order of the court by paying child support to the Petitioner.
2. Petitioner seeks a sanction of confinement.
3. Petitioner considers this sanction to be remedial.

Petitioner also moves the court for Judgment against respondent on account of Petitioner's reasonable attorney fees and actual costs incurred herein supported by petitioner's affidavit as set forth herein below.

DATED this _____ day of_____ , 20_____

Item # 15: Motion and Affidavit for order to Show Cause Re: Contempt

Deadbeat vs. Deadbroke

AFFIDAVIT

STATE OF [INSERT STATE NAME]

[Insert City Name] of [Insert County Name]

I, _____ , hereby swear the following to be true: I am the Petitioner herein. Respondent is my [former husband/boyfriend/wife/girlfriend]. We were divorced pursuant to a Judgment and Decree of Dissolution of Marriage entered herein on or about [Date], OR, we ended our relationship on or about (Date), and a child support order was issued by the court on or about [Date].

Paragraph 4 of the court's Judgment reads as follows:
"4, That the respondent is hereby ordered to pay support to the Petitioner in the amount of $_____ per _____ for the care, support and maintenance of said minor child, payable [Insert how child support was ordered payable], on the _____ day of each _____, until each child is emancipated in accordance with State Law, and is no longer attending school on a regular basis. All support payments shall be in the form of cash or check made payable to [Insert to whom child support is payable], with the first such installment to be paid on or before [Date]."

Respondent has failed and refused to pay any child support as ordered by the court despite repeated demand that he/she do so.

Based on the above, I believe respondent is in willful contempt of the decree of dissolution and therefore I ask that he/she be adjudged in contempt of court, In addition, I ask that the court impose all of the following sanctions, all of which I consider to be remedial in nature:

a. Requiring respondent to pay a sum of money sufficient to compensate me for loss, injuries, or costs suffered by me as a result of respondent's contempt of court.

b. Confining respondent in the [Insert your County Jail] or other appropriate facility for so long as his contempt continues or six months, whichever is shorter.

c. Requiring respondent to pay an amount not to exceed $500 or 1 percent of his annual gross income, whichever is greater, for each day that he/she remains in contempt of court. I ask the court that this sanction be Imposed to compensate me for the effects of his/her continuing contempt.

d. Any order designed to ensure compliance with a prior order of the court including probation.

e. Any other additional sanction if the court determines that the sanction would be an effective remedy for the contempt.

f. Awarding me judgment against respondent for all of my attorney fees, costs, and disbursements incurred in this matter.

_____Petitioner

SUBSCRIBED AND SWORN to before me this_____ day of _____ , 20_____

_____   _____
        NOTARY PUBLIC   My Commission Expires:

Item # 16: Affidavit

ORDER TO SHOW CAUSE, RE: CONTEMPT

IN THE CIRCUIT COURT OF THE STATE OF [INSERT YOUR STATE]
FOR THE COUNTY OF [INSERT YOUR COUNTY NAME]

[DOCKET NUMBER]
Docket Number

[INSERT YOUR NAME],
Petitioner,

And

**ORDER TO APPEAR TO
ANSWER CONTEMPT OF
COURT CHARGE - FAILURE
TO OBEY SUPPORT ORDER**

[INSERT OBLIGOR'S NAME],
Respondent

TO:

On the Motion of the Plaintiff,

YOU ARE ORDERED TO APPEAR in person before the Court, [Insert County Courthouse Name, Address, City, State], and show cause why you should not be adjudged guilty of contempt of Court for disobeying the support order entered in the above-entitled Court and cause.

_____
_____
_____
_____
_____

BE PREPARED TO TESTIFY REGARDING YOUR FINANCIAL POSITION, BRING WITH YOU ANY RECORDS YOU MAY HAVE IN CONNECTION WITH YOUR INCOME, ASSETS, EXPENSES, AND SUPPORT PAYMENTS.

NOTICE TO DEFENDANT: You are entitled to be represented by an attorney at the Court hearing. If you desire an attorney but cannot afford one, the Court will appoint legal counsel for you.

Dated this _____ day of _____ , 20_____.

_____
CIRCUIT COURT JUDGE

Item # 17: Order to Show Cause, Re: Contempt

chapter 12:

what the government can do for you

there are other methods of collection that can be utilized to get child support that is in arrears. These are methods that are only available to you through a government agency. You must have a current child support order and be using the state child support agencies to collect your child support in order for these government methods to work for you.

Tax refund intercept

Federal law allows for the interception of an obligor's federal tax refund if there is overdue child support in the amount of $150 or more. Think of it as a wage garnishment against a tax refund check. If you are receiving your child support through the state child support agency and you are due at least $150 from the obligor, tell your caseworker that you would like to have his tax refund intercepted. The caseworker will check to see if you have a child support order that is still in effect. If you do, you will be asked to sign an affidavit stating the amount of child support that is past due to you. The caseworker will also verify that the agency has the correct address for the obligor. If the address that you have is not current, the current address must be obtained before the intercept can take place.

When the address has been corrected, a letter is then mailed to the obligor advising him that the tax refund will be intercepted for the purpose of collecting past-due child support. Advising the obligor of the intent to intercept allows him an opportunity to contest the action. If the obligor decides to contest the interception, he can only have two defenses that can hold up in court:

1. The obligor can object because he does not owe the amount of child support that is stated. In this case, he would have to prove it by producing receipts of paid child support for the months that you say that it was not paid.
2. He can object because he is not the person that is named on the complaint. In this instance, the case of mistaken identity would have to be proven.

Your obligor may feel that because he currently is making timely child support payments and is slowly paying off past-due support, that a tax refund should not be intercepted. This is not the case, and it is not the law.

Unfortunately, most likely you will only be able to use the interception once as a means of getting past-due child support. Once your obligor is on to you, there is little chance that he will leave money in the hands of the federal government for you to get. Many obligors will at this time decide to change the status on their W-2 forms so as not to overpay taxes during the year. Instead, he would rather owe the government and make payment during tax time. Some may decide not to file their taxes at all.

If the obligor has filed taxes with a new spouse, the intercept will still be made. The spouse will then be able to contact the IRS and have the portion that is rightfully hers refunded. The portion will be determined by the amount of income shown on the income tax forms. (In the meantime, it would be nice to be a fly on the wall when that letter comes through.)

The IRS intercept has accounted for more than 20 percent of all child support collected since 1981. The beauty of it is that it works like a charm; the downside is that it is not always an automatically implemented tool—you must personally request that it be done. If you wait until the IRS decides on their own to implement it, you may end up waiting years. You must also request it many months in advance. Each state submits a case list to the IRS in August, along with the amount of the arrearages for an interception the following year, so you must plan far in advance. If your state or the state in which your obligor lives requires a state income tax to be filed, then check with your caseworker about intercepting that refund as well.

IRS Collection Procedure

This is a good method of collecting past-due support, but as with every other method, it is not without its downsides. For openers:

1. Your case must be handled by the state child support agency, or you must be on, or eligible for, welfare.
2. Your case must be at least $750 in arrearages and it must be at least six months since you last asked for IRS collection assistance.
3. You must provide identification information on the obligor and the IRS must have reason to believe that the obligor has assets that can be levied.

This is where some of your own investigation will come in handy – and necessary, because you are required to provide this information to the IRS before they will help you. They will not perform any asset searches or other investigations on your behalf. This is one of the benefits of having a child support advocate on your side. Remember the mom who learned that her ex was nearly a real estate mogul? With the pile of information that we dug up on him during an asset search, she was able to save herself from a downward modification and instead increase her child support award...all because her ex was behaving in selfish and greedy ways. If you provide the IRS with similar information, that would give them the green light to move ahead with procedures at their disposal. These procedures may be of great assistance to you.

Once this checklist has been completed, someone from the IRS will attempt to contact the obligor to make a satisfactory arrangement. Sometimes the contact of an IRS agent is all a deadbeat needs to whip into shape. He or she will suddenly go out of their way to find the money to pay you. After all, now that the IRS is involved, child support seems like a serious issue. If IRS contact doesn't shape him up, the agent will then send a notice of intent to levy any and all *nonexempt property* that the obligor may have. Exempt property essentially is property that you cannot take from the obligor. Non-exempt property is property on which you can place a lien and have the sheriff to seize and liquidate (sell), if it a non-cash item. Cash items would automatically be provided to you after the requisite period of time and paperwork. The guidelines of what constitutes exempt property vs non-exempt property varies state by state and your child support advocate would be able to help you sort through that information. Here is a rough guideline to follow, just to give you an idea:

Examples of Non-exempt Property

- Cash, bank account funds, and securities like stocks or bonds
- Valuable items like coin or stamp collections and antiques
- Musical instruments (unless the debtor is a musician by profession and uses the instrument)
- Second homes or vacation property
- Second cars, trucks, and other motor vehicles

Examples of Exempt Property include:

- Necessary items like clothing, furnishings, and household goods/appliances (up to a reasonable amount)
- Some motor vehicles, up to a specified value
- Jewelry, up to a specified value
- Tools or instruments of the person's trade, up to a certain amount
- Some unpaid earned wages
- Pensions
- Benefits such as social security, welfare, unemployment, if held in a bank account

This is the same as you executing on the obligor's personal and real property, only the IRS is doing it now. Very few obligees use this IRS collection procedure and fewer know that it exists. If your child support arrearages are on the high end and the assets that your obligor has are also on the high end, definitely consider using this method.

The IRS can also be used to locate the obligor and/or his assets. This can be done by doing a search on 1099 matches with names, Social Security Numbers, and wages. Those who are self-employed file 1099 forms with the IRS as opposed to W2 forms, for example. A 1099 is a means of reporting to the IRS your income and assets. If you have income from other sources outside of the wages that you earn (stocks, CDs, money markets, etc.) it would be reported on a 1099. It would also have the addresses that the obligor has reported to the outside source of income. This is useful because he may not report his correct address to the IRS if he knows that you are after him. He may report the correct address to the income sources, however, so as to receive statements and quarterly reports.

Now, let's say that the obligor is less that truthful when reporting to the IRS about additional income sources. Maybe he doesn't list them all, only listing ones that have old address information or that earn little money. The IRS has another procedure called the 1098. The 1098 reports to the IRS the interest that taxpayers pay on a certain account.

Deadbeat vs. Deadbroke

So even if the obligor doesn't report it, the IRS has a way of finding it, and through that they may uncover a correct address or an asset goldmine.

There are downsides to both the 1099 and 1098 information and asset location. You can only request that these searches be done if previous information has been requested of the IRS, but the obligor still has not been located. Also, the information can be used for location purposes only, and cannot be used to execute on found assets of the obligor. The way to get around this, however, is to subpoena the financial institution where the assets are located. The financial institution must at that time give you whatever information you request, even if it is information that you already have but cannot legally use.

chapter 13:
TANF & child support

the OCSE (Office of Child Support Enforcement), states in their fiscal year report (FY2012) that eighty percent of parents on TANF (Temporary Assistance to Needy Families, also known as welfare) do not receive child support payments. I don't think that I am making much of a leap here to say that these parents receive public services because the other parent of their children is unable or refuses to pay child support. In order to qualify for TANF, normally you must own less than a total of $1,000 in non-exempt property and have few resources and limited income. If you have any income at all while you are receiving public benefits, it is deducted from your monthly allowance to ensure that you pay the state back for any money that they give to you during your time of need. Consider it a signature loan. Just sign on the dotted line and you get the help that you need, but at some point in the future it must be paid back. If you own a home and are given a TANF grant, the state will attach a lien on your property for the amount that you have been given. When you sell your house, you will have to pay back the money that you received while on welfare.

Deadbeat vs. Deadbroke

The $50 disregard

The only exception to this rule is the "$50 disregard." The first $50 of any payment that you receive per month, from any income source is disregarded as income. Under these conditions, child support is considered income, as is any money that anyone gives to you as a gift. The welfare office considering child support as income is inconsistent with any other policy that I have ever heard of. Normally, child support is not considered to be income, unless you want it to be. If you apply for a loan or for credit of any type, in the area where you must list your income sources you will plainly see a statement which clearly says, and I am paraphrasing here, "you do not have to include child support" or "child support optional". Uncle Sam doesn't even count child support as income for tax purposes. The welfare office, however, says that child support is income. If you are able to get a part-time job earning $75 per month, you will be allowed to keep the first $50 of that amount while the balance must be given to the state. Likewise, if you are able to get any child support from the NRP while you are on public assistance, you will get to keep the first $50. Whether the NRP makes the payment in full or only a partial payment for the month is irrelevant, you get the first $50 either way. Yes indeed, the welfare office wants their money back. Consider this story which happened to clients of mine:

Bob and Jane (not their real names, of course) had two teenage daughters, Lillian and Beth. Lillian and Beth were 17 and 18 respectively. Both Lillian and Beth lived at home with their parents and both Lillian and Beth were teenage mothers. Lillian had one child and Beth had two children. The fathers of these children were brothers and lived at home with their parents as well and they both were college students without an income. Bob and Jane arranged for their daughters to receive public assistance to assist with the support that they gave to them. They provided a roof over their heads, clothes and diapers for their grandchildren and any and everything else Lillian and Beth needed for themselves or their children when the public welfare assistance didn't quite stretch far enough.

One day Bob and Jane received a letter in the mail stating that because they lived in a state which allowed for grandparent financial support, (as described earlier in Chapter 4); the state was taking them to court for child support for their grandchildren. Yes, you read that correctly. The same grandparents who were already financially supporting their grandchildren were now being sued by the state. Bob and Jane contacted me because the other grandparents had never helped with their grandchildren and now they were claiming poverty to the government, when Bob and Jane knew that they ran a successful event planning business for musicians and were paid mostly in cash. I worked closely with Bob and Jane and helped them to establish the other grandparents' income to the courts, so that they too would be on the hook for supporting their grandchildren. But what's really interesting is that after the state sued Bob and Jane for child support, Lillian and Beth each began to receive $50 "child support payments" each month from their parents. How crazy is that? The state kept the rest of the child support payment money to pay down the debt incurred from the girls receiving TANF benefits for the previous year or two. The end of the story is that shortly thereafter both Lillian and Beth dropped TANF, their parents continued to support them as they had done all along and they both received child support from the other grandparents which helped equalize the financial responsibility. The fathers of the children eventually graduated from college and found jobs...and then I heard from Bob and Jane again. As I said in the first line of the preface of this book, "Some things change slowly, some things change quickly, and some things never change at all. This certainly applies to those who have gone through the child support process only to find themselves going through it once more".

In-kind payments

If anyone makes payments on your behalf, say for your car, rent, or cable bill, they are not considered to be income unless the money touches your hands. If you are lucky enough to have someone who is willing to subsidize a better apartment for you or a safe vehicle to drive, have that person make the payments directly. Payments made to your accounts by someone else on your behalf are called in-kind payments. What an in-kind payment is and how it can affect you is important to understand because if it is perceived by the welfare agency that you are receiving additional "income" because someone is giving you money to make bill payments or anything similar, that additional money could add up and put you over the TANF income threshold. If that happened, you would no longer be eligible to receive benefits.

Further, there are some NRP who buy clothes, shoes and food for their children at times. They then claim that the purchasing of these items should be considered child support. By law, it is not.

Assignment of rights

If you are on TANF, you have assigned the rights of your child support case to the state. This is true whether you went to the state with a child support order already in place or if they are helping you to establish an order. The state now has control of your case. You are no longer the beneficiary of your child support, the state is. State employees are the ones who will now decide what happens with it or, more likely, what doesn't happen with it. They have the right to decide which collection method will be used to get money from your NRP and whether they want to go after him or her at all. They can do this without consulting you. If they are receiving any child support at all, whether it is the full amount or not, whether they can get more or not, they may decide that they don't wish to pursue the case anymore and settle for the small amount of money that they get. This of course does not work in your favor. If you are not able to receive more child support from the NRP because, for example, the state settled for an amount without requiring – or even requesting – that the NRP provide proof of income, you should absolutely consider receiving the additional money. That additional money could mean the difference between you being on welfare...or not. I have had tons of clients to transition from public assistance to independence simply because they were able to have their child support upwardly modified to an appropriate amount.

To be fair, it should be noted that the state agencies have more cases than they can effectively handle. It stands to reason that everyone doesn't get the best care this way. But that doesn't do your case any good and there is absolutely nothing that you can do about it. You can jump up and down, scream and shout, and tell your caseworker of the new job that the NRP just got, increasing their income $3000 a month. If the caseworker doesn't want to pursue it, they don't have to. They own your case. You can't get a modification, wage garnishment, or take the NRP to court unless the caseworker agrees to it. What's even worse, you may not be able to get the slightest bit of information on your case either.

When you apply for TANF benefits you won't be told that you are signing your rights away, although you are. If you had an attorney to represent you as you were signing up for benefits, he or she would have been able to tell you exactly what you were signing. It's all there in black and white. It's all also paragraphs and pages of legal language that most people would not understand or have the guts to question. But, of course, that's not the case since you probably needed every penny that you had at that time and you probably needed the assistance. I hate to be the bearer of bad news, but it's important that you know this before you try to start any kind of TANF proceedings. If you find yourself in this position, you can do one of three things:

1. Do nothing and accept your TANF benefits and your fate. If you are on welfare, you must need the assistance. You may not be in a position to refuse benefits and pursue child support on your own.

2. If you strongly believe that you can handle your case better than the state has and you are willing to take the gamble of relinquishing your TANF payments to pursue your child support—which could take months in some cases—then go for it. Many have succeeded this way.

3. Meet with your welfare caseworker. Explain your reasons for believing that if your child support case were pursued that you

would fare better financially. The only way to really make a case here is if you have reason to believe that you would no longer be entitled to receive welfare if you received your child support from the NRP parent. Otherwise your energy would be futile; it would make no sense for you to pursue the case. When you meet with your caseworker, tell him or her that you have read a great book which may help you to investigate on your own whether the NRP has an ability to pay or has an ability to pay more than he or she is currently paying. There shouldn't be a reason for the caseworker to turn you down. After all you are trying to make his or her life easier by doing some of the work. If you do happen to be turned down by your caseworker, remember that your caseworker has a boss. Ask your caseworker for the name of his or her supervisor and call that person with your same request. Remember that person has a boss. Keep going until you get to the person who is going to say, "yes".

The bottom line is this: You can't go after the NRP on your own if you are on welfare. Only you can decide if it will be worth your while to do without the benefits while you are chasing the other parent for money. When you are able to get child support from the NRP, will it be enough to sustain you? Will you be able to get it regularly or you will have to employ several collection methods to squeeze the money out of him or her? Find your answers, and then make your best decision.

chapter 14:
interstate child support collection

It is much easier to collect child support if the obligor lives in the same state as you do. If you know where he or she lives and works, a wage withholding is an easy method of collecting your support payments. If you choose to go that route, keep in mind that you will not have control over your child support case because a caseworker will have the responsibility of making day to day decisions on your behalf. Your other option will be to represent yourself, file all of your own paperwork and do all of your own follow-up. The time and energy invested is a price to pay for calling all of your own shots, and being "in the know" about your own case, but in my opinion, it is well worth it. You will have to make your own call. I like to remind my readers and my clients that your case is just that – a case – to your caseworker and to your attorney, if you have one. To you, your case affects your life. It IS your life. Your caseworker and/or attorney may care very much about your case, the outcome and its affect on your family but they do not have to live with it. At the end of the day, they go home to their own life.

If you do not know where the obligor lives or works, or if you need to do some sleuthing to find either the obligor or his/her assets, it's more difficult if they live far away from you if you are working with the agency

245

which handles child support cases in your state. The reason is because your state (known as the petitioning state) will have to "talk to" the state where the other parent lives (known as the responding state) and they will have to work together. I use the terminology "talk to" loosely because most times it is not people who are talking at all. Most of the communicating is done technologically. Instead of your state helping you directly, it has to ask the second state to help them to help you. Your state will be doing the asking – (ex: "do you know where this person is"? "Can you find this person"? "Will you please look for him or her and his or her assets"?) The responding state will be doing the answering – (ex: "No, we do not know where this person is located". "Does your petitioner have any information on the whereabouts of the subject"?) Needless to say, this can go on for a while. What's worse is that each state is allowed by law a certain amount of days in which to respond before the originating state can follow-up. The amount of time varies depending on the request which has been made but it is not uncommon for 30 or 45 days to be an allowable amount of time for a response. If you do the math, you may now understand why there are so many frustrated parents without information on their cases and why it sometimes takes so very long for seems to be a simple process of getting answers or enforcing a motion. This is another reason to cut through the muck and represent yourself.

There are some commonly known and widely used collections techniques you can employ if the obligor does not live in the same state as you and you decide to utilize the services of child support enforcement services. Of course, you will not be able to implement any of these yourself and will have to ask your caseworker to implement them for you, which he or she may or may not do you for…if you are able to get in touch with them.

Interstate wage withholding

The interstate wage withholding is the most popular method of collection. It works the same way that a wage withholding works if the obligor lives in the same state where you live. The only difference is that you must cross state lines in order to collect the money. The *originating state* (the state in which you live, also called the *initiating state or the petitioning state)* does not have *jurisdiction* over someone who does not live there, so it cannot withhold their wages. Instead, your state must petition (ask) the obligor's state to withhold wages for child support and forward them to the state where you live. If the state child support collection agency is collecting your support for you, they will receive the payment and then forward it to you. This often leads to more hold-ups. (If you are handling your own case and have filed against the employer directly, the payment will go directly to you). The drawback with this method is that most states do not respond immediately when petitioned for help on a child support case. The 30-45 day time-frame I mentioned before is quite the norm instead of the exception. You can see how these procedures can take months and can prove to be challenging. Additionally, the originating state is kept in the dark about whatever collection methods are, or are not, being used by the responding state. Generally, the responding state will send an electronic transmittal to the originating state once action has been taken on some collection method. But this is not guaranteed and even a small correspondence of this nature can take months. Some transmittals are still sent through the mail. Your caseworker and your state are left to wonder and so are you.

Even though your caseworker cannot take direct action on your child support case if it is out of state, the interstate wage withholding can still an effective method to use. It doesn't work well for everyone, so your decision at this point will still be whether you want to handle your case yourself, so that all of the correspondence must go to you, or whether you want the state agency to handle your case for you.

If you want to file for an interstate wage withholding yourself and you already have a child support order and an order for a wage withholding (if you do not, those must be your first action items), you must provide the following documentation:

1. Certified copy of the original child support order
2. Certified copy of the order for a wage withholding
3. An affidavit from you testifying to the amount of arrearage and the supporting documentation that goes along with it, or a certified copy of the payment record from the state agency that was collecting your support payments before you took over
4. The full name and current address of the obligor
5. The name and address of the obligor's employer
6. The name and address of the obligee (you)

This information must be provided to the responding state in order to file a *foreign order* of support. A foreign order of support, simply stated, is a support order that you have obtained that you would like to enforce in another state. A child support order that you received in your state is not good in any other state unless you have it registered in the state where you will try to enforce it. If the obligor moves from state to state, you will have to register your child support order in each state before you attempt to collect on it. Think of it as a vehicle registration. Your car may be properly registered in your own state, but if you move to another state, you must have it registered there before you can consider it legally registered. Unfortunately, this is how our child support system works right now.

The procedure to get a wage withholding on the income of an obligor who lives out of state if you intend to utilize child support enforcement services directly as opposed to having your own state facilitate for you, is as followed:

1. Send the above documents to the withholding agency in the state where the obligor works. (Although most states will accept this documentation from you, there are a small handful of states that will only accept it from a government agency. Check first.)
2. The support order will then be entered by the responding state.
3. You must then send notice to the obligor that you are intending to withhold his wages. If you need to refresh your memory on how to do this, see Chapter 10.

4. As long as the obligor does not contest the wage withholding, an order will be sent to the obligor's employer. The obligor can only contest the order on the grounds of mistaken identity. Otherwise, if contested, the order will be entered and a court date will be scheduled for other matters. (Most likely other matters in instances such as this would amount to the obligor now taking the opportunity to file for a downward modification or paternity test or something other which may help dismiss or lower his or her obligation).

The procedure to get a wage withholding on the income of an obligor who lives out of state if you are representing yourself, is as followed:

1. Contact the human resources department and get the name of the person who handles child support withholdings. If it's a small company, simply just call and ask management the same question. Some companies may tell you that you cannot do this on your own and that you must go through the child support agency. This is absolutely untrue. They probably are just unaware that this is your legal right because not enough people represent themselves for them to know this. If you get stuck in a tangle, contact me and I will provide you with the proper documentation which outlines your rights under the law. That should clear matters up quickly. Send the above documents directly to the obligor's employer.

2. You must then send notice to the obligor that you are intending to withhold wages. If you need to refresh your memory on how to do this, see Chapter 10.

3. As long as the obligor does not contest the wage withholding within the allowable period of time (usually about 20 days, depending on the state) you are free to send the order to the obligor's employer to begin the withholding. The only way that the obligor can only successfully contest the order and have it to stick is on the grounds of mistaken identity. Otherwise, if contested for other reasons, the order will be entered in the

interim, you will be able to being your withholding of wages and a court date will be scheduled to settle the other matters. (Most likely other matters in instances such as this will amount to the obligor taking the opportunity of your filing to counter file for a downward modification or paternity tests or something else which they hope will lower the obligation, dismiss it all together or stall the process).

4. The final support order will then be entered.

These procedures can seem very complicated to most people. Rest assured that if you follow them step by step, you will be fine. Some people will simply not have the emotional fortitude to take the bull by the horns and handle their own case, no matter how much assistance they can receive. Others, if they know that they can get assistance by contacting me or someone like me, may feel more self-confident. These are all very personal decisions.

Uniform Enforcement of Foreign Judgment Act

A *final judgment* is a judgment for a sum that cannot change—it is final. Ongoing child support payments are not final, they continue until the child reaches the age of majority, which means that they are emancipated. If you take an obligor to court for past-due child support and win your case, a judgment will be entered for the amount of child support that is past due at that time. That amount cannot change. If the obligor continues to add arrearages because he or she still does not pay, the amount that you are owed will continue to change, but the judgment amount will not. It is final. This becomes important when you are strategizing methods to enforce your order and collect your past sue sum because the amount you can collect will be based on how much your judgment says that you are owed. If you want to increase the judgment amount then you will have to return to court. If you have a final judgment for child support arrearages that you would like to collect under the Uniform Enforcement of Foreign Judgment Act, you can bring an action to enforce a foreign judgment in another state. (In simpler terms, you want to collect on your judgment in another state – perhaps by seizing an account or an asset, for example.) Just as you must register a wage withholding in the new state before you can withhold wages, you must register your judgment as well. The Uniform Enforcement of Foreign Judgment Act can only be used for final judgments. Following are the steps you must take to pursue an enforcement of foreign judgment:

1. Call the clerk of the court where the obligor lives and ask whether a copy of a certified judgment will be accepted, or whether it must be authenticated. Authenticated means that the clerk *and* judge of the originating state certify the document to be an authentic copy, as opposed to the clerk being the only one to certify, which is most often the case. According to the responding clerk's standards, obtain a copy of the judgment (see Item #19) and mail it. I always recommend that you send these documents certified so that not only is there proof of delivery, but you also have the name of the person signing so that there is some level of accountability. This holds true even when an entity such as a courthouse which receives a large amount of certified mail, does not actually sign for each individual envelope. They are 'signed" in bulk but the accountability remains the same.

2. File a statement with the clerk giving the name and current address of the obligor. You can send it in the same envelope.

3. The clerk will then notify the obligor that you have filed a foreign judgment and will supply a copy of the judgment.

4. The obligor will then have up to 20 (depending on the state) to contest the judgment. If he or she does not, you can then proceed with collection techniques.

5. As with the wage withholding, the obligor can only contest the order on the grounds of mistaken identity. Otherwise, if contested, the order will be entered and a court date will be scheduled for other matters.

Deadbeat vs. Deadbroke

Uniform Reciprocal Enforcement of Support Act

The *Uniform Reciprocal Enforcement of Support Act,* or *URESA,* is a law that allows you to file for current child support, back support, a modification of your child support award, medical expenses, and custody/visitation, all in a single motion and order. It is the same as applying for services through your local child support agency, asking them to collect support due from someone who lives in the same state as you do. The difference is that URESA only handles *interstate cases.* When you petition through URESA, they will file your documentation with the obligor's state and have someone represent you at the hearing where the absent parent/obligor resides. You can apply for services from URESA through your state child support collection agency. At that time you will be assigned a caseworker who will be the main source of communication between yourself and the responding state. You can also apply yourself, or through an attorney, by calling the family court in your area and asking where you must go in your area to apply for services. If you are representing yourself and you want current child support, back support, a modification of your child support award, medical expenses, and custody/visitation, and or other add-ons which you are entitled to, you must file for these on your own. A daunting thought, I know. Again, it comes down to how much you can stomach. In my opinion, it's still better to be in control of your own situation and destiny, but you may not agree.

Long Arm Statutes

Many people do not know about *long arm statutes,* though if they did, they could eliminate a lot of the heartache that goes along with collecting across state lines. You may remember that earlier I said that if your obligor lives out of state, you must have your judgment(s) registered in the state where the obligor lives before you can attempt to collect any money. I'm about to make tons of parents smile and click their heels by sharing an exception to that rule: Let's say that indeed your obligor lives out of state but he/she also has a vacation house (or an inherited house

252

left by parents, etc.) in the same state in which you live, which is the originating state of the child support order. If that were the case, you would not have to have the judgment(s) registered in the state where the obligor lives because the obligor has a legal residence in the state where the judgment was written. This means that the state has *personal jurisdiction* over the obligor. More examples of *personal jurisdiction*: If the obligor lives in another state, but works in your state (the originating state), the same would apply. Now let's say that the obligor lives 2,500 miles away and works in the same state in which he or she lives. They do not have any personal legal connection to the originating state. However, the company which he or she works for is a large company with branches in over twenty-five states, and one of those branches is in the state where you live. Since the state where you live, is one and the same as the state where the company is doing business, this means that the state has jurisdiction over the company and can cause them to do many things. Namely, one of those things is to pay your child support via a wage withholding order. In a case like this you could save yourself the time of registering your judgment somewhere else in order to get your support money. The way that Long Arm Statutes function can vary from state to state. It's important to know and understand the requirements of your state. Items such as the acceptable methods of delivering a Long Arm Statute, whether you can apply the Statue to internet businesses, how to properly serve a Long Arm Statute, etc., are all state to state matters. Each state decides their own rules. I have created a document which includes all of the nitty gritty requirements for all 50 states, plus Hawaii and Guam. If you need to get your hands on it because you are considering using this statue to help you collect your child support arrears, contact me. I will get it to you in the shake of a lamb's tail.

The following is an example of a notice to file a foreign judgment. If you ever need any help understanding any of the legal documents in this book, please contact me. These documents are not state specific, and can be used for any state.

NOTICE OF FILING OF FOREIGN JUDGMENT

IN THE CIRCUIT COURT OF THE STATE OF [INSERT YOUR STATE]
FOR THE COUNTY OF [INSERT YOUR COUNTY NAME]

[DOCKET NUMBER]
Docket Number

[INSERT YOUR NAME],
Petitioner,

NOTICE OF FILING OF
FOREIGN JUDGMENT

And

[INSERT OBLIGOR'S NAME],
Respondent

COMES NOW the petitioner and gives notice to respondent of the filing of the judgment rendered in the Circuit Court of the State of [State Name], a copy of which is attached hereto.

DATED this _____day of _____, 20_____.

_____
[Your Name], Petitioner

AFFIDAVIT

STATE OF [STATE NAME]

County of [County Name]

[Your Name], Petitioner, makes this affidavit under oath,

On [Date], a judgment was rendered by the Circuit Court of [State Name] styled "In re the Marriage of [Your It Name] in favor of [Your Name] in the amount of $_____

The name and last known address of the Judgment Debtor is as follows:

[Obligor's Name
Address
City, State Zip Code]

[Your Name
Address
City, State Zip Code]

SIGNED this_____ day of_____, 20_____

_____
[Your Name], Petitioner

Item # 18: Notice of Filing of Foreign Judgment

collecting from the self-employed, quasi-employed, cash-only-employed, street-hustlers, business owners (both real and shell) and others who try to go underground

If your obligor is self-employed, quasi-employed, works for cash, is a street hustler or a business owner, you have a unique set of issues and problems when it comes to child support enforcement. The self-employed obligor cannot have his wages withheld, because, under the law, technically he does not earn "wages." When you take him to court for child support, you may not be able to get a fair amount of support in proportion to his earnings because he may not report all business earnings. Unless you do some research, you may not even know that the obligor is running a business at all.

When it comes to self-employed obligors who don't want to pay, you have to pull out the heavy artillery. Strict enforcement techniques that have been outlined in Chapters 10, 11, and 12, will have to be used to collect from the unyielding self-employed obligor. Assuming that you have utilized all methods that you could on a personal level (or are in the process of doing so presently), the following are some methods that you can use to take money directly from the obligor's business if he/she owns the property himself/herself.

Keep in mind that you cannot put the obligor out of business. The obligor's business is exempt $12,000 from the various collection methods that you may use against him. So, if the obligor only has $12,000 in business assets (or less) you cannot take anything from the business. If he has more than $12,000, then you can put your plans into action. For example, if the obligor has $10,000 in business property and $2,500 in cash in an account for a total of $12,500, you will only be able to get $500 from the business. But, of course, that's $500 more than you had before and $500 less that he or she owes you. Furthermore, in the event you seize and/or garnish more than you will be allowed to keep (if you take $12,500 in the above example but you can only keep $500), you will succeed in making the obligor's life difficult for a few days while the courts free the money you have tied up. Personally, I like the idea. Aren't you being inconvenienced by having to chase the obligor for the money in the first place? And, if you are asked why you seized more money than you could keep, say what my daughter used to say when she was a little girl and made an honest mistake...whoopsie!

Onward and upward! The following methods are great ones to use against those who run their own businesses. Just keep in mind that this does not include those who run corporations, which are protected from the personal offenses of the obligor. If you find yourself in this situation, all is not lost, contact me.

Bank accounts

If the obligor is operating a sole proprietorship, he or she is using their own social security number for business tax records. Since that is the case, anything that the business owns, the obligor owns as well. This would include business accounts containing available cash.

Business property

You can also seize and sell business property. For example, if the obligor is running a local mechanic shop that has equipment worth a lot of money, re-read Chapter 10 and go to work on a seize-and-sell.

Company equipment is not the only sort of item that can fall prey to being seized and sold. Any kind of office equipment, inventory, and furniture can be seized for the payment of child support.

Till-tap

If the obligor is running a business with a cash register, have the sheriff conduct a till-tap. Remember to wait until the busiest season and the busiest time of day to reap the most benefit from this. One of my clients had an obligor who was a barber. He had his own shop, rented chairs to other barbers and had a full clientele, yet he cried broke and didn't make his child support payment for his two children. When the mom came to my office with her kids in tow, her oldest literally had one of his big toes sticking out from his sneaker. I mean, really. What kind of parent or person are you if you won't pay money so that you children can have proper footwear and you have the money to give? I encouraged my client to go for the gusto and had no sympathy when she scheduled the till-tap for Father's day weekend when all of the dads were there for their cut and shave. The sheriff showed up and the cash register was full. When one of the employees claimed to not know how to open the register for the sheriff and the obligor had stepped out to buy lunch for his entire crew, the sheriff simply removed the entire register from the shop and left. After fees were paid, my client yielded $1875 that day. It was far from the $8100 that he owed but the money was released to her in time for her to buy her children new clothes, shoes, books, backpacks and everything that they needed for school the beginning of September. She was also able to get them into day camp for two weeks before the summer ended. It never would have happened without the till-tap. She went on to other methods of collections afterwards.

Deadbeat vs. Deadbroke

Business suppliers

If you are fortunate enough to know who some of the obligor's suppliers are, you are ahead of the game. If you don't, do some research to find out. Then subpoena them for whatever information you can. If you find that the obligor is paying for shipments of goods, you can place a lien on whatever shipment(s) that the obligor has paid for. Of course, the obligor will be as mad as a lunatic, but after all, that's what you want. He will have no other choice but to pay you so that you release the lien, or watch his business go down the tubes. (You will, of course, attach a lien on every shipment with every supplier that he has until you are paid in full.) If the obligor does not pay you, you will then be entitled to sell the goods that you now own and keep the profit. If the shoe is on the other foot and your obligor is the supplier, you can garnish the payment that the obligor is due to receive from the company he or she is supplying.

The previous collection methods listed are methods that are used as *leverage* over the obligor. If you have leverage, the obligor may be willing to give you what you want just to get you off of his back. Some examples of leverage may be:

- If you are certain that the obligor is not reporting a portion of his income, you can threaten to gather proof and call the IRS. Also, the IRS has a child support department. You can reach them at: 386-274-0145 if you need to check up on an intercept pending or if you want to find out when an intercept will be delivered to you.
- If the obligor is an immigrant and his visa has expired, you can threaten to call immigration. I had a prospective client to call me today. She reported that her ex was from Nigeria and believes that he married her just to get a green card because as soon as he got it, he was as good as gone—leaving her with two babies to feed on her own. She has no idea what is current address is now, but guess which agency might know. You guessed it—the department of immigration.

You know the obligor better than I do. Find his soft spot and then go for the jugular. I would encourage you to not hold back and to not feel badly that you have caused so much misery for him. He isn't exactly being considerate of you and your children when you eat soup for supper every night or as you drain your bank account and IRA's, work two jobs to make ends meet...you get the picture. If that were the case, you would already have the child support money that your children need deserve and need.

Living off of the grid

There are whole hoards of people who are now living "off the grid". I'm a fan of it myself for plenty of reasons—everything from using alternative energy sources and home vegetable gardening, to hampering government intrusion, maintaining privacy, preventing and eliminating stalkers and much more. With the economic downturn, there have been plenty of other reasons to go gridless. Banks have upped their fees and are providing fewer services; the top brass of financial institutions are stealing our retirement savings and getting away with it...There are lots of good sound reasons to rethink our ways of life.

The downturn has also created perhaps the largest pool of people ever who do not have access to bank accounts. Businesses have failed, jobs have been lost, fortunes have been inched away and many have found themselves unable to either afford the fees associated with banking, do not want to afford them any longer as they scratch their way back to financial security and safety, or have lost access to banking accounts due to poor credit.

Parents who are looking for new and creative ways to avoid their child support have taken the opportunity and are using it for their own purposes. They are using the systems of non-bank banking created by the downturn and are avoiding transparency of income and assets. How are they doing it and what can you do about it?

Deadbeat vs. Deadbroke

Non-bank banking

NetSpend Corporation is the largest provider of prepaid debit cards to unbanked and underbanked consumers in the United States. NetSpend companies include: NetSpend pre-paid cards, PayPal, Metabank, Greendot, and Net10. Subpoena NetSpend with a copy of your certified judgment, the obligors name and social security number and listing of all of their companies which you like for them to check to see if the obligor has a deposit history with them. He or she could be depositing a paycheck electronically or making cash deposits. If this is the case, you would never know unless you check with them directly. Deposits such as these would never create a "hit" in the child support locator system.

The address for NetSpend is: 701 Brazos Street, Austin, Texas 78701

American Express has a similar prepaid card. Their contact address is: American Express Customer Relations, 4315 S. 2700 W., Salt Lake City, UT 84184

Chase Bank has a prepaid card as well. It is called Chase Liquid. Contact them at: National Bank by Mail, PO Box 36520, Louisville, KY 36520

You can collect from their lawsuit settlement

Lawsuit settlement money is considered income. Go to the court (or call and get a REALLY nice person on the phone to help you) and look in the court's computer for your ex's name under plaintiffs in the plaintiff/defendant index. That will give you the name of the court case and the case number. Once the case number is known, it can be presented to the court and the court clerk will provide the file. If you must do this over the phone, you can ask that a copy of the file be provided to you. Of course they will charge a fee but it should be minimal. The file will reveal if a settlement has been reached and the amount that your ex received.

You can collect from an inheritance

Money received from an inheritance is considered income. Go to the court (or call and get a REALLY nice person on the phone) and visit the probate department. Provide the name of the deceased and ask if there is a will on file and if so ask for the name of the executor. Once the will goes to probate, it becomes a public record. You will be able to obtain a copy of the will to see if your ex has received an inheritance in the will. If so, you can then contact the executor and file your lien directly with the estate for your share.

chapter 16:
collecting from the unemployed and underemployed

there are many obligees (the parents who are owed support) who complain that they cannot get any child support from the obligor (the parent who owes the support) because he or she doesn't have a job and therefore, no means to pay. The obligor may "support" himself or herself by living with a girlfriend or boyfriend who has been their benevolent benefactor for several years. Maybe they live with their parents and they provide for them. There are others who complain that they cannot get enough child support or that the arrearages will never get paid in full, because while the obligor may have a job, he or she does not make enough money to buy toothpaste, let alone, pay child support.

I saw a movie recently, where one person owed the other person a significant amount of money but the person who owed the money had a complete inability to pay. The person who was owed the money made no bones about it – he was going to get paid. He confronted him, telling him that every corner that he ever turned in life, he was going to be there holding out his hand for his share. Everytime. Every $5.00 that he earned -he was going to be there to collect $2.50. Then he told him that when he is finally beaten down from life and in jail somewhere because he could not make a living on the outside, and he was forced to scrub toilets in the jailhouse for .10c a toilet, and he was all smelly and sweaty and disgusting, he was going to be there collecting his .50c for the 10 toilets that he scrubbed that day.

Do you need to take it to that extreme? I can't tell you that. The choice is up to you. I can't make your decisions for you. I will tell you again, as I have many times in this book already that my function here is to tell you of your options and how to accomplish them. It is your job to decide if you need to take extreme measures, how extreme you need to be and your comfort level with the levels which you have chosen. I point this out because this happens to be a significant debate. When does child support collection become extreme? Does it? Is it any more or less extreme than any other bill collector coming to collect their due? As long as you act within the parameters of the law, when is it pushy and wrong to seize bank accounts and when it is the exercising of your rights and advocating for your children so that they either don't starve or so that they simply get what they deserve? Each child support judgment holder can only answer that question for himself or herself.

They say that they cannot get blood from a stone. I say that they have not learned the best way to squeeze. In more instances than not, though it may be a long wait at times, you can get child support—even from a stone. In this case, let's call the stone an unemployed obligor. The following outlines some of the many ways you can cash in on "other incomes" to get child support from someone who is unemployed or underemployed.

- **Unemployment benefits** - In most states, a portion of an obligor's unemployment benefits can be withheld for child support.
- **Disability benefits** - If the obligor is receiving disability benefits, you and/or your child may be entitled to benefits as well. Contact your local Social Security office for an appointment to find out.

- **Veterans' Benefits** – Receiving child support from Veteran's benefits can be tricky. They certainly do not make it easy for you. There is so much cloak and dagger and so many corn field mazes to navigate – and this is after they have you to take an IQ test and consent to a lobotomy. The VA procedure is maddening but I am going to try to break it down for you.

1. The first thing you must determine is the type of pay that the Veteran is receiving. That alone will determine whether you can get child support from his or her pay and how much.

2. You would think that if you are working through a state worker at a local CSE office that payment and address information would be readily available through the National Directory of New Hires (NDNH) database or the Federal Case Registry's (FCR) for automatic data matching, but alas— it is not. If you're working with a CSE agency, they will tell you that they must utilize their FPLS (Federal Parent Locator Service) to determine whether the obligor is receiving benefits through the Veterans administration. Now that might be okay, if only they didn't take so bloody long to get back to you. If you went on a hunger strike while waiting (and those of you who have used it know exactly what I mean), you will die, have been buried, become worm food, and have flowers growing on your grave before they get back to you. It is a process which takes not days or even weeks, but months. To add insult to injury, the VA still is not entirely operating on an electronic system. Most of what you are asking for is still located in paper files.

3. Generally speaking, VA benefits are not subject to withholding for child support, however there are some exceptions. If a Veteran has waived a portion of his/her retirement or retainer pay, in order to qualify for disability compensation, and received the disability compensation, *the*

portion which is considered compensation can now be garnished for child support (and alimony by the way). The portion of retainer or retirement pay which had not waived cannot be garnished.

4. Another exception to the rule is by using a clause which states that "if the veteran is not reasonably discharging his responsibility for his/her spouses' and children support then a certain amount can be apportioned towards them". What this means simply is that if the veteran is not financially supporting their family in a responsible manner that a portion (an *apportionment*) of their pay can be taken and sent to the family. The clause goes on to say that if the apportionment would create *"undue hardship"* to the veteran, then the apportionment would not be made. There lies the rub...there's always a rub. If the veteran hasn't been doing the right thing in the first place, you can almost count on him or her to continue on that course and not choose to do the right thing again. Fully expect that he or she is going to claim that the apportionment would create hardship and to object to the garnishment. No matter. Your job is to figure out the proper persuasive language to prove your case. You can do this, can't you? If you need assistance along the way, let me know.

- **Life Insurance Policies**- If the obligor has a life insurance policy that can eventually be cashed in, that policy can be garnished for past-due support. This type of policy is called a "whole-life" and it builds equity. The longer you own it, the more that it's worth. You can run a simple search to discover whether the obligor has one of these. With the economic downturn, many people have decided to no longer have those policies but that doesn't mean that everyone has done away with them. That being said, if the obligor is perpetually unemployed and underemployed, finding a whole life policy is probably going to

266

be a remote possibility, but check. Still check. Always check. "Term" life insurance policies, may as well just be called death polices because they are intended for the people and the debts that you leave behind. If you have one of those obligors who is living off of others and will probably always live off of others, can't keep a job to save their life, or due to other circumstances (poor education, poor health, past or current drug problems, mental health challenges, criminal history, etc.), you may have a child support order in the 5 or 6 figure range with no real possibility of it ever being paid. That is a real problem and a disservice to the parent who financially supported the children on their own and a disservice to the children who may have had fewer opportunities as a result of it. Life insurance can be a solution. By having the requirement of a life insurance policy written into your child support order for the amount of the arrears and, if your children are not yet emancipated; the calculation of the remaining child support that the obligor would have paid, if they were paying child support, up through and including the college years (if that is permitted in your state), may address the question of whether you will ever receive the full amount of support due to you for the benefit of your children. Because we are talking about a death benefit policy, we must also address the possibility that the obligor will outlive you. What good is a death benefit on the obligor if he or she outlives you? You will never be able to realize the relief and satisfaction that payment-in-full would bring. This is true. However, your judgment for child support is an asset and as such, it can be willed to your children. When the obligor passes, your children will be able to collect the death benefit policy. It will have come full-circle. How sublime. Before you discard this notion, consider for a moment how that windfall of cash – whatever amount it may be – may be able to benefit them in their 50's, 60's, 70', etc. It may benefit them – it may end up being a benefit to your grandchildren.

- **Assets-** If the obligor has assets that are worth you going through the trouble of seizing and selling (especially real estate), move to have liens placed on the property and then file to foreclose if it comes to it. The mistake that many parents make is that they will file a lien on the property but then take no additional action. They wait like a sitting duck until the obligor decides to sell the property. By that time, the crafty evaders have maxed out lines of credit against the property, and have taken out second and third mortgages because they know that the banks will be first in line to get paid. You may end up with little or nothing. Don't wait. The same rings true for large boats and small aircraft. Do the unemployed sometimes have homes, yachts and private plans? You bet that they do.

- **Inheritance-** This may seem morbid, but if you can't get any money from the obligor, you may get some from his parents or someone else who may leave him or her money in a will. You must continually update your judgment in court so that the proper amount is reflected at the time you can collect the money. When updating your judgment, be sure to ask for interest. Most states will allow you to receive interest from day one to the day you get your child support. Be sure to ask the judge for pre-judgment interest as well as post-judgment interest.

- **Lottery Winnings-** You don't have to be in it to win it. Most states will allow you to garnish the lottery winnings of those who owe child support.

Of course, these are only some of the ways that you can get blood from your own stone. If you think about it for a while, considering what you know about the obligor, I'm sure that you can think of some yourself.

chapter 17:
collecting from the military

If you are trying to collect child support from someone who is in the military, there is good news and there is bad news. The good news is that the military has policies towards family support and the policies are good ones. Each branch of the military, which includes the Army, Navy, Air Force, Marines, Coast Guard and National Guard, insists that its personnel support their families back home. The bad news is that it can be difficult to locate a military employee at times and when you do, superior officers are not always as helpful as they could be or should be.

Your first line of action, if the solider is on active duty should be to contact the Department of Veteran's Affairs Income Withholding and Veteran's Benefits office. Once you jump through a few hoops (remember that they still on a mostly paper system), they have something called an Income Withholding Order (IWO) that they use. The IWO would need to be sent to the regional office serving the veteran. You can contact the VA Regional office Inquiry Line: 1-800-

827-1000 for help. Because of all of the red tape and time that it may take to get anything significant accomplished, I wouldn't blame you one bit if you just skipped to the next advice for your line of attack. However, you may be asked to not pass go and to return to income withholding office for help before you up your ante. For that reason, it may make sense to see if they can and will do their job first before you pull out the bigger guns.

Bigger gun #1: If you know where the obligor is stationed, half of your battle is over. Write a letter to the soldier's commanding officer. Let him or her know that you have a judgment for a child support order. Supply your name, address, a copy of the soldier's name and his or her service number. Request that the commanding officer assist you in obtaining your support.

Bigger gun #2: In some instances, the commanding officer will help you by having the appropriate amount of child support withheld from the soldiers pay (without a wage withholding order) and forwarded to you. In other instances, you will be sent away and told to obtain a wage withholding prior to being helped. Once the wage withholding is received at the proper branch, you can expect to get payments after 60 days.

Bigger gun #3: If you are not using child support services and are getting stonewalled by the commanding officer, there are other people to contact who may help. If you are in a bind and need immediate financial assistance, contact the Red Cross and/or the Army Relief Fund. These organizations have emergency funds available to assist the families of military employees. You will need to provide your child support order, your name and address, and the soldier's name, address, and service number, if you have it. Also contact the inspector general. The inspector general is someone who can put pressure on the obligor's commanding officer for not doing his or her job properly, and can get your money on the way to you quickly.

Bigger gun #4: If you do not have a judgment for a child support order and you are married (thus the law can assume paternity) but separated from your spouse, you may be able to get child support anyway. Ask the commanding officer when you contact him/her.

If you do not know where the obligor is stationed, you can find out by contacting the recruitment office where the obligor enlisted. This information is a matter of public record. If you know where the obligor has been assigned, call the "installation locator" at that particular installation. Then call the number that you have been provided and ask for the soldier's unit of assignment.

If you still have not been able to locate the solider, try the military locator services listed in the back of this book.

chapter 18:
collecting internationally

Collecting child support can be challenging if you have to cross state lines. Imagine the difficulty you will have if you have to cross borders or oceans to other countries to collect your support payments. The United States is not the only country that has to deal with issues of child support or child support enforcement. Luckily for you, other countries have this problem as well. Because of this, and because their citizens sometimes cross the border into the United States seeking refuge from having to pay child support, they are, at times, willing to set up agreements to enforce foreign child support orders.

There are no formal agreements between the U.S. and other countries which require the payment of child support, although there are some countries that the U.S. has reciprocity with, and others with whom the U.S. is developing such a relationship. Many of the fifty states have been utilizing URESA for the collection of child support in other countries. Under URESA (Uniform Reciprocal Enforcement of Support Act) , a child support judgment from the United States is treated as a foreign judgment in another country. Once it is registered, the responding jurisdiction (in this case, the foreign country) will reciprocate by using URESA practices to sue the obligor for child support or enforce the existing order. As you learned earlier, if this action were to take place between two states it would be considered the enforcement of the Foreign Judgment Act. Between two countries it is *comity*. Comity is the practice of a country recognizing the law of another country within its own jurisdiction. It is a courtesy between countries; a sign of respect.

This is not to say that all countries will allow comity. There are a few countries that will allow the enforcement of a foreign child support order, but there are also many that will not. The rule of thumb is that if the country has the same or a "substantially similar law" in effect, they will probably allow comity. In many instances, when comity is allowed, there is a fee attached, payable to the reciprocating country, for the courtesy of registering your judgment and collecting your money.

Arrangements have been made with the following countries:

Australia

Canada

(separate agreements with 9 of the 10 Canadian provinces)
and with all 3 Canadian territories.

Czech Republic	El Salvador	Finland
Hungary	Ireland	Israel
Ireland	Netherland	Norway
Poland	Portugal	Slovak Republic
	Switzerland	

United Kingdom of Great Britain and Northern Ireland

I'm sorry to say that if your obligor has fled the country, you have a long road ahead of you when it comes to child support collection. This is not to say that it can't be done. I have had many clients who have been successful with international enforcement. This just means that it's time to buckle-up because it's going to be a long and bumpy ride.

The good news is that you can achieve success – just don't plan to play the bills with the support money just yet.

If you have the money, and if you are chasing a lot of money, you might consider hiring an attorney in the country where the obligor has fled (remember the home court advantage). If you are able, also hire an attorney in your state to represent you here. That means that you will be watching over two attorneys – one who is very far away from you. You will have to have nerves of steel, be vigilant and unwavering in your commitment, your approach and guarding the gate. Who's in charge? You're in charge. Whose money is it? It's your money that you spent caring for and supporting your child and you are the guardian for that child. You need to be reimbursed. Who is going to guarantee that the T's are crossed, the I's are dotted and the system of checks and balances are in place? You are. If you're ready for that— go get 'em, tiger.

If you don't have a lot of money to hire two attorneys, or if you want a referral to an attorney overseas, contact me directly. Either way you are going to need some assistance of someone across the pond to help you, but there may be ways to help you cut down on some of your costs.

chapter 19:
collecting from a federal employee

Collecting child support from a civilian federal employee can be one of the trickiest things you can attempt to do. The government bureaucracy makes it extremely challenging for anyone to attempt to get money from one of its own. Some of the problems I have heard and witnessed over the years: There have been reports of them returning court documents unanswered if information they want was not included. When they do accept the paperwork and process a garnishment, they will only allow it to be taken from the employee's net (take-home) pay, which includes other deductions like retirement, life insurance, medical insurance, savings plans, etc., rather than the employee's gross pay, which child support is based. When serving a federal employee, if the documents are not sent to the proper office and to the proper person, instead of forwarding them to correct person in their office, they will be returned. At the same time, the government has regulations that state that federal employees cannot be overdue in payments on a debt. **Any debt**. To any creditor. Their reputations must remain as clean as a whistle at all times. This is not to say that it doesn't happen all of the time. Tons of federal employees are in up to their eyeballs in debt – including debt to the IRS, ironically. That just means that the code/regulation is not always followed, or is only followed when someone wants it to be followed. The best thing that you can do when you are dealing with the federal government, or one of its employees, is to use their codes/regulations to your advantage and then you can beat them at their own game.

Prior to serving a wage withholding, visit your local library and ask the reference librarian to help you find Code Federal Regulation 5 CFR Part 581 (or located on my website). It has the address for every executive federal branch. Locate the branch where your obligor works. If you have been having trouble locating him/her previously, you will be able to use the address you have found to properly serve them. If you haven't a clue about the branch where the deadbeat works, try this number: (800) 688-9889. It is a general number for various government services but if you get the right person on the phone and with the right story, true, pretext or otherwise, they may function as a locator for you and provide the information that you need.

Mail the wage withholding notice itself by return receipt certified mail from the post office. Expect to pay a small fee of about $5 for this service. Although some of this information will already appear on the documents, along with your wage withholding, include the obligor's name, date of birth, social security number, civil service retirement number (if there is one), veteran's claim number (if there is one), and advise of the office where he works. Also include your name, address, a copy of the judgment, and the purpose of the judgment. Be sure to check this information before you use it because things sometimes change rapidly, but as of today this has been sourced as a good address for wage withholdings:

Garnishment Operations-HGA
P.O. Box 998002
Cleveland OH 44199-8002
Fax: 877-622-5930

Prior to faxing, check out the fax instructions provided by the government, by going to this website: http://www.dfas.mil/garnishment/fax.html. If you need to contact the office by phone with questions or want to confirm current mailing address (although the address at this point has been consistent for many years), use this phone number: 888-DFAS411 (332-7411). They are open 8 a.m. to 5 p.m. Eastern Time, Monday through Friday.

One way to possibly get some speedy action on your case would be to contact the civilian employee's supervisor by mail and request their assistance collecting your support. Gently remind them that Code Federal Regulation 5CFR Part 2635.809 prohibits the indebtedness of federal employees and subjects them to discipline for failure to pay their debts. Also remind them that Code Federal Regulations 5 CFR Part 735.203 prohibits conduct by a federal employee that may be prejudicial (damaging, disadvantaging) to the government. This may get you some action from the supervisor. Of course, in order for an employee to be disciplined for failing to pay his debts, it must somehow interfere with the employee's job performance. And, of course, it will, if the employee has to go to court several times for the non-payment of child support. And, of course, you will be sure to point out to the supervisor that is likely to happen when you unleash your deluge of motions upon the non-payor. You don't want to position this as any type of threat because you want the supervisor on your side. Merely, you are suggesting that this problem is likely to interfere with the employees work and that it seems to you that it meets the Code. No more. No less. And say it with a smile! Smiles actually do come through in your voice over the phone. Really. It's true. Honestly.

If the obligor is not a federal employee, but does business with the federal government by way of contract, you are out of luck. Unlike other contractors who do business with the government and you can garnish their payments— you can't with the Feds. Government contractors are exempt from garnishments of any type. Other methods of child support collection outlined in earlier chapters will have to be utilized.

chapter 20:
when an obligor files for bankruptcy

When I was working in collections for the bank, the people I was collecting from often told me that they were in bankruptcy. If a person files for bankruptcy, all collection attempts must stop <u>immediately</u>. This is called an *automatic stay*. If they continue, it can be construed as harassment and there can be penalties. This is true when it comes to child support collection as well. If the obligor files for bankruptcy, you can no longer pursue child support collection until you go to court to apply for a "relief" from the "stay." A person, or a company, can file for bankruptcy to either have all debts *discharged* (eliminated), or to have a "stay" from the collection procedures until the debts can be slowly paid off over time. Child support cannot ever be discharged, but it can be paid off at a slower pace. If your obligor has filed for bankruptcy, it will be handled in one of the following ways:

Chapter 7: Chapter 7 is the bankruptcy type where all of the debts are discharged. The obligor starts off with a clean slate with no debts.

Deadbeat vs. Deadbroke

Child support is an *undischargeable* debt. Seek immediate relief from the bankruptcy court by using the Motion for Relief from Stay (Item #20).

Chapter 11: Chapter 11 is mostly for businesses that are in over their heads. They can propose reorganization of the debts to the bankruptcy judge where they outline how their debts will be paid off. If the judge approves it, they then go into a Chapter 11. If the judge does not accept their proposal, then the bankruptcy becomes a Chapter 7.

Chapter 13: Chapter 13 is similar to the Chapter 11, but it is for individuals. It works the same way in that the individual filing for a bankruptcy must outline how all outstanding debts will be paid. If accepted, the individual can keep his personal property, if not, it is liquidated. In all three instances you are entitled to a relief from the stay. If the obligor has filed for a Chapter 13, all past child support owed will be reorganized under the plan. You cannot continue to attempt collection on that amount. Current child support and future child support cannot be reorganized, so those full amounts are still due to you. For example, if the obligor filed for bankruptcy on the first of the month owing you $33,000 with $500 in current support due the first of every month, and $350 additional towards the arrears, he/she will still owe you $500 when the next month rolls around. The past due $33,000 would still be owed by the obligor but the $350 towards the arrears would most likely be reorganized with the bankruptcy judge and lowered. You would have to accept whatever payment arrangement towards the arrears the judge decides.

The fees for filing for a relief from a stay costs varies from state to state but it would be fair to assume that it may cost somewhere between $50-$100.00 and it must be done at the clerk's office. If you cannot afford this fee, ask the clerk's office about filing for indigent status. You may or may not qualify but the clerk's office can provide you with the details. The clerk's office should provide you with proper filing instructions, but in addition to proving the court with your filing, you will need to serve a copy to the obligor, his attorney, if there is one, and the trustee. The notice that you receive informing you of the obligor's upcoming bankruptcy proceeding (as a creditor you are required to receive a copy) will provide you with the names and addresses of the people whom you need to serve. Bankruptcy is a federal action and is filed in federal court, unlike your petitions regarding child support, which are filed in state court.

MOTION FOR RELIEF FROM STAY

[Your Name
Your Street Address
City, State, Zip Code
Your Telephone Number]

IN THE UNITED STATES BANKRUPTCY COURT
FOR THE [INSERT YOUR DISTRICT] DISTRICT

In Re: **[INSERT OBLIGOR'S NAME]**,	Case No. [CASE NUMBER]
Debtor,	Contested Proceeding No .[CONTESTED CASE NO.]
[INSERT YOUR NAME], Plaintiff	**MOTION FOR RELIEF FROM STAY**
vs.	
[INSERT OBLIGOR'S NAME], Defendant,	

TO: The Honorable [Insert Judge's Name] Bankruptcy Judge:

COMES NOW Plaintiff [Insert Your Name] and moves the Court for an Order for relief from the automatic stay order so that child support may be collected in State Court proceedings from the earnings and assets of the Debtor which are not property of the estate.

PLAINTIFF [INSERT YOUR NAME] alleges, moves, and requests:

1. That on [Insert Date], the above-entitled Debtor, filed a voluntary Petition in Bankruptcy in above-entitled Court and was adjudged a Bankrupt on or about the same date.
2. The Bankruptcy Court has jurisdiction over this proceeding pursuant to 11 USC 362.
3. That the Debtor's Chapter 13 was confirmed by the Court.
4. The Plaintiff was listed as a creditor in the schedules of liabilities filed therein by said Bankrupt and was in fact as unsecured creditor of said Bankrupt at the date of the filing of said voluntary Petition in Bankruptcy in the amount of $_____.
5. That the nature of said unsecured debt owing by Bankrupt to plaintiff is child support arising out of an order issued [Insert Date], by the Circuit Court of the State of [Insert State Name] in and for the City of [Insert City Name, County Name]. By the terms of said judgment and order for child support the Bankrupt

Item # 19: Motion for Relief From Stay

was to pay $_____per month for the support of the minor child (ren) commencing [Insert Date], with an additional $_____ per month towards the arrears of $_____.

6. That Plaintiff, a Judgment Creditor of the Bankrupt debtor, received a judgment on [Insert Date], as set forth in paragraph 5 herein above plus interest thereon (if you have interest included in your pre or post judgment.

7. That the aforesaid Judgment and order is a judgment and order determining defendant Bankrupt debtor's obligation for present child support and past accrued reimbursement of child support and as such is non-dischargeable by virtue of 11 USC 523(a) (5) (A) as amended, 42 USC 656(b) as amended, and 42 USC 602(a) (26).

8. That between [Insert Date] and the date Bankrupt filed his voluntary Petition in Bankruptcy, the Bankrupt paid a total of $_____ on account of his said on-going above-mentioned child support obligation and $ _____ on account of said child support reimbursement arrearage obligation.

9. There was due and owing on the date of filing of the voluntary Petition in Bankruptcy by the Bankrupt the sum of $_____ principal plus interest thereon from [Insert Date], in child support reimbursement arrearages.

10. That the Charter 13 plan of the Debtor makes no provision for child support and for $ _____monthly to be applied to the arrears as a general unsecured claim.

11. The Bankrupt has sufficient income to make the scheduled monthly payment of $_____ to the Trustee of the arrearage and also pay said ongoing child support. Due to the automatic stay, plaintiff is unable to enforce the herein above-mentioned order for child support against the earnings and property of the Bankrupt which are not property of the estate.

It is therefore respectfully requested that plaintiff's motion be granted and the stay order previously imposed be partially vacated insofar as it operates to prevent enforcement by plaintiff of the hereinabove referenced order for child support in the State court against earnings and other property of the debtor that are not property the estate.

DATED this_____ day of _____, 20_____.

_____
Insert Your Name

chapter 21:
effective complaining

When all else fails and the child support enforcement agency is ineffective with your case, you can always complain. Complaining in an inefficient manner, or to the wrong people, will not get you anywhere. You may as well stay home and complain to your dog. Complaining effectively will help many people get to their end goal. This chapter is about the tools of complaining effectively and only to people who can help you.

Let me first give credit where credit is due. The caseworkers who manage the child support cases at CSE are overloaded, pure and simple. I have spoken to managers who say that their caseworkers have 800, 1000, sometimes 1500 cases to work. Let's think about that for a moment. How in the world can any one person effectively work on 1000 cases? At this moment it would take 1,594, 320 hours - or 182 years of labor power for CSE to collect the child support that's on the books right now in the U.S. I say this to say four things. First, now you know why you may not be getting the attention from your caseworker that you want, need and deserve. It's just not humanly possible. Two, most of those caseworkers work awfully hard every day and care very much about the families that they are working with. They do their best every day with the time that they have but they are also overworked and many times, unappreciated. That brings me to point number three. I interact every day with parents who complain that the system is broken. While I will not disagree with that, I will also say that the system is also BROKE. I guarantee you that if their caseloads were cut in half and their salaries were increased, you would see more productivity and less crankiness from those workers who could stand to be friendlier, and who are maybe not as helpful and productive as some of their peers.

Point four: Are you willing to wait 182 years for your case to really get the time and attention that it deserves? I say this tounge and cheek obviously, but the point remains. Albert Eienstein said that the definition of insanity is doing the same thing over and over again, but expecting a different result. Naturally, one of actions you can take if your case is in no-mans land is to represent yourself. This is not the best course of action for everyone and certainly is not for the faint of heart, but it IS an option, and one that I advocate.

Moving on—before considering a complaint to anyone, be sure that you have your facts in order and accurate records to support your positions. You must be attentive in your record keeping. Here is a short list of ways to keep impeccable records which will show that you are serious about your child support case:

Keep a log of every conversation that you have with a caseworker or anyone else with whom you may speak at the agency. The log should state what was said during the conversation, what action the caseworker promised, and when he/she told you to follow up (after you asked). It should also have the date and time that the conversation took place.

A case log may look something like this:

Day/month/year 9:30A.M. Spoke with Martin Oaks; he said that he does not have any new information on my ex. I told him that I was able to locate Dan's new home address and work address. Martin asked me to email the information to him and that he would get to work on a wage withholding, immediately. I asked Martin when would be a good time for me to follow up with him, just to be sure that the paperwork was sent to employer and that there was nothing else that he needed in order to proceed, and he suggested that I follow up in 2 weeks.

Day/month/year 9:45A.M. (two weeks later) Martin says that he hasn't had the opportunity to get to the paperwork on my case yet, but it is on his desk and he will get to it very soon. He told me that I could follow up with him in 2 weeks.

Day/month/year 3:25P.M. (two weeks later) Martin was not at his desk, so I left a message with Suzie.

Day/month/year 4:00P.M. (the next day) Martin was not at his desk, so I left a message on his voicemail.

Day/month/year 9:05A.M. (the next day) Martin said that he would check into the matter, but he didn't get back to me as he promised. I sent an email to him asking about the information that I provided and questioned why so much time has gone by without the wage withholding being sent to the employer. I also outlined his broken promises and failure to respond to the messages that I had left for him. I copied his supervisor on the email.

Day/month/year 10:40A.M. (three days later) Glenda Pickler, Martin's supervisor, called to say that a wage withholding has been sent to the employer and that I should begin to see payments in about two weeks.

This case log shows many things. It gives an account of what transpired between client and caseworker. If you keep a log like this, you won't have to rely on your memory to put details together, and you will also be better informed. By having the accurate dates of when you spoke with your caseworker the last time, you won't let too much time go by without a necessary phone call, email or other outreach. The time of day that you typically have been able to reach your caseworker gives you an indication of when he/she is likely to be reachable. It appears that Martin is more readily available in the mornings, rather than in the afternoon. When is the best time to reach Martin? In the morning. Plan your time and your contact accordingly.

This is a rather unflattering case log. Unfortunately, it is also a true one, which one of my clients provided to me after I suggested that she use a log to keep track of on-goings. It helped her to get the attention of the case manager and in the end, the caseworker who never snubbed her calls again. This is not to say that all caseworkers are like Martin. As I stated previously, there are very many, very good, caring caseworkers in every state.

Logs can be used for many child support and custody purposes and I strongly suggest that you use them when documenting day care expenses, child support received, parenting time, etc. Contact me for more information, log samples, etc., if you need to.

- Keep copies of anything and everything that you must forward to your caseworker, whether it is information on the obligor or a complaint letter that you sent to the caseworker/supervisor or whomever. Never send out a document— ever—without having made a copy first.
- When sending a complaint letter to your caseworker/supervisor, speed up the process by sending it by email if you have one available to you. An emailed document will get to your caseworker immediately, rather than waiting for "snail mail" through the post office. If you don't have an email address for the person you are contacting—then ask for it. If they do not provide email addresses to clients, then your next best bet is to fax it. Obtain the fax number by asking for it, and then use it. If you do not have a fax machine accessible to you, use (sigh) use the regular mail service. If you are faxing or using the post office to send your letters, then you must carbon copy ("cc") the supervisor at the bottom of the letter and then either fax the letter to the supervisor with the supervisor's name on the cover

letter, or mail a duplicate of the letter to the supervisor directly. To carbon copy the supervisor on the letter, you simply type "cc": [insert supervisor's name] and send that person a copy of whatever you have cc'd.

This accomplishes two things. First, it lets the caseworker know that you are keeping his supervisor informed; and second, it advises the supervisor of all proceedings with the case. In the event that you will have to complain, the supervisor should not be surprised and should be well-equipped to handle it.

- If you must send a complaint letter to someone higher than your caseworker's supervisor, send it by email or fax, but also send it return receipt certified mail from the post office. You will get a notice in the mail of when your letter was received at the child support agency and they will know that you mean business.
- When you do get the action on your case that was promised, be sure to write a quick thank you note to whomever it was that brought about the action.

The chain of command should go like this:

1. First bring your complaint to your caseworker (Item #21). If you are able to speak with him/her, ask them when would be a good time for you to follow up. Do not get off the phone without asking for a follow-up date no matter what they say. If they are not intending to blow you off, providing you with a follow-up date should not be a problem. Unless they are waiting for action from a responding state, a follow-up date generally should be no more than two weeks later. If the caseworker does not respond to you at all, wait two weeks before you take the next step.
2. If the caseworker does not do as promised, or if you are otherwise unhappy with the results that you have gotten, take your complaint to the caseworker's supervisor (Item #22). Follow the same steps and course of action. If the supervisor

does not prove helpful, wait two weeks before taking the next step up the rung.

3. The supervisor's manager is the next person that you would contact (Item #23). Telephone contact is usually the first method of contact, followed by any letters that you will send. If you end up sending a letter to the supervisor's manager, be sure to also "cc:" both the caseworker and the caseworker's supervisor, so that they know that they can expect to hear from the big boss. In my experience, many cases do not go beyond this point. In addition to contacting the proper officials who can get action on your case within the child support enforcement offices, also contact your elected officials (Item #24). Elected officials can put pressure on the child support enforcement office to get the job done. Begin with your state legislators such as your congressperson and/or senator.

Not only must you know the proper people with whom to lodge your complaint, you must also know the best way to write a complaint so that it does not fall on deaf ears and they realize that you are a person that will demand action. You must write your letter so that it gets the attention it deserves. Many obligees write long letters about how their ex left home, kicked the dog, smacked the kids took off in the car and left five dollars in the bank account. Sorry to say, but that information is best left for your therapist. There are probably about a hundred that come across his or her desk every day and half of them are probably worse than yours. The only information that your caseworker needs is the facts. Be short and sweet, but firm.

At this point it should go without saying that you don't have to put up with the merry go round most parents experience at the hands of CSE. Even though it should go without saying, I will say it anyway— you don't have to put up it. You can ditch CSE and go pro sé. It doesn't mean that life collecting child support will be rosy and without challenges, but it does mean that you eliminate the middle man and that puts you in charge of your own fate, destiny, freedom, whatever you choose to call it.

Deadbeat vs. Deadbroke

SAMPLE COMPLAINT LETTER TO CASEWORKER

Day/month/year

Caseworker's Name
Name of Child Support Agency
Street Address
City, State, Zip

Re: Case Number [Insert Your Case Number]

Dear [Insert Caseworker's Name]:

I spoke with you two weeks ago on [Insert Date], and you promised me that you would have a wage withholding done on my case. We agreed that I should follow up today. When I called your office you told me that you have not had a chance to do the wage withholding due to your large caseload. Since you promised to do this two weeks ago and did not, I would appreciate it if you would please be certain to do it now. I have been waiting far too long for my child support. If you need to reach me, please call me on my cell phone, [Insert Your Phone Number].

Thank you for your time.

Sincerely,

[Insert Your Name]
CC: [Insert Supervisor's Name], Supervisor

Item # 20: Sample Complaint Letter to Caseworker

SAMPLE COMPLAINT LETTER TO SUPERVISOR

Day/ month/year

Insert Name of Caseworker's Supervisor
Name of Child Support Agency
Street Address
City, State, Zip

Re: Case Number [Insert Your Case Number]

Dear [Insert Caseworker's Supervisor's name],

    I am writing to you for help with my case. On [Insert Date], I spoke with my caseworker [insert caseworker's name] and he/she promised that he/she would initiate a wage withholding against my ex, [Insert obligor's name] for child support. It is now a month later, a wage withholding has not been sent to the employer, and I have not been able to get [caseworker's name] on the phone.

    I understand that [insert caseworker's name] has a full caseload, but he/she did promise to get this done for me on that day. Would you please look into this matter for me and have the withholding done immediately? If there is a problem that prevents this from happening or if you need to speak with me for any reason, please do not hesitate to contact me. I can be reached on my cell phone and that number is: [Insert your phone number].

Thank you for your time.

Sincerely,

[Insert Your Name]
cc: [caseworker's name]

Item # 21: Sample Complaint Letter to Supervisor

Deadbeat vs. Deadbroke

SAMPLE COMPLAINT LETTER TO DIRECTOR

Day/month/year

Name of Director
Name of Child Support Agency
Street Address
City, State, Zip

Re: Case Number Your Case Number

Dear [Insert Directors Name]:

I have become very frustrated with the progress on my case and with your office, I am not receiving any action on my case, and I do not get a response from my caseworker or my caseworker's supervisor when I call or when I send an email.

At this time, I am requesting a copy of my case log so that I can review the activity on my case. I am also asking that a wage withholding be done on the obligor's income, I provided my caseworker with this information a month ago.

Thank you for your time,

Sincerely,

[Insert Your Name]
cc: [Insert Caseworker's Name], [Supervisor's Name]

Item # 22: Sample Complaint Letter to Director

SAMPLE LETTER TO ELECTED OFFICIAL

Day/month/year

Government Official's Name
Street Address
City
State
Zip

Dear [Insert Government Official's Name]:

    Enclosed you will find correspondence between the child support enforcement agency and myself. As you will see, there has not been much action on my case and I have provided everything that I can to the agency to enable them to enforce my order. It has been 120 days since I have asked them to utilize the state locator system to obtain a current address on my ex-husband. Although the law provides for 75 days to conduct a search, they still have not gotten back to me. Telephone calls and letters to their office remain unanswered.

Please help me with my case.

Sincerely,

[Insert Your Name]

CC: [caseworker's manager, [Insert county] child support office
Street Address
City
State
Zip

Item # 23: Sample Letter to Elected Official

appendix a:
glossary

Abnormal specimen testing A method of paternity testing that can be done on a deceased body to determine DNA matching for paternity.

Absent parent A parent who does not live with his/her children, but has financial responsibility for them. Also known as the non-custodial parent.

AFDC/ADC (Aid to Families with Dependent Children) Financial assistance (welfare) for families that have children who are deprived of the financial support of one of their parents by reason of death, disability, or continued absence.

Affidavit A written declaration, or statement of fact, made under oath, or in the presence of an officer authorized to make declarations under oath.

Appeal A request that a case be transferred to a higher court, for another hearing.

Arrearages Unpaid child support payments owed by a parent who has been ordered to pay.

Automatic stay The process by which a legal proceeding in progress must immediately come to an end.

Battle weary (War weary definition), utterly exhausted and dejected by war, especially after a prolonged conflict. With regards to child support collection of arrears, I use the term battle weary to describe parents who have been on the child support battle lines too long and are tired of being there. They lose hope and give up.

Buccal swab sampling A method of DNA matching, for the purpose of determining paternity, in which a large cotton swab is brushed along the inside of the cheek, collecting skin cells that can be tested for matching DNA.

Caretaker Authorization Affidavit A legal document which gives a grandparent temporary authorization to make decisions about a grandchild's care.

Chain of Custody The movement and location of physical evidence from the time it is obtained until the time it is presented in court.

Change in circumstances A change in the financial circumstances of either the non-custodial or the custodial parent, deeming the present child support order unfair.

Child grab A form of kidnapping which occurs when a legal custody order has not been established and one parent takes a child from the other and does not allow contact.

Child support award An amount of money that a non-custodial parent has been ordered by a court of law to pay for the upkeep of his/her children.

Child support enforcement agency A state-run government agency that collects child support for custodial parents.

Co-defendants A defendant who has been joined together with one or more other defendants in a single action.

COLA Cost Of Living Increase

Comity The practice by which one state or country recognizes the judgments or decisions of another, although they do not have to legally. It is a show of good faith.

Consent agreement Voluntary written admission of paternity, or responsibility for child support.

Consultation fee A fee charged to speak with a professional about your case.

Contingency fee A fee that only becomes payable if a case is successful.

Court-ordered Terminology used when the court has made a decision and handed down a ruling.

Creditor's bill A legal motion that must be filed with the court to prove that a person or entity is in possession of property that belongs to another person or entity.

Credit reporting agency An agency that reports one person's timely and late indebtedness to others, for the purpose of establishing credit-worthiness.

Custodial parent Parent with whom the child lives, and who has legal custody of the child.

Custody Legal determination that establishes with whom a child should live.

Defacto parent An individual other than a legal parent or a parent by estoppels who, for a significant period of not less than two years, (a) lived with the child and, (b) for reasons primarily other than financial compensation, and with the agreement of a legal parent to form a parent-child relationship, or as a result of a complete failure or inability of any legal parent to perform caretaking functions.

Default Failure of a defendant to file an answer, response, or appeal in a civil case within a certain number of days, after having been served with a summons and complaint. Results in an automatic judgment in favor of the plaintiff.

Default judgment Decision made by the court when the defendant fails to respond.

Deadbeat vs. Deadbroke

Defendant The person against whom a civil or criminal proceeding is begun.

Deposition A question and answer period that is conducted under oath.

Discharged The terminology used in bankruptcy when a debt is eliminated.

DIY Do It Yourself

DNA matching A method of familial relationship determination in which genetic chromosomal material is matched for its hereditary pattern.

Downward modification The terminology for a previously awarded child support amount being lowered.

Emancipation The age at which a child is no longer considered to be legally dependent.

Enforcement Forcing payment of a child support or medical support obligation.

Establish paternity The process of having paternity proved and established in a court of law.

Estoppel A law that says that once a decision has been made in a court of law, you cannot go back and ask that it be changed based on information that you had when the decision was made.

Execution Enforcement of a civil money judgment by ordering a sheriff to seize and sell the debtor's real or personal property.

Family calculation A method of DNA matching for the purpose of paternity testing in which immediate family members of the suspected father are matched along with the child in question. This is normally done when the suspected father is not available for DNA matching.

Federal Parent Locator Service (FPLS) A service provided by the federal government through the Office of Child Support Enforcement (OCSE) for the purpose of searching Federal Government records to locate absent parents.

Foreign order A judgment determined in a state or country other than your own.

Forensic paternity testing Methods of DNA matching for the purpose of paternity that can be done in the absence of the suspected father.

Garnishee The person, or entity, in possession of property that belongs to a debtor and upon whom a garnishment is served.

Garnishment A legal proceeding whereby a portion of a person's wages, or other assets, is withheld, and applied to payment of a debt.

Grandparents liability Part of the Welfare Reform Act, it requires grandparents to support the children of their minor child. 13 states have adopted this law.

Guardian One who cares for and protects

Guardian ad litem A person appointed by the court as a guardian to an infant or other person to act on his or her behalf in a particular action or proceeding.

Guardianship The position and responsibilities of a guardian

Guidelines Standard methods for setting child support obligations based on the income of the parent(s) and other factors as determined by state law.

Hearing An appearance before a judge, hearing officer, or administrative other.

Indigent A condition of being poor or needy. Also a person who is poor or needy.

Initiating state The state in which a proceeding is commenced and where the custodial parent is located.

Interstate case A child support case in which the custodial parent and the noncustodial parent live in two different states.

Interstate wage withholding A child support case in which a wage withholding is sent from one state to another to be processed.

Judgment A legal decision made by the court. Also known as an order.

Jurisdiction Legal authority that a court has over particular persons, certain types of cases, and in a defined geographical area.

Legal Custody When a parent has the right to make all decisions concerning their child's upbringing.

Legal father A man who is recognized by law as the male parent.

Legislation The making of laws.

Letter of consent Voluntary written admission of paternity or responsibility for support.

Leverage The use of power or effectiveness to enhance one's capacity.

Lien A claim upon property to prevent sale or transfer until a debt is satisfied.

Long arm statute A law that permits one state to claim personal jurisdiction over someone who lives in another state.

Medical support A legal provision for payment of medical and dental bills—can be linked to a parent's access to medical insurance.

Modify To change.

Motion An application to a judge for an order or a hearing.

Non-AFDC case A case where an application for child support enforcement has been filed and the family is not receiving public assistance.

Non-custodial parent The parent who does not have primary custody of a child, but who has a responsibility for financial support.

Obligation Amount of money ordered by the court to be paid by the responsible parent and the manner in which it is to be paid.

Obligee A custodial parent or guardian who has been awarded a child support order by the court.

Obligor A non-custodial parent who has been ordered by the court to pay child support.

Offset An amount of money taken from a parent's state or federal income tax refund to satisfy a child support debt.

Order A judgment handed down from a judge or other officer of the court.

Originating state The state from which legal documents originate.

Paternity Male parentage.

Paternity judgment Legal determination of fatherhood.

Paternity test A test that can determine male parentage.

Personal jurisdiction The power of a court over a person rather than subject-matter

Physical custody Looking after your children on a day to day basis

Plaintiff A person who brings an action, complains, or sues in a civil case.

POA Power Of Attorney

Deadbeat vs. Deadbroke

Pro sé The act of representing yourself during a court proceeding.

Psychological parent A person who a child considers to be his or her parent even though that individual may not be biologically related to the child.

Public assistance Money granted to individuals or families for living expenses, based on need.

Responding state A state receiving and acting on an interstate child support case.

Retainer A fee paid to retain an attorney's services.

Serve (service of process) The delivery of a summons or other notice to a person or entity.

Show cause A court order directing a person to appear and bring evidence to offer reasons why a court order should not be executed. A show cause order is usually based upon a motion and affidavit asking for relief.

State Parent Locator Service (SPLS) A service operated by the state to locate absent parents.

Subpoena An official document ordering a person to appear in court or to bring and/or send documents.

Summons A notice to a defendant that an action against him/her has commenced.

TANF Temporary Assistance for Needy Families

Title IV-D Title IV-D of the Social Security Act is the portion covering the child support enforcement program.

Title IV-D agency A state agency that collects child support for custodial parents under Title IV-D

Temporary physical custody A physical and legal custody agreement made by the parents or ordered by the court that is in place until after a final order from the court is entered. The courts final order may not be the same as the temporary order.

Transcript A typewritten copy of a deposition.

Undischargeable A debt that cannot be discharged under the bankruptcy law.

Unearned income Income that a person or entity receives that has not been earned by way of employment.

Uniform Reciprocal Enforcement of Support Act (URESA) A law which allows a custodial parent who lives in one state to establish and enforce a child support order against a non-custodial parent who lives in another state.

Upward modification The terminology for a previously awarded child support amount being increased.

Visitation The right of a non-custodial parent to visit or spend time with his/her children.

Volunteer agreements An agreement made between a custodial parent and a noncustodial parent for the payment of child support; made in lieu of a formal child support order.

Wage withholding Procedure by which automatic deductions are made from wages or income to pay a debt such as child support; may be voluntary or involuntary.

Writ An order issuing from a court and requiring the performance of a specific act, or giving authority and permission to have it done.

Written interrogatory A deposition that is conducted through the mail.

appendix b:

state child support enforcement offices

As of June 2014

ALABAMA
Bureau of Child Support
Dept. of Human Services
50 Ripley
Montgomery, AL 36130
www.dhr.alabama.gov
(800) 284-4347

ALASKA
Child Support Enforcement Div.
Dept. of Revenue
550 West 7th Ave., 4th Fl.
Anchorage, AK
www.childsupport.alaska.gov
(800) 478-3300
(907) 269-6900

ARIZONA
Child Support Enforcement
    Administration
Dept. of Economic Security
P.O. Box 6123/Site Code 776-A
2222 W Encanto
Phoenix, AZ 85005
www.azdes.gov/az_child_
    support
(602) 252-4045

ARKANSAS
Officer of Child Support
    Enforcement
Arkansas Social Services
P.O. Box 8133
Little Rock, AR 72203
www.childsupport.arkansas.gov
(800) 264-2445
(501) 682-8398

CALIFORNIA
Division of Child Support
    Department of Social Services
744 P Street/Mail Stop 9-011
Sacramento, CA 95814
www.childsup.ca.gov
(916) 464-5000

COLORADO
Department of Human Services
Division of Child Support
303 E. 17th Ave; Suite 200
Denver, CO 80203.1241
www.childsupport.state.co.us
(800) 374-6558

CONNECTICUT
Bureau of Child Support Enforcement
Dept. of Human Resources
999 Asylum Avenue
Hartford, CT 06105
www.ct.gov/dss
(800) 228-5437

Deadbeat vs. Deadbroke

DELAWARE
Division of Child Support
Dept. of Health 61, Social Services
P.O. Box 904
New Castle, DE 19720
www.dhss.delaware.gov
(302) 577-7171 (Customer service)
(302) 739-8299 (New Castle
    County)
(302) 856-5386 (Sussex County)

DISTRICT OF COLUMBIA
Office of Corporation Counsel
Child Support Enforcement
    Division
441 4th Street N.W. 5th Floor
Washington, D.C. 20001
www.cssd.dc.gov
(202) 442-9900

FLORIDA
Office of Child Support
    Enforcement
2410 Allen Road
Tallahassee, Fl 32399-0700
myflorida.com/dor/childsupport
(800) 622-5437

GEORGIA
Office of Child Support
    Enforcement
878 Peach Street N.E.
Atlanta, GA 30309
www.dcss.dhs.georgia.gov
(877) 423-4746

GUAM
Office of the Attorney General
Union Bank
194 Hernan Cortez Avenue
Agana, Guam 96910
www.guamcse.net
(671) 475-3360

HAWAII
Child Support Enforcement Agency
Department of Attorney General
601 Kamokia Blvd; Suite 251
Kapolei, HI 96805
www.ag.hawaii.gov/csea
(888) 317- 9081
(808) 586-1500

IDAHO
Bureau of Child Support
    Enforcement
Department of Health & Welfare
450 W. State Street, 6th Floor
Pete T. Cenarrusa Building
Boise, ID 83702
www.healthandwelfare.idaho.
    gov
(800) 356-9868

ILLINOIS
Bureau of Child Support
    Enforcement
Illinois Department of Public Aid
509 S. 6th Street
Springfield, Illinois 62701
www.childsupportillinois.com
(800) 447-4278

INDIANA
Child Support Enforcement
    Division
Department of Public Welfare
402 N. Washington Street
Room W360
Indianapolis, IN 46204
www.in.gov/dcs/support.htm
(800) 840-8757
(317) 232-4885

IOWA
Bureau of Collections
Iowa Department of Human
    Services
727 E. 2nd Street
Des Moines, IA 50309
www.childsupport.ia.gov
(888) 229.9223

KANSAS
Child Support Enforcement
    Program
Dept. of Social & Rehabilitation
    Services
P.O. Box 497
www.dcs.ks.gov
Topeka, KS 66601-0497

KENTUCKY
Division of Child Support
    Enforcement
P.O. Box 2150
Frankfort, KY 40602
www.chfs.ky.gov/dis/cse
(800) 248-1163
(502) 564-2285

LOUISIANA
Support Enforcement Services
Department of Social Services
P.O. Box 829
Baton Rouge, LA 70821
www.dss.state.la.us
(888) 524-3578

MAINE
Support Enforcement and Location
Bureau of Social Welfare
Department of Human Services
State House, Station 11
Augusta, ME 04333
www.maine.gov/dhhs/ofi/dser
(207) 624-4168

MARYLAND
Child Support Enforcement
    Administration
Department of Human Resources
311 W. Saratoga, 3rd Floor
Baltimore, MD 21201
www.dhr.state.md.us
(800) 332-6347

MASSACHUSETTS
Child Support Enforcement Unit
Department of Revenue/CSE
P.O. Box 4068
Wakefield, MA 01880
www.mass.gov/dor/child-
    support
(800) 332-2733

MICHIGAN
Office of Child Support
Department of Social Services
235 S. Grand Avenue
P.O. Box 30478
Lansing, MI 48909
www.michigan.gov/childsupport
(517) 373-7570

MINNESOTA
Office of Child Support
Department of Human Services
444 Lafayette, 4th Floor
St. Paul, MN 55155
www.dhs.state.mn.us
(651) 296-2542

MISSISSIPPI
Child Support Division
State Department of Public Works
939 N. President
Jackson, MS 39202
www.mdhs.state.ms.us
(800) 345-6347

Deadbeat vs. Deadbroke

MISSOURI
Child Support Enforcement Unit
P.O. Box 1527
Jefferson City, MO 65102
www.dhs.mo.gov/cse
(573) 751-4301

MONTANA
Child Support Enforcement
    Program
P.O. Box 5955
Helena, MT 59604
www.dphhs.mt.gov/csed
(800) 346-5437

NEBRASKA
Child Support Enforcement Office
P.O. Box 95026
Lincoln, NE 68509
www.dhhs.ne.gov/children_
    family_services/CSE
(877) 631-9973

NEVADA
Child Support Enforcement
    Program
885 E. Musser St., Suite 2030A
Carson City, NV 89710
www.nvemployers.com/CSE
(775) 448-5150

NEW HAMPSHIRE
Office of Child Support
    Enforcement Services
129 Pleasant St.
Concord, NH 03301
www.dhhd.nh.gov
(603) 271-4427

NEW JERSEY
New Jersey Division of Public
    Welfare
Bureau of Child Support &
    Paternity
P.O. Box 716
Trenton, NJ 08625
www.njchildsupport.org
(877) 655-4571

NEW MEXICO
Child Support Enforcement Bureau
P.O. Box 25109
Santa Fe, NM 87504
www.childsupport.hsd.state.
    nm.us
(800) 288-7207

NEW YORK
Office of Child Support
    Enforcement
40 W Pearl St., 13th Floor
Albany, NY 12260
www.childsupport.ny.gov/dcse
(800) 343-8859

NORTH CAROLINA
Child Support Enforcement Section
Division of Social Services
100 E. Six Forks
Raleigh, NC 27609
www.ncdhhs.gov/cse
(800) 992-9457

NORTH DAKOTA
Child Support Enforcement Agency
Regional Child Support
State Capital
P.O. Box 5518
Bismarck, ND 58506
www.nd.gov/dhs/services/
    childsupport
(800) 231-4255

OHIO
Bureau of Child Support
373 S. High Street
13th Floor
Columbus, OH 43215
www.jfs.ohio.gov/ocs
(800) 686-1556

OKLAHOMA
Division of Child Support
    Department of Human Services
P.O. Box 53552
Oklahoma City, OK 73152
www.okdhs.org/programsandse
    rvices/ocss
(800)-522-2922

OREGON
Recovery Services Section
Adult and Family Services
1495 Edgewater Street NW
Suite 290
Salem, OR 97304
www.oregonchildsupport.gov/
    services/pages/enforcement
(800) 850-0228

PENNSYLVANIA
Child Support Programs
Dept. of Public Welfare
1303 N. 7th St.
P.O. Box 8018
Harrisburg, PA 17105-8018
www.humanservices.state.pa.
    us
(877) 727-7238

PUERTO RICO
Child Support Enforcement
    Program
CALL Box 3349
San Juan, PR 00904
www.acf.hhs.gov/programs/
    css/state-and-tribal-
    child-support-agency
(809) 722-4731

RHODE ISLAND
Bureau of Family Support
77 Dorance
Providence, RI 02903
www.cse.ri.gov
(401) 222-2409

SOUTH CAROLINA
Child Support Enforcement
    Division
P.O. Box 1469
Columbia, SC 29202.1469
www.state.sc.us/dss/csed
(803) 898-9282

SOUTH DAKOTA
Office of Child Support
    Enforcement
700 Governors Drive, Suite 84
Pierre, SD 57501-2291
www.sd.gov/childsupport
(605) 773-7295

TENNESSEE
Child Support Services
Citizens Plaza Bldg., 12th Floor
400 Deadrick Street
Nashville, TN 37248-7400
www.tn.gov/humanserv/cs_main

Deadbeat vs. Deadbroke

TEXAS
Child Support Enforcement c/o
 Attorney General's Office P.O.
 Box 12017
Austin, TX 78711-2017
www.texasattorneygeneral.
 gov/cs
(800) 252-8014

UTAH
Office of Recovery Services
120 N. 200 West
P.O. Box 45011
Salt Lake City, UT 84145
www.ors.utah.gov/child_
 support_services
(801) 536-8636

VERMONT
Child Support Division
Department of Social Welfare
103 South Main Street
Waterbury, VT 05671-1901
www.dcf.vermont.gov/ocs
(802) 241-3110
(800) 649-2646

VIRGIN ISLANDS
Support and Paternity Division
Department of Justice
48B-50C Kronprindsens Gade
GERS Complex-2nd Floor
St. Thomas, VI 00802
www.pcsd.vi
(304) 775-3070 x5004

VIRGINIA
Division of Support Services
8007 Discovery Drive
Richmond, VA 23288
www.jupiter.dss.state.va.us
 /family
(800) 468-8894

WASHINGTON
Office of Support Enforcement
P.O. Box 9162
Olympia, WA 98507-9162
www.dshs.wa.gov/dcs/services
 /enforcement
(800) 457-6202

WEST VIRGINIA
Office of Child Support
 Enforcement
State Capital Complex
Building #6, Room 812
Charleston, WV 25305
www.wvdhhr.org/bcse
(800)249-3778

WISCONSIN
Division of Community Services
Office of Child Support
201 E. Washington Avenue, Rm.
 271
Madison, WI 53707-7935
www.dcf.wisconsin.gov/bcs
(608) 267-3905

WYOMING
Child Support Enforcement Section
Hathaway Bldg.
Cheyenne, WY 82002
www.dfsweb.wyo.gov/child-
 support-enforcement
(307) 777-6948

appendix c:

military locator service

United States Army
USA Enlisted Records &
  Evaluation Center
8899 E. 56th Street
Indianapolis, IN 46249-5301
www.hrc.army.mil
(866) 771-6357

United States Marine Corp
  Headquarters USMC MMSBIO
2008 Elliot Road. Suite 201
Quantico, VA 22134-5030
(760) 725-5171

United States Air Force
AFPC-MSIMDL
550 C Street
Randolf Air Force Base, TX 78150-4752
(210) 565-2660

United States Coast Guard
2100 Second Street S.W.
Washington, D.C. 20593
(202) 267-0581

Navy Personnel Command
Pers 312
5720 Integrity Blvd.
Millington, TN 38055-3120
www.public.navy.mil/bupers-
   npc/organization/npc/csc/
   pages/navylocatorservice
(901) 874-3388

index

about the author

Simone Spence is President and Founder of Child Support Solutions, LLC (CSS), an organization that helps parents collect unpaid child support payments throughout the US. Since CSS' founding, Spence's clients have been able to collect more than $15,000,000 in past due child support.

Spence learned first-hand about child support collection when she worked her way through the child support system to claim the payments to which she was entitled. Her efforts enabled her to support her own children and her victory led her to help other women who were unable to find success on their own. She explains, "I know it is difficult to navigate the system but my own experience gave me the ability to help other mothers. I find it incredibly rewarding to help mothers legally claim their outstanding payments and be able to provide for their children."

"We empower our clients by giving them the information and tools they need to provide for their children by recovering outstanding child support payments," says Spence. She adds, "We have an 83% success rate which we attribute to our understanding of both the child support collection process and comprehensive knowledge of an individual's rights."

Simone Spence is the author of *1-800-Deadbeats: How to Collect your Child Support* and *Deadbeats, What Responsible Parents Need to Know about Collecting Child Support*, published in 2000 by Sourcebooks and now, *Deadbeat vs. Deadbroke: A Guide to Getting Your Children All That They Deserve*. As a subject matter expert, Spence has been called on to appear on many television shows including but not limited to Fox News Channel's *Morning Show*, WOR-TV, Channel 9, TV Channel 21, Newstalk TV and she regularly makes appearances on talk radio. She is a sought after expert on child support and has written for Heart & Soul magazine and Essence magazine. She served as talk-radio hosts on both

321

Deadbeat vs. Deadbroke

WEVD and WGHT and for two years, wrote a weekly column "Diary of a Single Mom," for the North Jersey Herald & News. Simone Spence is an advocate, private child support consultant, trainer and coach.

Spence is a graduate of New York Institute of Technology, where she majored in journalism and communications. She has addressed U.S. legislative hearings for the Administration for Children & Families.

Among the many honors and awards Spence has received, former New Jersey Governors McGreevey and Corzine have honored Simone Spence with Proclamations for ending the cycle of hunger for families through her advocacy for child support enforcement. One of the greatest awards she was honored to have received was through *Events to Empower Humanity* when she received an honor for lifting a 4 time generational mother with 8 children from social services by teaching her how to collect her child support which helped her to become self-sustaining. This led to the Women Presidents Organization (WPO) inviting her to lead the key-note for their annual meeting in Toronto, Canada in 2005. Spence lives in the Southeast with her family. In her free time she enjoys nature and outdoor activities, writing poetry, painting, cooking gourmet Sunday meals, that she tops off with home-baked desserts and she loves to share them all with friends over a nice glass of red wine and scintillating conversation.

Visit her website at: www.dontgetmadgetpaid.com

CPSIA information can be obtained
at www.ICGtesting.com
Printed in the USA
FFOW02n1451030417
34183FF